THE
SIX WIVES
OF
HENRY VIII

THE SIX WIVES OF HENRY VIII

ILLUSTRATED EDITION

Antonia Fraser

Picture Research by Julia Brown
Abridgement by Gila Falkus

Weidenfeld & Nicolson
LONDON

For my parents
Nonagenarians extraordinary

Text copyright © Antonia Fraser 1992 and 1996

First published in 1992 by
George Weidenfeld & Nicolson Ltd
The Orion Publishing Group
Orion House
5 Upper St Martin's Lane
London WC2H 9EA

First published in this abridged, illustrated format 1996

A CIP record for this book is available
from the British Library.

ISBN 0 297 83567 X

Designed by Leigh Jones
Printed and bound in Italy

CONTENTS

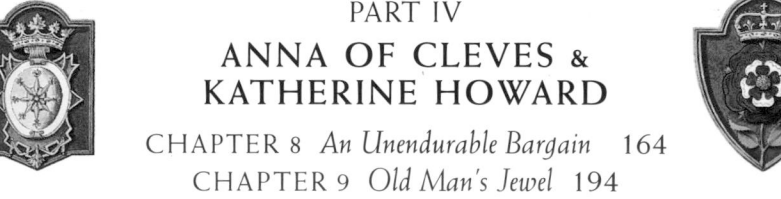

PROLOGUE

'DIVORCED, BEHEADED, DIED ... divorced, beheaded, survived ...': so the six wives of Henry VIII have become defined in a popular sense not so much by their lives as by the way their marriages ended. In the same way their characters are popularly portrayed as female stereotypes: the Betrayed Wife, the Temptress, the Good Woman, the Ugly Sister, the Bad Girl and, finally, the Mother Figure. The perils of such stereotyping were forcibly illustrated to me on a visit to Hever Castle when I listened to a knowledgeable schoolchild pronounce on a presumed portrait of Anna of Cleves: 'That's her, the ugly one.' To which his companion agreed: 'That's right, she's dead ugly' – except that they were both looking at a picture of the 'Temptress' Anne Boleyn.

A more sophisticated example is provided by the treatment of the six women in religious terms. Catherine of Aragon is crudely assumed to have been a bigoted Catholic (though in her prime distinguished for her patronage of Erasmian humanism – 'the New Learning'); Anne Boleyn displayed strong Protestant tendencies long before Rome blocked her marriage to the King and made her the natural ally of the reformers; Jane Seymour, who has gone down in history as the Protestant Queen, adhered in fact to the old ways in religion; Anna of Cleves, married for her 'Lutheran' connection, was a natural Catholic; Catherine Parr was the true Protestant Queen. The truth – as so often where the female in history is concerned – is both more complicated and more interesting than the legend.

My first aim in writing this book has been to look at the women behind the stereotypes – how far if at all did they deserve such labels? – as well as relating six life stories which are fascinating in themselves. With this in mind, I have tried wherever possible to avoid hindsight. Although *we* know that Henry viii will marry six times, we must always remember that he did not.

My second aim has been to illumine certain aspects of women's history through the lives of these celebrated exemplars – celebrated in the first place through marriage. But then that is the point. Marriage was the triumphal arch through which women, almost without exception, had to pass in order to reach the public eye. And after marriage followed, in theory, total self-abnegation. Here is the contemporary view expressed by one of those most sympathetic to

Fortune's wheel was a favourite image in the culture of late mediaeval Europe, recurring constantly in romances and histories. It was certainly an appropriate one for the six wives of Henry VIII.

women, the Spanish philosopher Juan Luis Vives: 'A wife's love for her husband includes respect, obedience and submission. Not only the traditions of our ancestors but all human and divine laws agree with the powerful voice of nature which demands from women observance and submissiveness.' Even Thomas More, regarded as a prominent patron of women's learning, expressed the hope that the coming child of his daughter Margaret would resemble her in all but 'the inferiority of her sex'. Behind the liberals Vives and More marched ranks of people, both men and women, who took for granted woman's inferiority – and her subordination to her husband.

7

If this were true of ordinary wives bowing before ordinary husbands, how much more awe-inspiring must the power of a royal husband have been! We are dealing with six women who were married in turn to the supreme power in the land, the royal head of state and, from 1534, the self-constituted head of the church as well. No wonder Katherine Howard, young and incredulous, was convinced that the omnipotent King must be able to overhear the very sins mentioned in the confessional. Catherine Parr, one of the very few women in this period whose works were printed, was explicit on the subject: 'Children of light . . . if they be women married, they learn of St Paul to be obedient to their husbands.'

It is now that the wonderful paradox emerges that makes the study of women's history so fascinating and even exhilarating, not merely a pathetic chronicle of suffering. Rich, feisty characters flourished in this atmosphere of subjection: one might note that even the naïve Katherine Howard was not suggesting that certain sins should not be committed – only that they should not be mentioned in the confessional. The other five wives exhibited remarkable degrees of spirit and defiance.

Although this is the story of six very different women (to that extent the varied stereotypes are correct), it is essentially a composite narrative. This reflects the important linkage which existed between the six women. In terms of court ceremonial, Anne Boleyn waited on Catherine of Aragon before supplanting her, Jane Seymour waited on Anne Boleyn, Katherine Howard on Anna of Cleves, Anne Parr on Katherine Howard, thus bringing her sister Catherine into court circles. King Henry certainly did not pass easily from one marriage into another (as a modern serial divorcé may at least hope to do). The stability of his early married life to Catherine of Aragon – for nearly twenty years, a much longer period than is sometimes realized – gave way to an era of marital tempest in which there were all too often two women alive who either were or had once been Queen of England. If her fate does not compare in poignancy with that of Catherine of Aragon, Anna of Cleves' protracted survival at the English court in the honorary role of the King's 'good sister' is certainly one of the odder episodes in the story.

Other transfers were of course achieved with less serenity. Jealousy permeates this story, not only the desperate jealousy of the Queens who found themselves abandoned, but also the sexual jealousy of the King who discovered himself betrayed. Rivalry was also inevitable when the stakes were so high in the great game of marrying the King of England; for the woman concerned, and also for her country if she was a princess, and her family if she was a commoner. This is however no reason for a biographer to perpetuate those rivalries nearly five hundred years later. I myself have not developed any particular favourite among the six Queens – unlike King Henry VIII for whom Jane Seymour remained his 'true wife', the one who was 'entirely beloved' – because she gave him a son.

I have, on the contrary, attempted to deal with each woman with the sympathy I feel they all deserve for having had the unenviable fate of being married to Henry VIII. At the same time I have tried to practise the detachment which recognizes that this is an eminently modern judgement; not one of the King's six wives married him against her will. I have also hope to practise that detachment towards the King himself: the gigantic Maypole at the centre of it all, round which these women had to dance. But this is not his story. It is theirs.

THE PLANTAGENET DESCENT OF HENRY AND HIS QUEENS

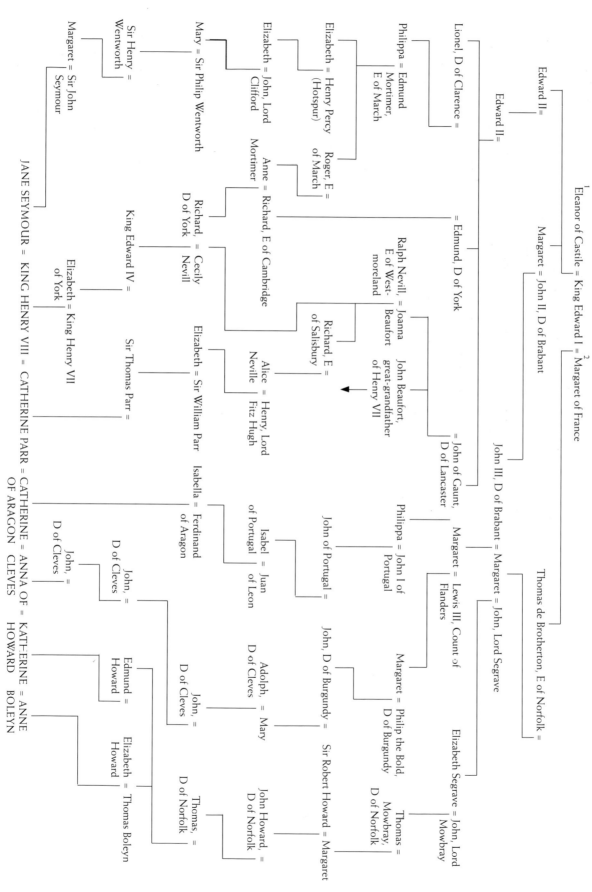

Eleanor of Castile = King Edward I¹ = Margaret of France²

THE TUDORS AND THEIR RIVALS

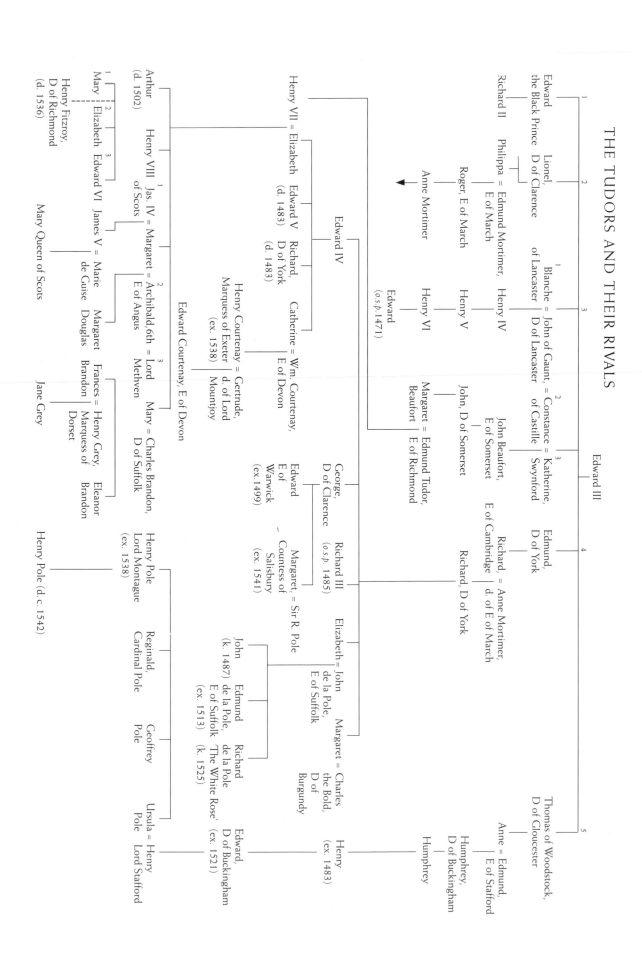

PART I

CATHERINE
OF
ARAGON

CHAPTER 1

Princess of Wales

THE STORY BEGINS in Spain. On 16 December 1485, a few months after the battle of Bosworth Field at which Henry Tudor secured the throne of England, a princess Catherine (or Catalina) was born. She had an unusual parentage for she was the daughter of not one but two reigning monarchs, Isabella of Castile and Ferdinand of Aragon – the 'Catholic Kings', as they would be designated by the Pope. For the first fifteen years of her life (nearly half the life expectancy of a woman of that time, and as it turned out nearly one third of her own life) Catherine lived alongside her older brother and three older sisters under the tutelage of her remarkable mother. Isabella's unique position as a queen regnant was matched by that combination of pious character and military achievement which made her the wonder of Europe. As Europe was indelibly impressed by the image of Isabella the Catholic so too was her daughter Catherine.

An illuminated manuscript showing Queen Isabella, Catherine of Aragon's celebrated mother, being presented with a book by the author Marcuello. Isabella's active patronage of learning led to a general revival of classical studies in Spain.

Isabella had come to the throne unexpectedly, thanks to the accident of her half-brother's death without a legitimate heir. She had been raised in a secluded convent without any of the skills needed by a statesman – male or female – on the European stage. In particular she knew no Latin, still the language of international diplomacy, and had therefore been obliged to learn it as an adult: a traditionally painful task. Where her daughters were concerned, Queen Isabella was determined that they should be given the advantages that had been denied to her. In this she acted not only as a prudent mother but also, in agreement with Ferdinand, as a prudent monarch.

Once the male succession was assured, the birth of a princess, who through a powerful marriage could act as the ambassadress of her parents, was not seen as a disaster. The birth of Catherine meant that Isabella now had four of these potential envoys. She was determined that they should be well trained. As a result Catherine studied not only her Missal and the Bible, but also classical literature. She learnt to speak good classical Latin with great fluency. Then a knowledge of both civil and canon law was thought appropriate, as well as heraldry and genealogy.

Music, dancing and drawing – the traditional and graceful spheres of Renaissance feminine accomplishment – were naturally not ignored. But Queen Isabella also passed on to her daughters another more universal feminine tradition of basic domestic skills, all the more poignant perhaps, since the wives who practised them would be married to kings and archdukes, not merchants and farmers. It was said that Isabella insisted on making all King Ferdinand's shirts. Certainly her daughters were taught to spin, weave and bake; Catherine in turn would see it as both her duty and her right to embroider her own husband's shirts.

There were other personal legacies which Isabella passed to her daughters which had important emotional consequences. With Isabella's strength of public purpose went a private wifely submission to the husbandly authority of Ferdinand and a profound belief in the divinely ordained nature of all marriages – and hers, which had brought about the fruitful union of two countries, in particular. A husband was sent by God. A wife, whatever her royal rights, submitted to her husband and was of course bound to him for life. Two of Isabella's daughters – Juana as well as Catherine – were to show, in their very different ways, an obsession with the husband given to them for reasons of state, but surely also by the will of God.

King Ferdinand of Aragon, known as the 'wily Catalan', was determined to negotiate useful dynastic marriages for his five children. He did not fully commit Catherine to a Tudor alliance until he was confident that the dynasty was firmly established.

It is hardly surprising that such a pious woman as Isabella was also chaste. Indeed, it is noticeable that among the princesses of Europe who were descended from her, personal chastity like wifely submission was another characteristic: not for them the hot-running blood of the Tudors – Catherine's future sisters-in-law – who on several occasions allowed their hearts or physical appetites to rule their heads. Personal chastity, on the other hand, was not the watchword of Catherine's father, Ferdinand. His amours angered Isabella – as such things generally do – without diminishing her devotion, let alone her feeling for the divinely instituted nature of her marriage. She might be furious; jealous too on a purely human level; but she would never consider that the position of mistress could or would be converted into that of wife. That to Isabella – or her daughter – was quite unthinkable.

As for Ferdinand, his intelligence and his ability to survive were probably his greatest legacies to Catherine. There was a streak of unbalance in Isabella's family, coming from her mother, a Portuguese princess, which may have had its origin in depression following childbirth. This would emerge tragically in Catherine's sister Juana but in Catherine such hysterical feelings were for the most part kept well under control; through all her tribulations she retained Ferdinand's fierce sanity. Catherine, with that strong sense of family inculcated by her upbringing, greatly admired her father: his constant hostility to France, for example, based on the geographic position of Aragon, was one of his attitudes which certainly formed her own. His deviousness she saw merely as suitable regard for his national interests.

It was to be expected that the marital alliances planned by King Ferdinand for his children would reflect his preoccupation with the neutralization of France. The key players in this game of dynastic chess were Burgundy and Austria. In 1477 their houses had been joined by the marriage of Marie of Burgundy to Maximilian of Austria.

The convenient birth of a son and daughter to this royal Habsburg couple, of an age to be matched with a prince and princess of Spain, put Ferdinand within reach of his most brilliant coup. In August 1496 Catherine's sister Juana, not quite seventeen, married the Archduke Philip of Austria; in April the following year her eighteen-year-old brother the Infante Juan was married to the Archduchess Margaret.

At first sight England was a minor power compared with this mighty trio of Spain, France and the Habsburg Empire (as it became). Nevertheless England enjoyed certain natural advantages in any diplomatic or military game. There were already dynastic links. A strong dose of Plantagenet blood flowed in the royal Spanish veins. There had once been talk of Queen Isabella herself marrying an English Yorkist prince – Edward IV perhaps or the Duke of Clarence. Then England's value as a potential ally was greatly enhanced by her geographical position. Both Spanish and Burgundian merchants needed the protection of English ports if France was barred to them. Furthermore in the

Catherine's sister Juana married the Archduke Philip of Austria and became the mother of the Emperor Charles V. Both she and Catherine were to show, in their very different ways, an absolute obsession with the husband given to them for reasons of state, but also, they believed, by the will of God.

Portrait of Henry VII in a black coat and black hat painted at about the date of the wedding of Arthur Prince of Wales to Catherine of Aragon.

Opposite, top: The family of Henry VII with St George and the Dragon by an unknown artist of the Flemish school. In the foreground the King is kneeling with three sons on the left and, on the right, is Elizabeth of York with four daughters. Their marriage ensured that their children would inherit the claims of both Lancaster and York.

1480s – not so very long after Agincourt in terms of folk memory – France was the hereditary foe of England as well as the natural enemy of Spain. Although only Calais remained of the English possessions in France, ancient English claims to French territory and the throne of France itself were still bellowed forth on appropriate occasions.

The real problem with an English royal marriage, from Ferdinand's point of view, was the shaky nature of the new dynasty. In August 1485 Henry VII had established himself on the throne at the point of the sword. But undoubtedly there were other individuals with a superior dynastic claim – not only his Queen, Elizabeth, daughter of Edward IV, but other representatives of the house of York (see 'The Tudors and their Rivals' family tree). Nonetheless, the first overtures concerning the marriage of Henry's son Arthur to Ferdinand's daughter Catherine probably came as early as 1487 when Arthur (born in September 1486) was under a year old and Catherine not yet two. On the surface there was steady progress. In April 1488 a commission was given to Dr de Puebla, a middle-aged Castilian with a decent record of government service and an excellent grasp of languages, to draft a treaty of marriage.

There was much courtly rejoicing – particularly on the English side. The Spanish reactions were somewhat cooler. It was no part of the policy of Ferdinand, known for good reason as 'the wily Catalan', to marry one of his well-trained ambassadresses into 'a family which might any day be driven out of England' as he wryly put it. When the English began to quibble about terms – over the dowry to be given to Catherine or her rights of succession to the throne of Castile – the Spanish commissioners suggested that 'bearing in mind what happens every day to Kings of England, it was surprising that Ferdinand and Isabella should dare give their daughter at all.' But for Henry VII the value of the marriage was sufficient to make it well worth swallowing an insult or two. The Treaty of Medina del Campo between England and Spain in March 1489 represented his first major breakthrough in terms of a European alliance. It was of the essence for Henry that Yorkist pretenders would no longer find refuge on Spanish soil; and both Ferdinand and Henry were relieved to be united against the French. Furthermore Henry had secured the promise of a bride for his son, grander than any English consort since that French princess whom Henry V had wed, Catherine de Valois.

Below: Bust of a child believed to be Henry VIII as a boy, attributed to Guido Mazzoni, c. 1500.

Where royal marital bargains were concerned, however, a promise was a long way from performance. The great heiress Marie of Burgundy, for example, had been betrothed no less than seven times before she married Maximilian of Austria. In the dynastic game, formal betrothals, even proxy marriages which theoretically allowed a princess to sail for a foreign country already with the status of a wife, were none of them foolproof moves. Catherine of Aragon was just over three at the time of Medina del Campo, but negotiations for the betrothal of the young pair, as provided for in the treaty, were not begun until late 1496, shortly before her eleventh birthday. At this date, given the various twists and turns of the international situation in the intervening years, the marriage currently suited both parties to the treaty. Moreover Dr de Puebla was impressed by the growth of internal stability in England. So in August 1497 Arthur and Catherine were formerly affianced at Woodstock, with de Puebla 'standing in' for Catherine. If such a betrothal *per verba de praesenti* (i.e., one with immediate present effect, as opposed to a betrothal *per verba de futura*, for some future date) was consummated, it had the force in church law of a marriage. Of course there was no question of such a consummation with Arthur in England and Catherine in Spain. But from now on Catherine was officially termed the Princess of Wales.

One of the vexed questions raised by treaties of marriages concerned when the betrothed princess should set out for her fiancé's country. This in turn related to the delivery of her dowry – another perennially vexed question, especially where parents such as Ferdinand of Aragon and Henry VII were in dispute; if the one was rapidly becoming a byword for diplomatic trickery, the other was gaining a distasteful reputation for inordinate meanness. While negotiations dragged on a series of instructions about life at the English court were despatched to the 'Princess of Wales' from her future mother-in-law, including a request for Catherine to accustom herself to drinking wine. 'The water of

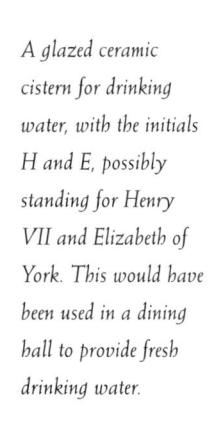

A glazed ceramic cistern for drinking water, with the initials H and E, possibly standing for Henry VII and Elizabeth of York. This would have been used in a dining hall to provide fresh drinking water.

England', wrote Elizabeth of York sadly, 'is not drinkable, and even if it were, the climate would not allow the drinking of it'. Meanwhile King Henry VII loved to speak about, even drool over, his little Spanish daughter-in-law.

On 19 May 1499 the first of the wedding ceremonies that were to bind Arthur Prince of Wales and Catherine of Aragon took place at Bewdley Palace in Worcestershire. Prince Arthur spoke 'in a loud and clear voice' according to de Puebla, declaring that he was pleased to contract 'an indissoluble marriage with Catherine Princess of Wales'. He was acting not only out of obedience to the Pope and his father 'but also from his deep and sincere love for the said Princess, his wife'. (The reference to the Pope arose from the papal dispensation that had been granted in order for Arthur to make his vows – he was not yet fourteen and thus below the age of consent.) De Puebla's own role, a conventional one by the standards of the time, was that of the bride; as such he not only took the prince's right hand in his own and was seated at the King's right hand at the subsequent banquet, but also inserted a symbolic leg into the royal marriage bed. But for Ferdinand's part, so little did he trust the bargain that he instructed another Spanish envoy to watch de Puebla like a hawk, fearing that the doctor had been suborned by Henry VII. He was to keep his ears open for rumours of another match being negotiated for Arthur with a rival princess and ensure that at all times Catherine was styled 'Princess of Wales'. A further practical precaution was a second proxy marriage at Ludlow Castle once Arthur had actually reached the age of consent.

It was finally agreed that Catherine should set off on her journey towards England shortly before her sixteenth birthday. The royal family of Spain during this last year of her girlhood was very different from the confident unit in which she had been brought up. In October 1497 Catherine's adored brother, the Infante Juan, newly married to the Archduchess Margaret, had died after a short illness. There was now no direct male heir to Aragon where by Salic law a female could not succeed, while the Castilian succession passed to Isabella's eldest daughter, Isabel, Queen of Portugal. But fate had not finished with the 'Catholic Kings'. Isabel herself died in childbirth in the summer of 1498, her baby son following soon after. The succession now passed to the Catholic Kings' second daughter Juana, wife of the Habsburg Archduke Philip of Austria who in February 1500 gave birth to a son, Charles. It became apparent that this infant Habsburg heir was the most likely candidate to succeed to the Spanish throne as well as the empire of his grandfather Maximilian. All Ferdinand's brilliantly planned dynastic marriages, far from elevating his own royal house, now looked like handing over the throne of Spain to the Habsburgs.

The last months of Catherine's residence at her mother's side must indeed have been melancholy. Catherine's stately journeyings north-west across Spain through the summer of 1501 were scarcely more cheerful. There were further delays. A fresh Moorish uprising threatened Ferdinand's farewell to his daughter. Catherine herself suffered en route from 'a low fever', a phrase which covered a multitude of indispositions in modern terms, from influenza to a bout of (understandable) adolescent depression. One of her last stops before her embarkation at Corunna on 17 August was at Santiago de Compostela, where she spent the night in prayer at the hallowed shrine of St James. But her prayers did not spare her yet another ordeal once she was aboard the ship. A vicious storm in the Bay of Biscay drove her back to Spain. It was not until the end of September that Catherine was able to re-embark for an England increasingly impatient for her arrival. At last on 2 October 1501 the Princess of Wales arrived at Plymouth Sound.

'The Princess could not have been received with greater joy had she been the Saviour of the World', wrote a member of Catherine's Spanish entourage. This reception began with the spontaneous welcome given by the people of the West Country, who were moved by the gallantry, as well as the charm and dignity of the young princess. After so many delays and frustrations, King Henry VII's own excitement equalled that of his subjects. At the last moment, he decided not to wait at Richmond, as had been planned, but to sally forth to meet her, first taking in tow Prince Arthur, coming from Ludlow. It would be pleasant to see the King's uncharacteristic impetuosity as being inspired by that quasi-paternal affection to which his letters had borne witness. But something more calculating was in fact at the bottom of it all. Like Doubting Thomas, King Henry needed to see his son's bride with his own eyes, to make sure she was healthy, nubile – so far as the eye could see, and appearances were held to count for a lot in this respect – and preferably goodlooking as well.

Fortunately he was enchanted by what he saw. With a mixture of relief and delight, the King was able to say of Catherine that he 'much admired her beauty as well as her agreeable and dignified manners.' Even allowing for tactful hyperbole, it is clear that Catherine, now on the eve of her sixteenth birthday, did have the kind of youthful prettiness and freshness that charmed observers. It was partly a question of her complexion: her naturally pink cheeks and white skin were much admired in an age when make-up – 'paint' – was scorned. A fair complexion like Catherine's was thought to indicate a more serene and cheerful temperament than a 'brown' (sallow) one. Catherine's hair was also fair and thick, with a reddish-gold tint. Her chief disadvantage was lack of height. All the grace of her bearing, inculcated over many years, could not conceal the fact that she was extremely short, even tiny. She was also on the plump side – but then a pleasant roundness in youth was considered to be desirable, a pointer to future fertility. In contrast Catherine's voice was surprisingly low and 'big-sounding' for a woman; and that no doubt contributed to the impression of gracious dignity she left on all observers.

Catherine, for her part, might have been less enchanted by the sight of her bridegroom. Arthur Prince of Wales was now fifteen, but he was so small and undeveloped that he seemed much younger. He had been born prematurely – by at least a month, probably two – and had never recovered from that debilitating

start. When it came to height, Catherine might be short, but Arthur was half a head shorter still; the longed-for male heir to the houses of both York and Lancaster gave the impression of being a mere child – and a delicate child at that. He too was fair-skinned like his bride, but without her healthy pink cheeks the result was a worrying pallor. At least the prince had received (like his bride) an excellent classical education. Latin had been the language of their correspondence, but unfortunately Catherine's pronunciation of Latin, however fluent, turned out to be different from that of King Henry and Prince Arthur, so that she still could not make herself understood. Only the English bishops were able to persevere and make some sort of contact. Nor could the prince and princess dance together. Their training in this respect – important as it was at any Renaissance court – was once again completely different. So Catherine was content to dance a Spanish dance, while Arthur danced in the English manner with some ladies of the court instead.

Opposite: A recently rediscovered portrait of Arthur, Prince of Wales. This is the only contemporary likeness of him and is thought to be his marriage portrait, painted when he was fifteen.

None of this was felt to matter in the slightest, given that Arthur had at last successfully set eyes on his 'dearest spouse'. By the standards of a royal marriage at the time, it was really already a remarkably happy venture, with the couple roughly the same age, some of the dowry already paid up, the contract virtually completed. In an optimistic mood, King Henry swept his son and daughter-in-law towards London for the wedding ceremony at St Paul's.

There on 14 November to the sound of Spanish trumpeters Catherine of Aragon and Arthur Prince of Wales were married. If coming events truly cast their shadow before, then Catherine should have been aware of some tremor as she was escorted up the aisle by her husband's younger brother, Henry Duke of York, her hand

London.

in his. He was only ten years old, but with his long legs and broad shoulders had already far outstripped Arthur, five years his senior. But there is no evidence that she felt any such tremor. On the contrary, all Catherine's concentration was bent on pleasing the man whom she had been trained to accept as her new 'father': Henry VII. Arrangements at the wedding banquet were significant. Catherine sat on the right hand of the King while Prince Arthur sat at a separate children's table with Prince Henry and his sisters, the twelve-year-old Princess Margaret in cloth of gold and Princess Mary, aged five in crimson velvet trimmed with fur. Not only during the banquet itself but for the whole period of official celebration which followed, Arthur was not considered to have any particular role.

A view of London from Richard Pynson's Cronycle of Englande, 1510.

25

Margaret Tudor married James IV of Scotland when she was fourteen, two years after her brother Arthur's marriage to Catherine of Aragon.

There was just one exception to Prince Arthur's non-participation. This was the ceremony of the wedding night which, like the banquet, took place at Baynard's Castle, the historical London residence of the house of York. The symbolic leg that de Puebla had first placed in the prince's bed over two years earlier was now to be replaced with the real thing. Thus, at the end of the banquet, the Princess of Wales was formally bedded with her husband by a host of courtiers, English and Spanish; the attendants then withdrew and they were left to lie there together. By an ironic twist of fate, the question of the sexual relationship – if any – between these two innocent adolescents would become of paramount importance nearly thirty years later. By then one of the two had been dead almost as long; the other was facing the most desperate crisis of her life. There is no contemporary record of Prince Arthur's views and one must surely leave aside the vulgar gossip produced so conveniently years later by courtiers hoping to serve the interests of their master. One is therefore left with Catherine's unwavering assertions, dating from 1502 onwards (not from the late 1520s like the courtiers' tales), that the marriage was unconsummated.

There was however a third person ready to express a first-hand view on this delicate if vital point: Catherine's second husband, Henry VIII. He, after all, had either found her to be a virgin on their own wedding night (as he used to boast in his youth) or had not. It can be argued that Catherine herself, like Henry's

A mid-sixteenth-century view across the Thames. Baynard's Castle, where the wedding banquet for Prince Arthur and Catherine of Aragon was held, is on the left, in front of St Paul's Cathedral.

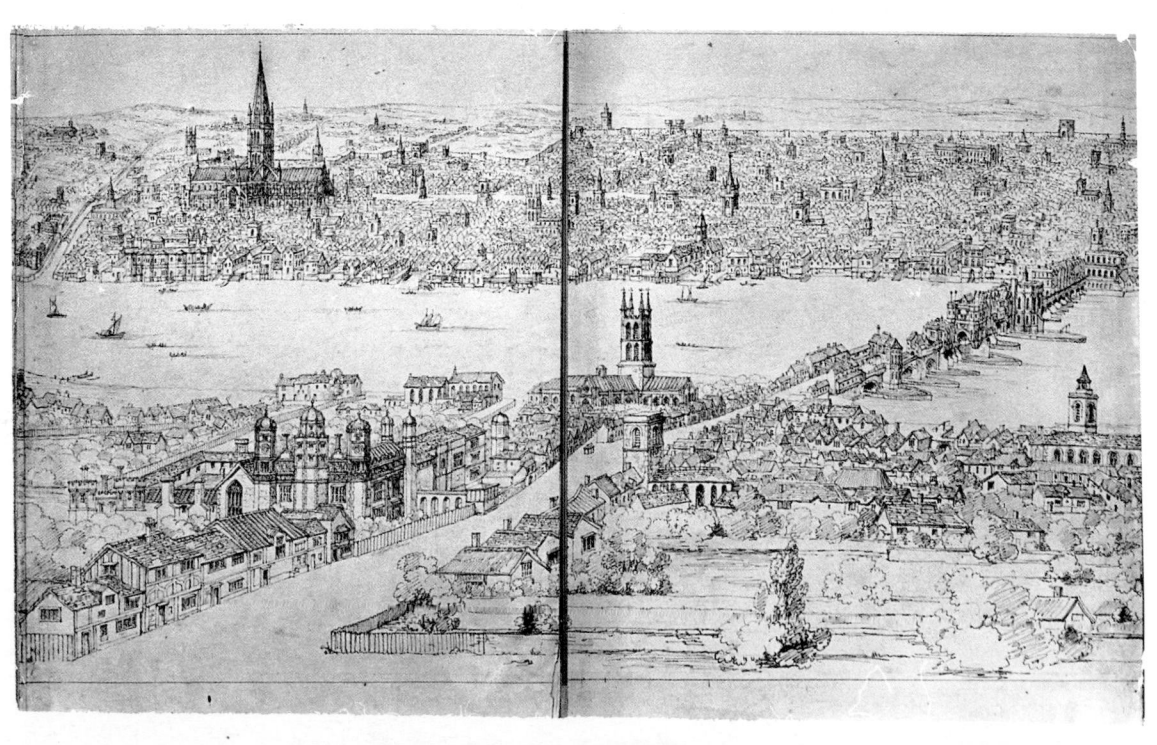

courtiers, was not an unbiased witness. In that case more convincing evidence of non-consumption is provided by the fact that Henry VIII himself in later life never gave Catherine the lie on the subject when publicly challenged to deny that he had found her 'a maid'.

A Flemish tapestry, now in Magdalen College Oxford, showing the marriage of Prince Arthur and Catherine of Aragon. Richard Mayhew, President of the College from 1480 to 1506 was one of the envoys sent to meet Catherine on her arrival in England in 1501.

But what really stands against the notion of the consummation of the union, all subsequent allegations apart, is that custom was all against it. In an age when marriages were frequently contracted for reasons of state between children or those hovering beween childhood and adolescence, more care rather than less was taken over the timing of the consummation. Once the marriage was officially completed, some years might pass before the appropriate moment was judged to have arrived. Anxious reports might pass between ambassadors on physical development; royal parents might take advice on their offsprings' readiness. The comments sometimes remind one of those breeders discussing the mating of thoroughbred stock, and the comparison is not so far off. The siring of progeny was the essential next step in these royal marriages, so endlessly negotiated.

In the case of Arthur and Catherine, all four parents apparently agreed that nothing should be rushed. Henry VII and Elizabeth of York were anxious to protect their son's health, while Ferdinand and Isabella sent assurances that they too would 'rather be pleased than dissatisfied' if consummation was delayed. The plan therefore was for Catherine to remain in London, under the tutelage of her mother-in-law while Arthur continued his growing-up, undisturbed by the distractions of a wife, at Ludlow Castle. But this plan, which had an agreeably human side to it – Catherine would learn to know her new family, and also learn English, before she attempted to forge a proper relationship with her husband – was not carried out. Instead, Catherine set off for Ludlow Castle in December 1501.

The change, which infuriated the Spaniards, came back to the question of Catherine's dowry. In principle payment of the dowry by the bride's parents was made in return for promise of full financial support from her husband's estate later. Thus Ferdinand had agreed to hand over 200,000 crowns on Catherine's marriage on condition that, if widowed, she would receive one-third of the revenues of Wales, Cornwall and Chester. Of the promised 200,000 crowns, however, Ferdinand had so far only delivered half. He suddenly announced that a substantial portion of the remainder – 35,000 crowns – was in fact being consigned in plate and jewels. This was definitely stealing a march on the English King for whom, like most monarchs of the time, cash was an essential but elusive commodity.

It did not take Henry VII long to come up with a Machiavellian counter-plan – in this respect Ferdinand and Henry were well-matched. Supposing the Princess of Wales was sent to Ludlow the establishment of her household there would inevitably involve the considerable deployment of plate and jewels, commensurate with that status on which the Spaniards were so keen. To do this, she would have to use her own plate. This in turn would make it difficult for the Spanish King to have 'these same, now second-hand jewels and plate' re-emerge as part of the dowry. And so to the Marches of Wales Catherine went, with a considerable Spanish train, including the redoubtable Doña Elvira

A view over Ludlow, the capital of the Marches of Wales, showing the castle where Prince Arthur and Catherine of Aragon spent the winter of 1501-2.

whom Isabella had put in charge of Catherine, and a Spanish chaplain.

There, at Ludlow, roughly 150 miles from London, Catherine and her Spanish attendants sat out the winter of 1501-2. On the Welsh borders the following spring the weather was notably cold and wet, as a result of which sickness of various types was rife. Towards the end of March 1502 Prince Arthur's fragile health began to give way. He may have been suffering from tuberculosis; there was also an outbreak of plague in the neighbourhood, and an epidemic of another scourge of the times known as 'the sweating sickness'. This disease was much feared for its mysterious course: victims did recover but others died 'some within three hours, some within two hours, some merry at dinner and dead at supper'. The sweating sickness seems the most likely diagnosis since Catherine also collapsed. She was still seriously ill on 2 April when Prince Arthur died. Catherine of Aragon, at the age of sixteen and three months had become the Princess Dowager of Wales.

The news of Arthur's death reached the court at Greenwich late on the following day. The Council had the sensitivity to summon King Henry's confessor, a Franciscan Observant friar, to break the news. Henry then sent for the unfortunate boy's mother and told her himself. Elizabeth of York behaved with great courage; she did not break down, but pointed out that the King's own mother 'had never no more children than him only, and that God by his grace had ever preserved him, and brought him where that he was.' They too had a son, Henry, Duke of York, as well as two princesses, Margaret and Mary. Besides, the Queen added, their family was not necessarily complete: 'we are both young enough'. Elizabeth did in fact conceive again a month after Arthur's death. What she did not foresee was that the child would be a daughter, that the daughter would die, and that she herself would die too, shortly afterwards, as a result of her ordeal.

On the death of her boy husband Catherine of Aragon became a problem of state – in two countries. Little thought was spared for the personal feelings of the girl who now found herself convalescent in a country whose language she spoke sparingly if at all, surrounded by possessive Spanish attendants whose intention was to cut her off still further in the name of the honour due to her. Those close to her were more interested in practical problems, including, of course, the question of the dowry. The obvious solution was that Catherine should be married – or at least betrothed – to 'the Prince of Wales that now is', as Ferdinand described the young Henry. This occurred to both sets of parents almost immediately. In Spain Isabella and Ferdinand were predictably shocked by the news of Arthur's death; when Ferdinand wrote on 12 May that 'the affliction caused by all their former losses had been revived by it', we may believe that for once there was real sincerity beneath the conventional condolence: the deaths of the Infante Juan and Queen Isabel of Portugal were still raw to their parents. Yet an alliance was imperilled and so their first thought must be to stabilize the rocking balance of power.

Prince Arthur was buried in Worcester Cathedral. In the chantry subsequently raised there, the heraldic allusions of the roses of York and Lancaster, the Beaufort portcullis and Catherine's badge of an arrow-sheaf provide a sad echo of the marriage celebrations only six months earlier.

Then there was the question of money. In theory – Spanish theory – it could all now be beautifully simple. The money already paid for the first marriage could count towards the second; the Anglo-Spanish alliance would remain intact. This renewal of negotiations was not necessarily unwelcome to the English King, since he knew himself to be in a strong position. First, he indubitably did have the widowed Princess of Wales there at the English court. Secondly Prince Henry, who was only eleven, was a ripe candidate to take part in one of those betrothals which could, if necessary, be repudiated once he reached the age of consent. Besides that, it would be against nature for Henry VII to return any money already paid. Returning then to the question of Catherine's dowry, what would be the proper provisions for the next marriage treaty? At this point things, theoretically so simple, turned nasty.

When Ferdinand, shortly after Arthur's death, set himself to establish whether his daughter's marriage had been consummated or not, he was not interested in her physical wellbeing. The fact was that the Princess Dowager of Wales had the right to demand back the 100,000 crowns paid as the first instalment of her dowry, even before she received the stipulated one-third of the revenues of Wales, Cornwall and Chester, if the marriage had been completed in this respect. But as we have seen, it had almost certainly not. And Doña Elvira swore categorically to that effect. It is important to bear in mind for the future that when Doña Elvira swore so firmly that consummation had not taken place, she was not giving the answer then most convenient to Spain. Nevertheless her version convinced Ferdinand: 'God has taken Arthur to himself too soon'. By the beginning of July 1502 he was quite certain that 'our daughter remains as she was here', i.e. a virgin. It was on this basis that Ferdinand instructed his representative to negotiate for the new marriage.

Catherine spent the years of her widowhood at Durham House in the Strand, the mediaeval London house of the bishops of Durham.

The treaty of betrothal between Prince Henry and Catherine was signed the following summer, on 23 June 1503. The projected match required special permission – a dispensation from the Pope. According to the rules of the church, the marriage of Arthur to Catherine had created an 'affinity' between Catherine and Henry. It was as though Catherine had become Henry's actual sister, rather than his sister-in-law, through this earlier union: brothers and sisters being related 'in the first degree collateral', were forbidden to marry. It was the sexual union between husband and wife, not the marriage ceremony, which was held to create this affinity. As we shall see, a man who had made love to one sister might require a dispensation to marry another, even though no ceremony had been involved in the first (clandestine) relationship. A different kind of dispensation was required in the case of an unconsummated marriage: one on grounds of 'public honesty'. Notwithstanding the lack of consummation, a first marriage had taken place in the public eye: this fact had to be acknowledged before the second marriage was publicly seen to be legitimate. Given that the entire point of such dispensations was to establish a lawful unquestionable marriage, from which – even more importantly – legitimate offspring would flow, more thought was generally given to the future of the second marriage, rather than to the facts about the first.

Thus when the Spanish King asked for a dispensation from Rome for Catherine to marry Henry, he asked for, and was granted, a dispensation which referred to her first marriage having 'perhaps' (*forsitan* in Latin) been consummated. A great deal of trouble would later be caused by this little weasel word 'perhaps'. At the time – with Ferdinand quite convinced that the marriage had

31

not been consummated, Catherine herself, to say nothing of Doña Elvira, passionate in her denials – what was taking place was clearly a Spanish manoeuvre. Such a dispensation – for a man to marry his brother's widow – was unusual, but it was certainly not unknown. Catherine herself could hardly have regarded it as exceptional, since King Manuel of Portugal had married her two sisters Isabel and Maria in quick succession. There were various biblical texts on the subject, one of which – from Leviticus – forbade such a marriage, and one – from Deuteronomy – explicitly enjoined it as bounden duty on the part of the second brother. These texts, which, like the little word 'perhaps' and the events of the wedding night of two adolescents, were to be analysed exhaustively nearly thirty years later, featured little if at all at the time; this was yet another game of power politics, with youthful royal brides and grooms as the pawns.

There were however some significant new pawns on the matrimonial chessboard. Catherine of Aragon's claim, as a princess of Spain, to represent the most powerful alliance available to Henry VII, had been considerably eroded since that original Anglo-Spanish treaty nearly fifteen years earlier. There were, for example, the grandchildren of the Emperor Maximilian, the growing family of his son Philip the Handsome and Catherine's sister Juana: if Charles, Catherine's nephew born in 1500, was the greatest male matrimonial prize in Europe, his sisters, Eleanor and Isabella, also represented interesting possibilities as brides. Nor was Catherine the only widow on the European scene. Her former sister-in-law the Archduchess Margaret, who had gone on to marry Philibert of Savoy, had recently been widowed for the second time.

October 1504 saw the death of Catherine's own mother, Isabella. The unity of the kingdoms of Aragon and Castile was now in jeopardy and Ferdinand for diplomatic purposes had been transformed into an eligible bachelor. Promptly the next year he married Germaine de Foix. Apart from being the niece of the King of France, she was also his own half-great-niece. She was eighteen; he was fifty-three. Such mercurial turnabouts boded ill for Catherine. By the summer of 1505, as the fourteenth birthday of Prince Henry approached (the date at which he reached the official age of consent, when Catherine might expect their actual marriage to take place), a very different set of rumours was sweeping Europe. King Henry VII was believed to have set his heart on a triple marriage to link his own family to the imperial house of Habsburg. His daughter Princess Mary would be betrothed to Charles, the heir to the Habsburgs and to Castile; King Henry himself would wed Charles' twice-widowed aunt, the Archduchess Margaret; and Henry, Prince of Wales would be espoused to Charles's sister, Eleanor of Austria. On 27 June, the day before his birthday, Henry formally repudiated his betrothal to Catherine.

Even before this blow fell Catherine's state had become increasingly wretched. Nor had the betrothal two years earlier substantially affected her welfare as might have been hoped; on the contrary it made the pointed requests of King Henry – where was the rest of her dowry? – all the more exigent. Such demands were accompanied by polite but firm refusals to provide anything but minimal maintenance for her himself. By the spring of 1504 Catherine reported that she did not even have enough money to buy food for herself and her household. As the first stages of the much-desired betrothal of Charles of Austria to Princess Mary were reached, so Catherine's anxiety about her own future sharpened. Not only present poverty but ultimate rejection seemed to threaten her, though with a courage that did her credit, she told King Henry that she regarded her marriage to Prince Henry as 'irrevocable'.

Silver-gilt effigies of Henry VII and Elizabeth of York by Torrigiano in Henry VII's Chapel in Westminster Abbey.

As the uncertainty dragged on it was hardly surprising that Catherine's health gave way and she suffered persistent attacks of 'low fever' – once again this was likely to be a form of depression as any other feverish ailment. In the spring of 1507 she told her sister Queen Juana that she had recovered and was bearing her adversity with fortitude. But by August Catherine burst out to her father that 'no woman of whatever station in life' could ever have suffered more. Put against this, King Henry's protestations a month later that he had just sent her £200 (her servants must have stolen it) and that he loved her so much that he could not bear the idea of her 'being in poverty' have a hollow ring.

In the spring of 1509 Catherine's spirit finally gave way. In a letter to her father of 9 March, she broke down and told him that she could no longer combat the petty persecutions of Henry VII. She was ready to return to Spain where she wanted to spend the rest of her life serving God. This was the final expression of despair on the part of Queen Isabella's daughter who had been trained to believe that life on the throne, not in the convent, was the destiny for which God had sent her on earth. The next month Fuensalida, the Spanish ambassador, began the process of despatching Catherine's belongings to Bruges. And then, suddenly, Catherine was no longer in King Henry's power. On 21 April, after a short illness, he died. It was almost exactly seven years since the death of Prince Arthur.

CHAPTER 2

Harmonious Wedlock

*The opening of
the tournament roll
of 1511 displays
the royal initials of
the King and Queen,
the Tudor rose and the
Spanish pomegranate.
Every public
opportunity was taken
to blend the initials of
Henry and Catherine
(H and C or K) from
the mock castles erected
for pageants down to
the love-knots on the
King's armour.*

SIX WEEKS AFTER the death of the old King, on 11 June 1509 Henry VIII married Catherine of Aragon in the oratory of the friary church just outside the walls of Greenwich Palace. He was about to be eighteen; she was twenty-three. The ceremony was small and private; Catherine wore white, with her hair long and loose as befitted a virgin bride. Describing the wedding night which followed, King Henry liked to boast that he had indeed found his wife 'a maid', although years later he would attempt to pass off these boasts as 'jests'. On Midsummer Day a more public and splendid celebration took place when, at the orders of the new King, his bride shared in his coronation at Westminster Abbey. The coronation of a queen was more than a good opportunity for loyal subjects to feast their eyes on a great deal of glittering gold and white – and to inspect her charms. It was also a deliberate act of state, one which did not necessarily coincide with marriage to the King: Elizabeth of York had only been crowned after the birth of a son and heir.

Why had this miraculous transformation in Catherine's fortunes taken place? One suggestion was that the King's Council had advised Henry that the marriage would be 'honourable and profitable to his realm' simply because they wished to hang on to Catherine's dowry. There was also the need to secure King Ferdinand as an ally against France. And of course there was the nervous dynastic situation in England where, if King Henry had died in an accident at one of the coronation tournaments in 1509, it was not at all clear who his heir would be. An adult bride was far more attractive in terms of founding the new dynasty than, for example, the eleven-year-old Eleanor of Austria. But the truth is more romantic. Although the various arguments in favour of the marriage may also have played their part – especially where the King's counsellors were concerned – they were essentially justifications of a decision which the new King took himself. And he took it for reasons of love, not politics, ruled by his heart not his head. After all, it was hardly difficult to find arguments to support a union to which he had been committed officially for six years, one that had obvious material and diplomatic advantages.

Portrait of Henry VIII after Joos van Cleve. Henry loved to
wear lavish clothes and jewels. The Venetian ambassador
described his fingers as 'one mass of jewelled rings'.

All his life King Henry VIII had a happy capacity for falling in love: happy at least from his own point of view, given that he was able to secure the object of his passion with reasonable speed. Of his six marriages, four were made for love, and one for affection, bordering on love; the only marriage which was made for pure reasons of state was an instant disaster. In the summer of 1509 Henry was a young man, ardent, chivalrous, moved by the sufferings of the girl he had been brought up to consider his 'most dear and well-loved consort'. It was not difficult to love the graceful, appealing Catherine, with her sweet nature and evident devotion to 'the prince her husband'.

For Queen Catherine, her new life certainly had all the elements of a fairy story, including the presence of a handsome young prince. Never is it more important to get away from the popular stereotype of King Henry VIII – Bluff King Hal, the bloated monarch of the later years – than when considering the man whom Catherine of Aragon married in 1509. Few kings have been endowed by nature with such dazzling physical qualities as the young King Henry. From his earliest years he had excited admiration for having what was deemed to be the perfect princely appearance. Apart from his colouring – the golden hair with a glint of red, the blue eyes and fair skin which received universal praise – his build was heroic. The King was six foot two inches tall, with broad shoulders and fine, long muscular legs, in an age when men were certainly smaller than they are today, if not quite as small as is sometimes suggested. The sheer physical energy of the young Henry, forever leaping, dancing, riding, hunting, wrestling, tilting, jousting, and masking, amazed the world. A vast love of life and pleasure in all its forms exuded from him, which was so agreeable to contemplate in a charming young man – particularly one who had inherited a prodigious fortune from his careful father.

The elaborate chamfron (head protection) worn by Henry VIII's horse.

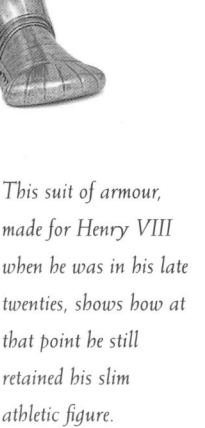

This suit of armour, made for Henry VIII when he was in his late twenties, shows how at that point he still retained his slim athletic figure.

Illuminated design on a set of motets by Richard Sampson, Bishop of Chichester and later of Coventry and Lichfield. The motets were preceded by a hymn in honour of Henry VIII.

Illuminated design on a set of motets by Richard Sampson, Bishop of Chichester and later of Coventry and Lichfield. The motets were preceded by a hymn in honour of Henry VIII.

Music played an important part in Renaissance court life and the ability to play and sing was an essential accomplishment for both men and women.

Yet for all the King's impatience at any activity which involved staying still for too long – writing letters, for example – this was no handsome but mind-less athlete. Henry VIII had been extremely well educated; he was an avid read-er and he had a naturally quick intelligence; theological debate was an area of real interest. Music was another passion: in 1515 he was described as being able to play almost every instrument and compose tolerably; another report had the King able to sing 'from a book at first sight'. He would leave a legacy of over thirty songs and instrumental pieces which he had either composed or arranged himself. It would be easy for any woman to love such a man as Henry now was, and Catherine of Aragon was not any woman – she had for many years been his wife in the eyes of God – as she firmly believed.

At the same time, Catherine herself had not escaped unmarked from her seven-year ordeal of hardship and humiliation. It was not – fortunately – her looks that had suffered. She was after all not yet twenty-four. It was the inner

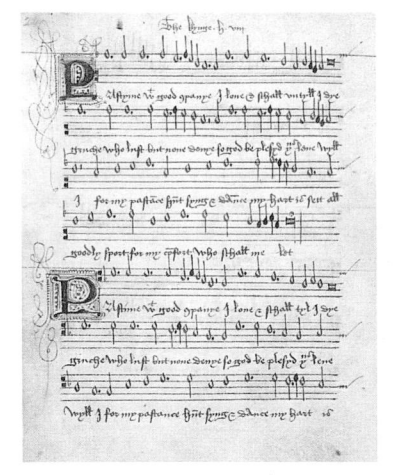

woman who bore the marks. Like a mediaeval saint, she had undergone a series of harrowing experiences, only to prevail. Her prayers had been answered. But these privations were not without effect on her character – how could they be? Catherine of Aragon was stamped as much by her tribulations, as she had been earlier formed by her happy childhood. She was no longer the tremulous young girl who had arrived seasick, if still dignified, in England. She was much stronger, of course, as people who surmount adversity generally are. The depth of her religious devotion, by consoling her, had probably saved her where another princess might

Above: Henry VIII's song Pastance with Good Company. *Henry left a legacy of over thirty songs and instrumental pieces which he had either composed or arranged himself.*

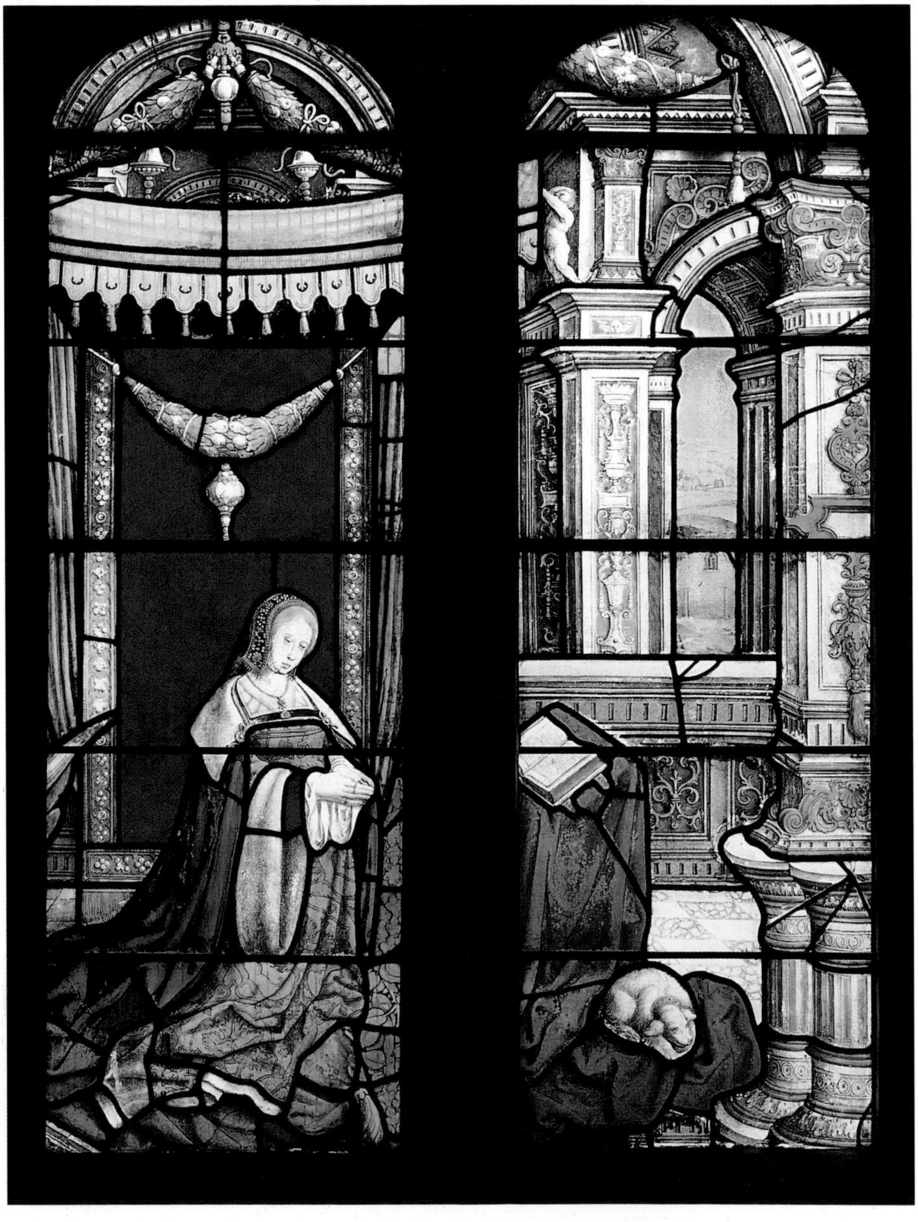

Right: Catherine of Aragon's piety excited general admiration. During her later years she followed a regime of increasing rigour, rising at midnight to attend matins and then spending much of her day at prayer. This image of her is from The Vyne in Hampshire.

have collapsed, but the effect was to give her a somewhat narrow, black-and-white view of morality. Catherine of Aragon had not broken, but she had also not learnt how to bend.

For the present the English court spent its time, as Catherine wrote to her father, in 'continuous feasting' and in an endless series of tournaments, masques, and ceremonial rejoicing. Masques – including elaborate disguises which fooled of couse no one – were a passion of the King; as such they quickly became the passion of the whole court. Everyone joined in, especially the King's young male friends and the numerous girls of fairly good family who had come to court hoping to secure a profitable marriage – and along the way enjoy a good time. The Queen's role in all this was not so much to be fun as to be astonished, full of wonder, definitely not recognize the King, suddenly recognize the King, and finally congratulate him with lavish praise. This she did very well.

According to custom the young King and Queen lived in two parallel households with their own officers. For this reason the presence of a queen was much welcomed after a gap of more than six years, since it substantially increased the amount of places available at court. The layout varied from palace to palace, but their suites were generally on the same floor, with the bedrooms close together. It was a way of life which did not preclude cosiness – the King would bring visitors without warning to dine late in the Queen's chamber (his third large meal of the day) or would suddenly decide he that needed a meat meal himself, causing her to scurry about like any wife proud of her housekeeping. The domesticity of Catherine's life with her ladies was the counterpoint to her more formal role

This piece of embroidery, recently rediscovered and thought to be the work of Catherine of Aragon, has been made up into a chasuble.

presiding over tournaments as the official 'lady' of Sir Loyal Heart. A good deal of time was spent making and embroidering the King's shirts, often in black and white, the colours of Castile – another activity on which Catherine prided herself and which, like her admiration of his dancing and jousting, cannot have been displeasing to her husband.

There was of course no privacy. Even the King's natural functions were not performed in private: the role of Groom of the Stool, responsible for the maintenance of the royal close-stool (as well as the King's linen and goods when he travelled) became in consequence one of the most important posts at court, because it involved the ultimate proximity to the King's person. When King Henry VIII decided to make love to his wife, the curtains of his bed were drawn back, his night robe (or dressing-gown) was sent for, and an escort of pages and Grooms of the Bedchamber was summoned to accompany him with torches down the passage to the Queen's chamber. The evidence indicates that King Henry took that conjugal route with great regularity. He was young and healthy: in the tradition of St Augustine Erasmus declared that the purpose of marriage was not to gratify 'lusts' but to procreate children – but who was to prevent a man doing both at the same time? The King needed heirs; he thus had every reason to make love to his wife with assiduity. Given his original affection for Catherine and the fact that she was neither old nor charmless, it was a duty of state, but it was also an agreeable one.

Queen Catherine did in fact conceive her first child with suitable speed after her wedding. Four a half months later the King was able to write to Ferdinand not only that the Queen was pregnant but 'the child in the womb was alive'. The 'quickening' of the baby at four months or thereabouts was always an important moment; up till then the midwives were never absolutely sure that they were dealing with pregnancy rather than some other condition. It was not that they did not understand the relevance of a woman's monthly cycle and its stopping; just that hopes of conception were always so desperately keen in high-born ladies that a great deal of unwarranted optimism was encouraged. The quickening of the baby made hope an established fact.

This baby, a daughter, was stillborn at seven months on 31 January 1510. For some time Catherine did not tell Ferdinand and when she did she begged him

not to be angry since 'it has been the will of God'. In any case, by the time she broke the news on 27 May, she was already about seven weeks pregnant, although, by the custom of the time, it was too soon to mention the fact. By the end of September yards of purple velvet were being ordered for 'the King's Nursery'. And joy of joys, a son, named Henry for his father, his grandfather, and a long line of mediaeval royal Henries, was born on 1 January 1511.

The baby prince was christened on 5 January (the Archduchess Margaret was his godmother). It was a measure of his august position that despite being fed at the breast by a wet nurse, Prince Henry was immediately considered to need a carver, a cellarman and a baker. At Candlemas, on 2 February, an elaborate tournament took place to celebrate this great event which had, as it seemed, ensured the Tudor succession. But only a few weeks later, the royal accounts, which had been full of payments for scarlet and crimson velvet for the tournament, were recording payments for black cloth for the burial of Prince Henry. He had lived a mere fifty-two days. The cause of his death was never stated, but in an age of such high infant mortality this particular death might have been a tragedy but it was not of itself extraordinary. According to Hall's *Chronicle* the Queen took it far worse than the King: she 'like a natural woman, made much lamentation', while Henry 'like a wise Prince, took this dolorous chance wondrous wisely'.

No doubt the King did comfort his Queen, as Hall suggested, so that by 'his good persuasion ... her sorrow was mitigated'. Nevertheless things had not gone according to plan. The world was, momentarily, not quite so golden. It was fortunate for Henry VIII that foreign policy existed to distract him from domestic tragedy; and given that Henry's foreign policy was heavily entwined with that of Catherine's father, fortunate for Catherine that she too could share in the enterprise. Henry's belligerence towards France was something that struck all observers. It was the Venetian ambassador who drew the obvious corollary: he would shortly invade the country. This belligerence – or martial spirit as it was more flatteringly viewed – was neither surprising in a monarch nor unwelcome to Henry's subjects. The cultivated Lord Mountjoy, expatiating to his friend Erasmus on the wonders of the new reign deliberately contrasted the avarice of Henry VII with his son's heroic ambition: 'Our [new] King is not after gold, or gems, or precious metals, but virtue, glory, immortality.' War was the ultimate tournament, in which an energetic young man could win renown in the eyes of his royal peers as well as his native court.

One of the most important of King Henry's preparations for the invasion of France was to designate the Queen as Regent in his absence. It was a natural step in one sense because before the rise of the King's super-servant Wolsey, Catherine was Henry's closest confidante. But the appointment of the King's consort was by no means automatic, so it was also a tribute to Catherine's intelligence and diplomatic ability. Besides, her work was not expected to be purely formal: the King and his Council, wrote Hall, 'forgot not the old Pranks of the Scots, which is ever to invade England whenever the King is out.'

Given that the King's war was undertaken in alliance with Spain, given his confidence in Catherine, how much did his expensive martial foreign policy owe to his wife's 'Spanish' influence? At first sight, the Queen's five-year seniority coupled with her devotion to her father would seem to indicate that she had exercised a considerable sway in directing her husband towards Spain. But this view of the Queen's paramount influence is to reckon without two important arguments pointing the other way.

The first concerns Catherine's near-fanatical devotion to her husband: duty to him, enjoined by God, came before her duty to her father. She was indeed so careful in her behaviour in this respect that by December 1514 the Spanish ambassador to the Provincial of Aragon was complaining that the Queen of England needed some discreet and intelligent person to point her in the right direction – towards the interests of Aragon. The second argument concerns the character of King Henry himself, a young lion increasingly confident of his own strength. Time would show that the most successful campaigns to influence the King in a particular direction only took place when in fact he had wanted to go in that direction all along.

The King departed for France in June 1513. While he was there Thomas Wolsey, currently the King's almoner, made an excellent conduit for the Queen's anxious messages, since the King himself found life too short (and exciting) to write letters. She told Wolsey that she would worry all the time about the King's health: there could be no rest for her while the King was near 'our enemies'. Henry led his 'army royall' in the successful sieges of Thérouanne and Tournai and in the Battle of the Spurs (where the French fled). As a matter of fact he was never anywhere near the front of the action – unlike François I and Charles V, and indeed his own father, Henry VIII never actually fought – but reading the Queen's letters is to get a different picture.

In the meantime, when not worrying about her husband (did he have enough clean linen?), the Queen was playing her part as Regent with energy and determination. The Scots – led by the King's brother-in-law James IV – did indeed take the opportunity to indulge in 'the old Pranks' and attacked England's northern border. 'In imitation of her mother Isabella' Catherine then made a splendid oration to the English captains, telling them 'that the Lord smiled upon those who stood in defence of their own', and they should remember that English courage excelled that of all other nations. The men were said to be 'fired by these words'. The Queen had even intended to go north herself, but before she could set out news was received of the colossal Scottish defeat at Flodden on 9 September. The flower of the Scottish nobility were among those lying dead on the battlefield and the King of Scots too was killed. The victory of Flodden removed the Scottish threat for a generation by this slaughter of its leaders; the eighteen-month-old James Prince of Scotland who now nominally succeeded to the throne was the nephew of the English King, the Regent was his sister, Margaret.

In contrast the Battle of the Spurs, although part of an expensive campaign, was forgotten the next year when the King abruptly turned his foreign policy on its head. For in 1514 King Henry, furious at King Ferdinand's cynical self-interest, executed a complete diplomatic volte-face. Turning his back on Spain, he began to negotiate for the union of his sister Princess Mary to the recently widowed King Louis XII of France. Their proxy marriage took place on 13

Portrait of the marriage in 1514 of Henry VIII's sister, Mary Tudor, to the elderly King Louis XII of France.

August 1514 and Catherine was among those who travelled to Dover in October to see Princess Mary off on her journey to her new country. Since Mary had been formally betrothed to Charles of Austria for the last six years it was hardly surprising that the Habsburg representatives spoke 'shamefully' of the marriage of 'so fair a lady' and 'so feeble, old and pocky a man'. The Princess

The marriage portrait of Mary Tudor and Charles Brandon (later Duke of Suffolk). Their wedding took place — without the consent of Henry VIII — in 1515, soon after the death of King Louis XII.

was eighteen her bridegroom fifty-two. He was to die on 1 January 1515 whereupon Mary promptly (and without her brother's consent) married the man she had fallen in love with before she left England — big, handsome, straightforward Charles Brandon, Duke of Suffolk.

What were the implications of this volte-face for Queen Catherine? The French match did not itself represent a diplomatic reverse: she had never argued publicly in favour of the pro-Aragonese alliance, but merely acted as the obvious conduit for negotiations between her husband and father. True, in the

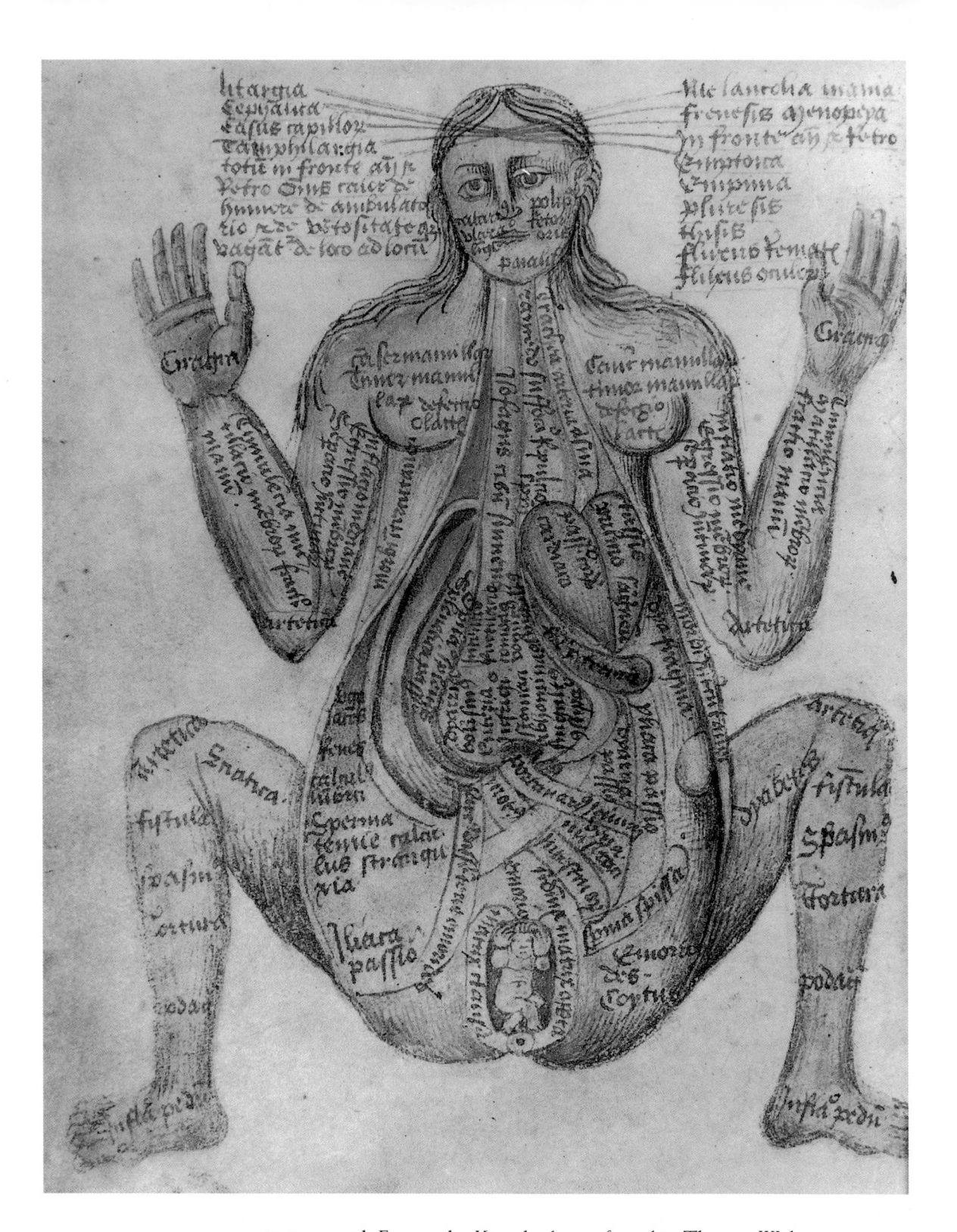

negotiations with France the King had now found in Thomas Wolsey a servant whose habits of industry matched his own pattern of work – energetic commands, restless execution – in a magical way. Furthermore Wolsey's origins as a butcher's son in Ipswich ensured that he owed everything to royal advancement.

But Wolsey did not at this point dictate policy and he did have – for good practical reasons – an excellent relationship with the Queen. Nor did the French alliance mark the end of Catherine's political closeness to the King, who continued demonstrably to value both her loyalty and her good sense.

In other ways their relationship showed every sign of prospering. It was true that the expected heir had not materialized. Yet the Queen's fertility was not in question: she conceived again in the spring of 1513, just before the King went to France, although she lost the baby in October. In early February 1515, as she told her father, she did give birth to a son at full term: a 'prince which lived not longer after'. Nevertheless it is important not to judge this tale of gynaecological woe by modern standards, let alone with any prejudicial knowledge of the end of the story. It has been estimated that in aristocratic families in England during this period only two out of every five births resulted in living children. With such high infant mortality, the ability to conceive was the important thing. And at the beginning of 1516 Catherine was looking forward to the birth of another child.

On 18 February 1516, at four o'clock in the morning, Queen Catherine gave birth to a daughter who was named Mary. The labour had been long and hard, although the Queen endeavoured to protect herself against the pangs of child-birth by clutching a holy relic – a girdle – of her patron saint. Whatever the sufferings of the mother, the baby herself was healthy, even robust. As at every royal birth at this time, a prince had been confidently expected. The arrival of a princess meant that celebrations were suitably scaled down. But King Henry was in buoyant mood. 'Sons will follow', he told the Venetian ambassador Giustinian, pointing out that 'the Queen and I are both young'. The King was glad and he was right to be so. There was indeed good cause for rejoicing at the birth of a daughter, leaving aside his not unreasonable prediction that sons would follow. Although he continued to hope for a Prince of Wales, King Henry undoubtedly now had a new and useful card to play in the game of European matrimonial alliances. We should take care to view Queen Catherine's successful delivery of a healthy princess as it was seen then – including by King Henry: as a piece of good, or at least promising news, from which important diplomatic consequences might flow. King Henry certainly needed every kind of diplomatic asset – a quiverful of princesses could have been employed – if he was to hold his own on behalf of England.

Queen Catherine never had the opportunity to tell her father that God had at last sent her a healthy child, albeit a daughter. The news of King Ferdinand's death on 23 January 1516 had in fact been kept from the Queen – and thus from public announcement at the English court – in case her grief start her labour prematurely. Although Catherine had not set eyes on her father for over fifteen years, he had occupied a primal place in her affections. Now symbolically enough, the birth of her own child had occurred within a few weeks of his death. Henceforward it was the young Princess Mary who would provide the

Opposite: A late fifteenth-century English illustration of a pregnant woman from a treatise entitled Diseases of Women. *Two of King Henry's wives were to die of complications following childbirth.*

focus for her mother's hopes and familial loyalties, while Catherine's sense of reverence for the Spanish royal house from which she had sprung transferred to her nephew, Charles of Austria.

In many ways the next few years were a time of satisfaction for Catherine. It was true that ambassadors no longer commented on her beauty – rather the reverse. One report went so far as to call her more 'ugly than otherwise'. 'Ugly' was certainly an exaggeration: her bright complexion continued to receive tributes. Another report, written much later, describing Catherine as 'if not handsome, certainly not ugly', was probably nearer the truth. Nevertheless, the Queen's numerous pregnancies had not helped her figure, always on the plump side. By now she was unquestionably quite fat, a stout little woman on the wrong side of thirty, compared with her glamorous, atheletic husband, six years her junior.

Queens however were not expected to be great beauties. Queens were expected to provide connections and a rich dowry on marriage, and carry out the functions of consort with requisite dignity thereafter. All this Queen Catherine did, and more. Her dignity was imperturbable. Even at the height of her troubles in the future she would be praised for having 'always a smile on her countenance'. At this date the particular flavour she imparted to the court, not

Opposite: Catherine of Aragon in middle age. By the second decade of her marriage the age gap between her and King Henry, six years her junior, began to attract attention.

Below: Portrait of Erasmus by Holbein. Erasmus wrote more letters to Catherine of Aragon than to any other woman.

only by her graciousness but by her learning and piety, excited general admiration. It was Erasmus who hailed the court of Henry VIII in 1519 as 'a model of Christian society, so rich in men of the highest attainments that any university might envy it'. The Queen's interest in and patronage of the learning termed 'humanism' was an important part of the process which formed this society, as the books dedicated to her indicated.

Basically humanism involved the use of the recently rediscovered classical texts to enhance religious appreciation, rather than obliterate faith. It proved of natural interest to both the King and the Queen since each was endowed with an excellent classical education, and also, in their different ways, a sincere desire to deepen their own spiritual understanding. Humanistic interests became the hallmark of many courtiers and scholars surrounding the

An engraving of Thomas Linacre, physician and humanist. Henry appointed him royal physician, and in his last months Linacre acted with the Spanish scholar Vives as tutor to Princess Mary.

royal couple, including Erasmus (who addressed more letters to Catherine than to any other woman), Thomas Linacre and Thomas More. The Queen's chamberlain, Lord Mountjoy, had been the pupil of Erasmus, and had maintained contact with him ever since while the Queen's physician, Dr Fernando Vittoria, was another humanist.

Erasmus indeed rated Queen Catherine's scholarship more highly than that of King Henry: her patronage, he believed, was more consistent. It is true that Catherine was more unrelievedly serious-minded. Henry in his twenties continued to enjoy every aspect of life, from the dance to the learned argument. The Queen in her thirties no longer danced – there are many references to her withdrawing early – although she played her official part fully at state banquets and in the reception of ambassadors. In 1520 Erasmus wrote in praise of the English court: 'What family of citizens offers so clear an example of strict and harmonious wedlock? Where could one find a wife more keen to equal her admirable spouse?'

The spectacle of a royal lady interesting herself in scholarship was not a novelty in England. In one sense Queen Catherine was merely continuing the tradition of her husband's grandmother, Margaret Beaufort Countess of Richmond: as one patroness died, another took her place. But if in one sense Catherine's patronage looked back to the late mediaeval tradition of Margaret Beaufort, in another it was very much of its own time: the brief, glittering period of the humanist court in England, whose short span should not consign it to obscurity. There were significant differences in the personal attainments of the two royal ladies. Margaret Beaufort, for all her large library of English and

French books, was no classical scholar: in fact she had never been taught
Latin and could only read the Latin
headings in her prayer book. And
when Margaret Beaufort interested
herself in the question of education –
in terms of learning – she was think-
ing of young gentlemen. Margaret
Beaufort, the mother of an only son,
never had any practical reason to
interest herself in the higher education of girls. But Queen Catherine
had to set about the important task of
educating a royal daughter. It was an
important distinction.

Like her interest in learning, the
Queen's piety increased with the
years, as happens to most people of a
natively religious temperament. Time
– and sorrow – would bring about a
religious routine which might by
many standards have been considered excessively severe. But the
Queen, who was for so many years
the cheerful consort and 'bedfellow'
of Henry VIII, initially had no need
of such austere practices, which were
brought on by later desolation. In the
contented years of their marriage,
Queen Catherine pleased her hus-
band rather than otherwise by her religious observance. Henry VIII was no
exception to the general rule that a pleasure-loving man is happy to have a
devout wife – provided she does not interfere with his pleasures. Royally born,
intelligent, pious and gracious, Queen Catherine incarnated in all ways but one
– the provision of a male heir – the ideal of the early sixteenth-century consort.

*Margaret Beaufort,
grandmother of Henry
VIII and an earlier
patron of education.*

*Overleaf: Illumination
from a Bible made for
Henry VIII and
Catherine of Aragon,
c. 1509. The emblems,
initials and arms of the
King and Queen can be
seen in the borders.*

CHAPTER 3

Without an Heir Male

The accession of François I to the throne of France in 1515 marked the beginning of an intense personal rivalry between the two young kings.

I N 1518 IT LOOKED as though Queen Catherine would remedy her single deficiency and present the King with an heir. Some time in the spring – probably in late February – she became pregnant again. The timing had a particular piquancy since on 28 February 1518 the French Queen presented her husband with a son, following the birth of two daughters. Outwardly, the King of England rejoiced and accepted the role of godfather. Inwardly the competi-

tive feelings he harboured concerning King François must have made him relieved that his own wife was pregnant again after a two-year gap. But there was of course another angle to the birth of a French prince, when an English princess of roughly the same age existed – the diplomatic one.

The proposed betrothal of the baby Dauphin to the two-year-old Princess Mary was the symbolic expression of a new accord between their respective countries, finally expressed in the Treaty of London of 4 October 1518. This accord was to be England's – or Wolsey's – answer to the Peace of Cambrai in March 1517 when the Emperor Charles and the King of France had agreed to go to each other's assistance if attacked – leaving England unpleasantly isolated. The timing of the Treaty of London the following year, signed during the late stages of Queen Catherine's pregnancy, is important because with the usual optimistic conviction that Catherine would shortly give birth to a healthy prince, Mary was not at this point

viewed as the heiress to the English throne.

The French alliance was Wolsey's dream, not the Queen's; he was now the King's closest confidant on matters of policy, as well as his assiduous servant. The Cardinal (as Wolsey had become in 1515) understood very well how to make his will work in harmony with the King's so that it was difficult at the time – and remains so – to decide how much these French initiatives sprang from the King, and how much they were sprung upon him. But clearly King Henry favoured the treaty as a way of getting back into the European game, while both King and Cardinal – and the French King – seem to have been genuine in their desire for a relaxation of hostilities. As to the Queen's position,

obviously her political prestige was greater when England was pursuing a pro-Spanish policy than when the mood was in favour of France, the hereditary enemy of her family. For the same reason, it was hardly her dearest wish to see her daughter married to a French prince: her Habsburg-Spanish nephew Charles was after all still the most eligible bachelor in Europe. Yet she too seems to have accepted the peaceful aims of the treaty as being genuine.

Then on 18 November tragedy struck. The 'prince' so confidently expected turned out to be a princess – and was born dead.

Privately the Queen's grief can only have been compounded by the fact that

Henry VIII was soon to become the father of an illegitimate son. The dashing Bessie Blount, one of the ladies of the court, had become pregnant by the King very shortly before her own sad experience. King Henry had known Bessie Blount for some years: she had been a girl-about-court since 1513 and a favoured royal dancing partner. Bessie Blount was exactly the type of girl described by Anthony Fitzherbert in *The Boke of Husbandrye* of 1523 as being most attractive to men: 'hard of words' yet 'merry of cheer', 'well paced' and 'easy to leap upon'.

Bessie's baby son was born at the beginning of June 1519. Catherine, with her usual composure, made no comment but instead attended (with the rest of the court) the festivities that the King arranged to celebrate the birth. The baby was given his father's Christian name and the traditional surname of a royal bastard which pointed proudly to his parentage. It was another mark of official favour that Cardinal Wolsey acted as Henry Fitzroy's godfather, just as he had acted as godfather to the baby's half-sister Mary nearly three and a half years earlier.

Whatever Catherine's private distress, in public terms the election of her nephew as the Emperor Charles V about the time of the birth of Henry Fitzroy at least meant that Spain was once more a potentially valuable ally. The extraordinary extent of the territorial sway of the new Emperor – virtually surrounding France – could not fail to threaten French interests, and at the same time affect the attitude of France's new ally, England. It was a situation that Queen Catherine was well placed to exploit. The French alliance sat uneasily with a great many of the English nobility; then there was the position of Princess Mary as the betrothed of the Dauphin. Although at the beginning of 1520 hopes of the Queen giving birth to a male heir had not yet been totally abandoned – Catherine was only thirty-four – at the same time Princess Mary was now her father's only living legitimate child. Matters had been different when the Treaty of London was concluded. To secure a meeting between her husband and her nephew now became a prime object of the Queen's diplomacy. It made perfect sense in family terms (she had still never met her sister's son) and it made sense also in terms of an Anglo-Spanish rapprochement, perhaps even some kind of closer family alliance.

The Queen's desire to bring about such a meeting became more acute as preparations for a splendiferous formal encounter between the official allies, the Kings of France and England, got under way. The Field of Cloth of Gold, as this majestic enterprise would be known to history, was the focus of an extraordinary amount of English artistic energy, coupled with English money, throughout the early months of 1520. At the same time the Queen bent her energies to persuading the Emperor to visit England en route from Spain, so that at least this Anglo-French jamboree would be to some extent neutralized. Queen Catherine did not manage to impede the mammoth court progress which started to lumber in the direction of France in late May. That was scarcely within her power; she acted as ever as the petitioner and as such knew her

The Field of Cloth of Gold by an unknown artist. The size of King Henry's retinue was officially estimated as just under 4,000 people and just over 2,000 horses.

limits. But by the same tactics she did secure the arrival of the Emperor Charles. The Emperor landed at Dover on 26 May, the last possible date before the English court embarked.

Catherine's political instincts proved correct: the brief meeting between the Emperor and the King of England was highly successful. The grave, rather clumsy boy, with his long chin and jutting Habsburg lower lip, whom she embraced with rapture on the outskirts of Canterbury, accompanied by a cavalcade of her ladies, presented a diffident air to his magnificent uncle. A long breakfast took place – a family breakfast at which not even Wolsey was present

— and the subject of the peace of Europe was discussed. It is quite possible —
although there is no record — that on this occasion the betrothal of Princess
Mary to her cousin Charles was also touched upon.

It is true that Mary was officially affianced to the Dauphin: but unbreakable
contracts had been known to melt away with remarkable suddenness when reasons of state demanded it. Charles himself had already been betrothed to two
French princesses and to the elder Mary Tudor whom he would now shortly
meet for the first time at a ball given for him at Canterbury. Otherwise the most
conspicuous feature of the visit was the modesty and respect that he maintained

59

towards King Henry. By going further and referring to Henry as his 'good father', Charles V struck a yet more welcome note. Henry agreed to a further meeting with the young Emperor, this time on the other side of the Channel, following the Field of Cloth of Gold.

Compared with the Emperor's perfect manners, King François' behaviour towards Henry VIII proved a good deal less satisfactory. It was certainly not deferential. How could it be? And indeed why should it be? With some reason,

Queen Claude of France (centre) with Eleanor of Austria and three of the French princesses. An illustration from the Hours of Catherine de Medici.

François was extremely suspicious of King Henry's imperial involvement. They were two sovereigns, two energetic and competitive men in their late twenties – in their prime, one might say – who were equals. And as such they were inevitably rivals. The ballyhoo surrounding the Field of Cloth of Gold should not distract attention from the fact that this was an enormously expensive party which not everybody enjoyed (as is the case with many enormously expensive parties). Queen Catherine was surely among those who did not relish the experience. However, clothed in all the hieratic glory of her rich garments, precious jewels and pearls (which were voted the finest of all), with a Spanish headdress over her famous, still abundant, long hair, she played her part. If King Henry was dining with Queen Claude, then you might be sure that at that very moment Queen Catherine was entertaining King François, sitting opposite him under a costly canopy at Guines. When the two kings were in conclave, then the two Queens were busy paying each other visits, or, on one occasion, praying together at Mass. It was convenient for Queen Catherine who no longer cared to dance that Queen Claude, although many years younger, was also unable to dance. Convenient but also poignant: for at the age of twenty-one the French Queen was heavily laden with her fifth pregnancy.

There were a few unscheduled happenings, some of which went off more successfully than others. When King François decided to pay a surprise visit – in disguise – to Queen Catherine, this veteran of King Henry's boyish pranks was well able to cope with the situation. She had no difficulty in recognizing him and no difficulty either in graciously pretending not to do so. When King François paid a similar unexpected visit to King Henry, however, the outcome was less fortunate. 'Come, you shall wrestle with me', Henry suddenly called to the French King. It was a challenge that no English courtier would have declined; but, like Queen Catherine, the courtiers would also have known exactly how to behave. King François, however, proceeded to throw his brother of England heavily to the ground. The incident was glossed over but it was one of those seemingly unimportant little moments that linger in the memory. It all ended on 24 June with protestations of undying friendship. But François

would go on to use his gorgeously ornamented pavilions and encrusted tents for his military wars; while King Henry set off to Calais to meet his nephew the Emperor for the second time.

There Charles, mercifully not interested in boisterous wrestling games, continued to display that delightful filial obeisance which had so pleased his uncle. Besides, there was business to be done – or at least discussed. With a duplicity that was perfectly commonplace Henry allowed the leisurely talks concerning the marital fate of his daughter Mary to continue, for all her betrothal to the Dauphin; just as his father had discussed Henry's own marriage to Eleanor of Austria, notwithstanding his proxy marriage to Catherine of Aragon. The possibility of a Spanish marriage for her daughter was a great deal more welcome to Catherine than what had recently transpired on the sumptuous Field of Cloth of Gold. Her political star was rising again.

In the early 1520s, insidiously, the succession question began to permeate the politics of the English court. Giving up hope of conception is, after all, an insidious process in itself. But optimism about the birth of a future 'prince' gradually waned after 1518. The court, the King, and perhaps last of all the Queen, began to face reality: Henry VIII did not have, and was not likely to have, a legitimate male heir. It was a situation to arouse atavistic uneasiness in a country where memories of civil unrest, rebellions by claimants to the throne had by no means died away. There were obvious, if unspoken, fears concerning the King's way of life – he was never cautious about physical risks, hunting and jousting as energetically as ever. Given that his daughter suffered from the double handicap of being both female and a child, who was to succeeed him in the event of some accident? Then there was the more discussable question of the succession following the King's death in the fullness of time.

The very different dynastic maelstrom of the 1530s should not blind us to the fact that in the 1520s the solution sought always involved Princess Mary and her putative husband. It is an important point to grasp for it demonstrates how committed the King was during these years to finding this solution within his long-established marriage to a Queen he respected, if he had not loved her in any romantic sense for many years: a Queen who also happened to be the aunt of the all-powerful Emperor.

At the beginning of 1521 Princess Mary was still technically betrothed to the Dauphin. More and more, however, King Henry leaned towards what he regarded, understandably, as a more magnificent destiny: her marriage to her first cousin the Emperor Charles V. The enthusiasm of the Queen in this respect fell upon fertile ground. The single previous example of female succession in English history was that of Henry I settling his dominions on his daughter Matilda when civil war with Matilda's cousin Stephen had followed. What was, however, incontrovertible was the fact that the eventual succession had gone to Mathilda's son and Henry I's grandson, Henry II. Now Henry VIII began to encourage dreams of his grandson, the child of Mary and Charles V, who would preside over a large proportion of the Old World, including England, and a great deal of the so-called New World across the seas.

Negotiations for Princess Mary's splendid match proceeded apace, affording both the King and the Queen much happiness. In August Cardinal Wolsey, at Bruges, negotiated the marriage treaty as part of the 'Great Enterprise' by which Henry and Charles were to make war against François. The wording made it clear that at least the possibility that Princess Mary would succeed her father was being envisaged even though dowry arrangements were, as ever, fiercely discussed: 'Should, however, the King of England die without an heir male, and the Princess Mary become Queen of England, the Emperor elect is not entitled to any marriage portion.'

One of the earliest portraits of Mary Tudor, the only surviving child of Henry VIII and Catherine of Aragon.

In the meantime the visit of Charles V to England in June 1522 – his second to the country, his third meeting with Henry VIII – constituted a triumphant occasion for Queen Catherine. (She could hardly have anticipated that it was to be the last purely enjoyable public occasion in her life.) The Emperor arrived with a train of 2,000 courtiers and 1,000 horse at Dover where the King greeted him and showed him his ships, which the Emperor sedulously praised. The

Queen awaited them at Greenwich. There on 2 June this great Emperor knelt to Catherine and asked her blessing: 'for that is the fashion of Spain between Aunt and Nephew'. Queen Catherine knew that the two of them were joined – as she put it later – not only by consanguinity, but also by 'love'.

Furthermore this omnipotent prince was one day to become the husband of the little girl brought to Greenwich to meet him. At the age of six Princess Mary presented her fiancé with gifts of horses and hawks. For his part, he viewed her 'with great joy'. Following the Emperor's visit, the language of the English, including that of Cardinal Wolsey, makes it clear that the idea of the marriage became even more attractive with the passing of time. Above all, the dream grandson, ruling over Europe, was to be the 'magnificent compensation' to Henry VIII for his son-less state. Henry now habitually spoke of Charles as his son, and it was specially fortunate that Charles V had no living father to

compete with Henry's claims to be his *'bon père'*. Charles V responded in kind. On 10 May 1522, for example, he promised to do all he could for Henry VIII: 'as much as a good son should do for a father'.

For Catherine the imperial marriage promised much and threatened nothing. It certainly aroused no fears of national extinction in her breast. This was not only on account of her own Spanish blood, but also because she had grown up in the firm belief that the marriage of a queen to a king – Isabella of Castile to Ferdinand of Aragon – brought felicitous unity in its wake. Why should not the union of Mary of England and Charles of Spain do the same? Neither the Queen nor the King seem to have paid much thought to the sixteen-year difference in age between the bridal couple, although it might have occurred to them that Charles V's practical need for an heir would make the waiting period rather long. Princess Mary's twelfth birthday (the minimum age of cohabitation supposing the girl was physically mature) was not until February 1528. Queen Catherine dismissed such thoughts in favour of educating her daughter to be Queen of Spain, as once Isabella had educated her to be Queen of England.

In general, this took the form of supervision and appointment of teachers rather than direct teaching. They did, however, study Latin together, since after Mary was sent to Wales, the Queen referred to it in a letter: 'As for your writing in Latin, I am glad that you shall change from me to Master Federston,

Juan Vives, the Spanish philosopher whom Catherine of Aragon consulted about the education of her daughter.

Mary Boleyn, Anne's elder sister. Mary briefly became Henry's mistress in about 1520 and then married William Carey, a gentleman of the Privy Chamber.

for that shall do you much good to learn by him to write aright'. Rather wistfully, the Queen asked Mary sometimes to pass on her exercises when Federston had corrected them: 'For it shall be a great comfort to me to see you keep your Latin and fair writing and all.' The scholar the Queen chiefly consulted, the humanist Juan Luis Vives, was a Spaniard like herself, although he had been educated in France and had lived in Flanders. Vives' book *The Instruction of a Christian Woman* was dedicated to Catherine. In his preface, Vives explained that he was moved to write it 'by the favour, love and zeal that your Grace beareth to holy study and learning.'

Quite apart from its relevance to Princess Mary, this is an important document. For one thing, its emphasis on the need for real (classical) learning in any female likely to face responsibility – including the upbringing of children – demonstrates the trend introduced into England by the Renaissance princess, Catherine. Vives denied that learning had ever made women 'cunning' (i.e. wicked) and appended a long list of learned women from history, all of impeccable character. He concluded the list, naturally, with the 'chaste' but well-educated daughters of Queen Isabella. If it is not absolutely certain that Vives taught Princess Mary personally – it may be that his precepts were merely passed on by Thomas Linacre who did – it is clear that the princess was brought up to value her own intellect.

However at the same time Vives' work reveals the extremely low estimate of the moral nature of women – their sheer inferiority to men – which was current at the time, even among male scholars who believed in their education. Vives wrote eloquently of the need for female obedience, and, even more, for female silence. Woman, he wrote was 'a frail thing, and of weak discretion, and may be lightly deceived, which thing our first mother Eve sheweth whom the Devil caught with a light argument'. This should not be regarded as Spanish intransigence: it was a universal attitude. And such an attitude subtly but steadily affected the whole question of female succession: was one of these inferior creatures to be allowed to rule over a nation of men? Women were not intended to rule. When God worked mysteriously in allowing a woman to inherit a throne, the obvious answer was to install a man – a husband, a protector – at her side; hence the concentration on a suitable bridegroom for Princess Mary.

In 1524 Catherine commissioned a work on the subject of marriage from Erasmus via her chamberlain Lord Mountjoy. This has sometimes been interpreted as a gesture of despair over her husband's infidelity. It was more likely to have been an intellectual interest of her own and a help to the preparation of her daughter, for whom marriage certainly lay ahead. When King Henry replaced Bessie Blount (now married) with a young woman called Mary Boleyn, Catherine gave no outward sign of annoyance. At the end of her royal fling Mary Boleyn married – on 4 February 1521 – a gentleman of the Privy Chamber called William Carey. The Queen attended the wedding festivities, just as she had graced the celebrations for the birth of Henry Fitzroy.

The affair with Mary Boleyn was to have unlooked-for consequences, given that sexual intercourse as well as marriage created an affinity between two

Henry VIII's writing desk, made from painted walnut and gilt leather depicted the royal coat of arms and badges of Henry VIII and Catherine of Aragon.

people: in the case of two sisters, in the first degree collateral. At the time the affair seemed only to repeat the pattern established by Bessie Blount: here once again was a vivacious young girl, an energetic dancer and masker, taking the fancy of a man with an older, more serious-minded, wife. Both Bessie and Mary Boleyn were among the maids of honour at court; there seemed no reason why King Henry should not continue to take his pick from among these willing young women, confident of the resigned acceptance of his Queen.

Presents continued to come from the Emperor in Spain to signify his serious intentions: two mules with crimson velvet trappings and marvellous garnishing of silver and gilt for King Henry, and mules with equally rich trappings but 'after the Spanish fashion', for the Queen. Catherine went on writing lovingly to her nephew and future son-in-law. (He did not answer.) But to the King and Wolsey the manoeuvrability of Princess Mary was like a valuable golden coin: further bargaining with it would not affect its value, so long as it was not actually given away. In this manner, serious negotiations began between the English and Scots for a very different union: that of Mary and her first cousin on her father's side, the young James V, King of Scots. At Christmas 1524 the imperial ambassador, noting the Scots ambassadors at the English court, enquired pointedly where this left the imperial treaty. Both the King and Wolsey assured him that they had no intention of breaking the alliance: the game was simply to prevent James V from marrying a French princess. And that seems to have been the truth.

It was the Emperor, not King Henry, who was about to break his word. Charles V's colossal victory over the French at Pavia in northern Italy on 24 February 1525 only increased the English King's lust for the alliance. News of

Isabella of Portugal, niece of Catherine of Aragon, became the wife of Charles V in 1526. Portrait by Titian.

the victory reached London on 9 March, early in the morning, in the form of a triumphant missive from the Archduchess Margaret, describing how 'the whole power of France' had been 'discomfited'. The casualties were enormous and the French King was himself captured. Queen Catherine cried out in ecstasy at the news. She wrote to her nephew on 30 March to congratulate him, blaming 'the inconstancy and fickleness of the sea' for the fact that she had not received any letters from him in reply to her own. A more hurtful explanation was to hand, but she rejected that, while admitting that 'nothing would be so painful as to think that your Highness had forgotten . . . your good aunt Caterina.' For the past three years the thought of her daughter's Spanish marriage had been a lodestar, shedding a brilliant guiding light on a life that was otherwise drifting into a melancholy middle age.

Yet the truth was that for some time the composed and secretive Emperor had been turning away from the English project. He needed a wife who could satisfy his Cortes and pacify his Spanish subjects; he needed a large dowry; and lastly, he needed a wife sooner rather than later, so that he could set about procreating a family. His eventual choice fell upon another first cousin: Isabella of

Henry VIII by Lucas Hornebolte, c. 1525.

67

Portugal, daughter of Catherine's sister Maria. Charles V was betrothed to Isabella officially in July 1525, having withdrawn from the English match in May, and married her the following year. Isabella was intelligent, mature and sensible; to crown it all she soon presented Charles V with a male heir (the future Philip II). From the Emperor's point of view, Isabella of Portugal represented an excellent choice.

Matters were a good deal less happy from the point of view of King Henry and Queen Catherine. Regardless of the fact that poor Catherine felt herself quite as betrayed as King Henry (where was that love and consanguinity which bound aunt and nephew so closely together?), the King's terrible frown now turned in the direction of his wife. Indeed, the behaviour of Henry VIII following the Emperor's abandonment of the marriage treaty shows a new aspect of his character: a tendency to lash out when thwarted – not necessarily in the direction of the guilty party – but with the object of relieving his own pent-up wrath.

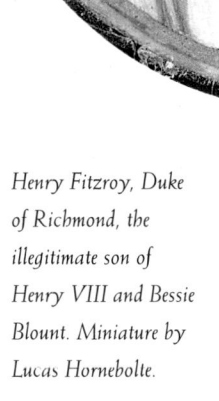

Henry Fitzroy, Duke of Richmond, the illegitimate son of Henry VIII and Bessie Blount. Miniature by Lucas Hornebolte.

Shortly after he heard of the Emperor's defection, King Henry suddenly arranged the public exaltation of his six-year-old illegitimate son, Henry Fitzroy. This exaltation was to be in two parts. The first ceremony, which took place on 7 June 1525, had to do with Henry Fitzroy's installation as a Knight of the Garter: in St George's Chapel at Windsor he was given the second stall on the sovereign's side. Catherine of Aragon watched from the 'Queen's closet', decorated with her pomegranate badges, overlooking the high altar. Two weeks later the little boy was created Duke of Richmond. Letters patent gave Richmond precedence over all the dukes already created or to be created in the future – except those born legitimately of the King's body, or the body of his legitimate heirs. Large estates were settled on the new duke, and in addition he was made Lord High Admiral, Lieutenant-General North of the Trent and Warden of All the Marches towards Scotland. To the north Henry Duke of Richmond would now go, to be brought up in the elaborate state commensurate with his position.

Queen Catherine was furious. Since all her hopes for the future were now concentrated on her lawfully conceived daughter, she could hardly fail to feel mortified at this celebration of the male bastard. Yet in the past she had swallowed similar insults: the public festivities at Henry Fitzroy's birth, for example, less than a year after her own child had been stillborn. Now there was a difference. The Queen, after years of dealing with her husband by diplomatic methods of outward submission, displayed open resentment, making it clear that she was strongly dissatisfied.

How far was the Queen's indignation justified? The first thing one should note is that her anger recalls the hysterical letters of her unhappy youth as Princess of Wales. Her health was not good now, as it had not been then, and it may be that the Queen simply felt too ill to maintain her usual dignified serenity, that much-praised smiling countenance. At the same time, the very fact that the Queen did lose control is in itself proof that the timing of the two ceremonies was deliberate and that she knew it. She was being punished for the treachery of her family.

That still leaves the question of what King Henry actually intended by the elevation of his son. He certainly did not intend the immediate demotion of his daughter Mary. There was one report that the King granted Richmond precedence over 'everybody', but since future 'Dukes' who would be the King's lawful issue were to take precedence over Richmond, according to the deed of creation, Mary's position was clearly not affected. On the contrary the King made a further move to treat Mary as 'Princess of Wales'. She had been tacitly treated as Princess (or Prince) of Wales by outsiders, although never formally given the title.

Now Princess Mary was sent to Ludlow, capital of the Marches of Wales, as titular administrator of the Welsh kingdom, even as Arthur Prince of Wales had been despatched. She was given a magnificent household – 165 people with a total of over 300 catered for – suitable to a Prince of Wales. Princess Mary thus had both the substance and, informally, the style of 'my lady prince's grace', as the title accorded by her Council. To many people, untroubled by the exaltation of the illegitimate son, Princess Mary's removal to Wales was further proof of her eventual succession. For all the Queen's distress at her departure, she recognized the duty of a princess. Mary, by being constituted her father's delegate (as the new Duke of Richmond was similarly established in the north), was following in the tradition

Catherine of Aragon painted by Lucas Hornebolte.

Edward Stafford, Duke of Buckingham. He was descended from Edward III and was the most prominent adult male of royal descent after the King. As Henry became increasingly obsessed with the question of his succession, so he became increasingly paranoid about any possible rival. Buckingham was executed in May 1521.

by which English kings ruled through the ceremonial installation of their off-spring. This was at least a recognition of her daughter's status.

The autumn of 1525 saw the King and Queen reconciled. The Queen's health got better, as she told Princess Mary in a letter. Of the Princess, it was reported to Wolsey that she was 'of her age as good a child as ever I have seen, and of as good gesture and countenance'. As her fortieth birthday passed on 16 December 1525 Queen Catherine looked forward to a tranquil life of ever greater piety, even more pilgrimages. And then something happened to pull down this carefully constructed and, not totally unhappy, world around her ears. In the spring of 1526 the King fell in love.

PART II

ANNE
BOLEYN

CHAPTER 4

The Dart of Love

THE OBJECT OF the King's affections was a graceful, black-eyed girl called Anne Boleyn. She was born around 1500 or 1501, probably at Blickling in Norfolk where she certainly spent part of her childhood; her actual birthday seems to have been at the end of May or in early June. Therefore in the spring of 1526 Anne Boleyn was probably twenty-five or twenty-six. With her ancestry we are on firmer ground. The family into which she was born was not one of the grandest, but it was by no means inferior. Later it became fashionable to laugh at her self-invented pedigree, but that mockery was the product of the violent jealousy Anne Boleyn would arouse on many different levels. In reality, Anne Boleyn was well-born enough to make a claim that she was 'descent of right noble and high thorough regal blood' perfectly legitimate, and only a slightly partial picture. Among her great-grandfathers she could number a duke and an earl – as well as a self-made man, Sir Geoffrey Boleyn, a wealthy mercer who became Lord Mayor of London in 1457.

Hever Castle in Kent, the home of the Boleyn family.

It is, however, to the character and accomplishments of Anne Boleyn's father, Thomas, that we must look for the most important influence on her career. He was a remarkable man. Thomas Boleyn was born in 1477, making him fourteen years older than Henry VIII. He made an advantageous marriage to Lady Elizabeth Howard, eldest daughter of Thomas Howard, 2nd Duke of Norfolk and his appearances at court went back to the marriage of Prince Arthur and Princess Catherine in 1501; he had escorted the then Princess Margaret to Scotland in 1503 to marry James IV. He was Squire of the Body at the funeral

Thomas Boleyn, father of Mary and Anne. Drawing by Holbein.

of Henry VII, and was knighted at the new King's coronation. He was an expert jouster and took part in the 1511 tournament to celebrate the birth of the ill-fated baby Prince Henry. Thomas Boleyn also had a remarkable talent that set him apart from most of his contemporaries. This was a talent for languages, and thus, by extension, for diplomacy.

It was as a result of his first mission, to the court of Archduchess Margaret, that Sir Thomas Boleyn was able to arrange for his younger daughter Anne to be educated there. She was then about twelve or thirteen, the minimum age for a *fille d'honneur*. An undated letter from the Archduchess Margaret to Anne's father sings her praises – 'I find her so presentable and so pleasant, considering her youthful age, that I am more beholden to you for sending her to me, than you to me … ' Even allowing for the politeness of princes, the excellent impression made by the young Anne Boleyn does much to explain why her father made the effort to send her in the first place. Anne Boleyn at thirteen was quite old enough to have demonstrated a particular brightness, sufficient to convince him that here was a child worth backing – some kind of star, in terms of parental hopes. She

Detail from a sixteenth-century French tapestry of a nobleman hawking in a forest. Anne Boleyn eagerly joined Henry VIII on his hunting and hawking expeditions.

was, for example, of a very different character from her giddy sister Mary; far more intelligent and far more applied.

From the household of the Archduchess Margaret, in 1514 Anne Boleyn transferred to that of the King's sister Mary 'the French Queen', and thus she went to France where she joined her own sister Mary. The manner of Anne's transfer is not clear since only Mary Boleyn would return with 'the French Queen', now Duchess of Suffolk, to England the following year after the death of Louis XII. Anne stayed on in the household of the new French Queen, Claude, and remained in France for the next six or seven years. She may well have been present at the Field of Cloth of Gold. She became, in effect, a Frenchwoman, or one who would be regarded as such by an English court, already predisposed to be dazzled by all things French, from clothes to manners. She also conceived a great love of things French, not only the language, which she could speak 'ornately and plain', but French poetry and music.

It is true that there were other less agreeable aspects of the French court: the lechery of King François, for example, was of a very different degree from the mild, jolly affairs indulged in by King Henry. The household of his wife Queen Claude to which Anne was attached was, however – perhaps predictably under the circumstances – extremely strict. Certainly Anne Boleyn learnt the art of pleasing at the French court, but it was the art of pleasing by her wit and accomplishments – sophisticated conversation, rallying remarks, flirtatious allusions, these were her weapons; there was courtly promise, perhaps, but no question of fulfilment. When Anne Boleyn returned to England there were then no louche whispers surrounding her name.

Anne Boleyn's recall to England, around 1521, concerned her marriage. Although she was by now about twenty, there was no urgency in terms of her age: only great heiresses were married off in extreme youth and the Boleyn girls were certainly not heiresses. It was a question of solving a tricky dispute over the Butler-Ormonde inheritance after the death of her great-grandfather, the Earl of Ormonde, in 1515. The old earl had died without a son and left his two daughters Lady Margaret Boleyn (Anne's paternal grandmother) and Lady Anne St Leger as co-heiresses. The title itself was claimed by a distant cousin, Sir Piers Butler, who became the 8th Earl but certain properties were disputed between Sir Thomas Boleyn and Sir Piers Butler, while Sir Thomas had by no means given up on claiming the Ormonde title itself. Since the son of Sir Piers was roughly the same age as Anne Boleyn, the marriage of the young couple appeared an equitable solution. While the matter was sorted out, Anne Boleyn was placed in the household of Queen Catherine as a maid of honour. Her first recorded appearance at court was at a masque on 1 March 1522.

What did she look like, the girl who danced at that masque? We must obviously discount venemous propaganda: stories of a goitre disfiguring her neck and a grotesque array of moles or warts (wens). Such a monstrosity would hardly have won the love of a king. She did have a few moles, although she was hardly disfigured by them; on the contrary they acted as beauty spots. But Anne Boleyn was not a great beauty. The Venetian ambassador pronounced her, 'not one of the handsomest women in the world'. One of her favourite chaplains gave the opinion that Bessie Blount was better looking; Anne Boleyn was only considered moderately pretty.

Some of this lukewarm praise may have been due to the fact that her looks did not accord with the fair-haired, blue-eyed ideal of the time. In theory, dark looks were regarded with suspicion and Anne Boleyn's looks were conspicuously dark. Beautifying lotions involved the whitening of the skin and the lightening of the hair, by the use of such diverse preparations as nettle-seed, cinnabar, ivy leaves, saffron and sulphur. It would have taken a great deal of saffron and sulphur to lighten Anne Boleyn's olive complexion. Her hair, thick and lustrous as it might be, was also extremely dark and her eyes were so dark as to be almost black. But then the theory of public admiration was one thing – blondes were supposed to be of cheerful temperament – and the practice of physical attraction was quite another. Clearly Anne Boleyn exercised a kind of sexual fascination over most men who met her; whether it aroused desire or hostility, the fascination was there.

Anne Boleyn was of 'middling stature' and she seems to have been quite slight or at any rate not full breasted – the Venetian ambassador remarked that her bosom was 'not much raised' (fashion made the 'trussing' of breasts up high another preoccupation). Possibly Anne Boleyn did have a vestigial sixth finger on her left hand, which understandably she took some pains to conceal. But a much more important aspect of her appearance was her elegant long neck; this together with the deportment she had learned in France – 'your ivory neck is raised upright', wrote a panegyrist – gave her a special grace, especially when dancing.

The projected Butler marriage did not prosper but meanwhile Anne Boleyn became involved in a romantic relationship with the young Henry Lord Percy, heir to great estates and an ancient name, whose own betrothal – to Lady Mary Talbot – had also foundered. Their dangerous love affair took place against the background of the Queen's household and the danger at this point, of course, lay in the fact that Lord Percy was one of the most eligible bachelors in England whereas Anne Boleyn (with a brother to inherit her father's wealth) was no kind of heiress. Percy began by going to the Queen's chamber 'for his recreation' and ended by being deeply enamoured of Anne, an affection which she returned. According to Cavendish, Cardinal Wolsey's gentleman-usher who wrote his master's life, it was Wolsey who put a stop to the romance – hence Anne Boleyn's subsequent hatred of him – at the request of the King (whose motive was said to be his own predatory intentions).

Cavendish was wrong to ascribe royal opposition to the match to the King's own lustful feelings (1522 is much too early for this). But what is important about Cavendish's account is his suggestion of a precontract. According to him, Anne and Lord Percy 'were ensured together'. There is other evidence too that something of this sort took place. Lord Percy was hastily married off to Lady Mary Talbot, a marriage which – perhaps predictably – proved unhappy. According to Lady Percy in 1532 her husband had told her he had been precontracted to Anne Boleyn – which would have made their own marriage invalid. As we shall see, there was a degree of official nervousness over Anne Boleyn's marital status in the testing early years of her relationship with Henry VIII – had she or had she not been precontracted?

There was another liaison too. Anne Boleyn's premarital relationship with Sir Thomas Wyatt is a more nebulous affair. There are clues in his poetry (whose significance has been hotly debated), but no solid evidence as to its exact

nature, beyond the fact that he was briefly imprisoned in the Tower at the time of her fall, but did not forfeit the King's favour thereafter. But by 1520 Wyatt was already married. Even though he was separated from his wife, he was in no sense an eligible match. Whatever the extent of his romance with Anne Boleyn, it belonged to the important but separate tradition of courtly love: conventional, if ardent poetical professions, not the more down-to-earth world of the marriage market.

The King's love of Anne Boleyn started with great suddenness, most probably in the jovial atmosphere of Shrovetide 1526. Henry was now in his thirty-fifth year – a dangerous age, it might be thought – and he had been married to Catherine of Aragon for seventeen years. But although middle-aged by the standards of the time, the King remained capable of boyish enthusiasm and what he at least felt to be boyish desire. He was still energetic, still handsome, his build still athletic rather than corpulent. Yet for all Henry's fresh vigour, he no longer bore any real relation to the secluded youth who had fallen in love

One of the passionate love letters that Henry VIII wrote to Anne Boleyn. This one begins: 'Mine own sweetheart, this shall be to advertise you of the great elengness [loneliness] that I find here since your departing...'.

with Catherine. That Henry had long ago vanished – except perhaps in the Queen's tender memories. Here was a confident, and at times ruthless sovereign, who regarded it as his natural right to have his own way in all things.

The violence of Henry VIII's passion for his wife's lady-in-waiting is attested by the sequence of love letters that he wrote to her. All are handwritten. Indeed, their very existence is a proof of passion, since the King greatly disliked writing letters and very few other handwritten letters of his have survived, with the exception of brief notes to Wolsey. But Anne Boleyn's absence from court from time to time, for a variety of reasons, proved intolerable and drove him to his pen. There are seventeen letters altogether; none of them is dated. Although various internal references help to place the letters in some kind of order, this can only be approximate. Nine are written in French, probably as a security precaution since few Englishmen enjoyed the fluency in the language possessed by both Henry and Anne. The King's letters mysteriously ended up in the Vatican Library in Rome (where they surfaced in the late seventeenth century and still are today) while Anne Boleyn's replies have disappeared. No doubt – again for reasons of security – the King destroyed them.

A miniature gold whistle belonging to Anne Boleyn, and believed to be the first present given to her by Henry VIII. Such trinkets were sewn onto his pageant clothes.

Yet for all their textual and dating difficulties, the letters do clarify an important point beyond the mere existence of the King's passion. These are the letters of a lover who aspires to his 'mistress's' favours – the word did not then necessarily have a sexual connotation, rather a courtly one – but has not yet received them: the pleas of a suitor. In a letter written when Henry had, by his own account, been 'for more than a year, struck with the dart of love', he describes himself as having been poring over Anne's own letters with 'a great agony, not knowing how to understand them'. He beseeches her to let him know her true intentions. He is still not yet sure whether he will fail in his quest 'or find a place in your heart and affection'.

Of course the King's love did not remain secret for long. It was true that the courtly conventions of the time – where the relationship of 'mistress' and 'servant' might be playful rather than sexual – did help to mask what was really going on. If the King paid court to a maid of honour, chose her for her dancing, no one could be absolutely sure at first whether she was another Bessie Blount in the making. But this state of affairs could not last long. Anne Boleyn was after all a member of the Queen's household. The cramped conditions, the lack of privacy must be stressed; then there was the acute interest inevitably felt by the courtiers (and ambassadors) in every aspect of their sovereign's life.

And Anne Boleyn, capricious fascinating 'Brunet', was not to be another Bessie Blount, let alone another Mary Boleyn, quickly, easily seduced, pedestrianly married off thereafter. At some point, the exact moment of which can never be known for certain, but it occurred some little time before May 1527, the King had decided that it was God's will that he should have, as it were, a second chance in life. His conscience told him that he should get rid of his first 'wife' (to whom, it transpired, he had never really been married) and procreate a new family with the aid of a 'fresh young damsel'.

Although the word divorce is generally used concerning the King's 'great matter', what he actually sought was not a divorce in the modern sense of the word, which recognizes that a marriage has taken place before splitting it in two. He wanted a declaration that his marriage was invalid (in modern parlance an annulment). This would mean not only that Henry was unmarried in 1527 but that he had never been married in 1509. Catherine's status would once more be that of the widow of his brother Arthur – as it always should have been, according to this agreement.

Divorce was by no means such an unthinkable prospect, nor such an uncommon occurrence then as is sometimes supposed. Looking no further than Henry VIII's own family, we find that both his sisters were involved in somewhat murky marriage arrangements. Among the English nobility, it has been observed that the repudiation of a wife was a 'nearly daily occurrence'. If the nobles in question were not to have their wives killed, but nevertheless needed to get rid of them for financial or philoprogenitive reasons, they had no option but to discover some flaw in the original marriage contract. Some awkward affinity, some hitherto unsuspected precontract, some incorrectly framed dispensation sufficed to end the unwelcome union.

The dramatic consequences of the divorce of Henry VIII from Catherine of Aragon – its relationship to the English Protestant Reformation – have tended to mask the fact that such a divorce might well have gone through comparatively painlessly if certain circumstances had been different. One of these circumstances was undoubtedly the domination which Catherine's nephew Charles V exercised over the papacy. But the coincidence of two women of unexpectedly iron character on the scene – Anne Boleyn as well as Catherine of Aragon – was another.

The exact moment when the King began to be afflicted by the scruples of conscience concerning his marriage to Catherine which caused him to question its validity can only be estimated. Afterwards, various official explanations were given for these scruples, none of them particularly satisfactory. Let us suppose

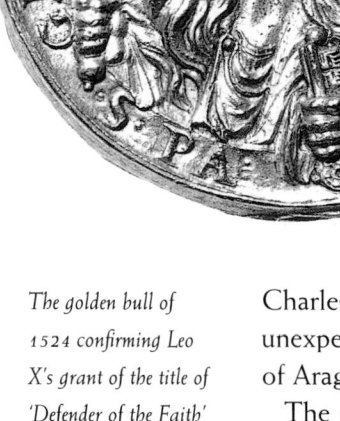

The golden bull of 1524 confirming Leo X's grant of the title of 'Defender of the Faith' to Henry VIII.

that the real beginning of it all was like this: that the King's dissatisfaction with his son-less state, dulled into acceptance over the years, flared up again in view of his passion for the young (and presumably nubile) Anne Boleyn.

Much has been made of Anne Boleyn's denial of her sexual favours to the King and his consequent frustration which led him to jettison his marriage – and a good many other things as well – in order to achieve consummation. Certainly she did not allow the King to make love to her (fully) for several years after he first began to pursue her, although 'liberties' of an increasingly intimate nature were probably allowed to the King. Some form of *coitus interruptus* seems indicated: with the interruption occurring at an increasingly late stage of the proceedings.

Much later the King would be said to explain his passion by reference to sorcery: he had been bewitched by Anne Boleyn. That was not literally true. She was not a witch – whatever malicious tongues would pretend – and cast no spells and devised no potions to capture the King's love. But in another sense Henry VIII was bewitched: not only by Anne's youth, grace, and liveliness, but by the promise she offered of a proper fertile marriage (with sons to follow him – like François I and Charles V); somehow he had been robbed of this. Anne Boleyn's personal role is attested by the timing: the crucial fact that the King had never contemplated divorce before he fell in love with her. Up to the mid-1520s, King Henry's attempts to marry Princess Mary to some kind of alternative successor are incompatible with a plan for a divorce from her mother. Yet within a year of being struck by the 'dart of love' fired by Anne Boleyn's black eyes, King Henry was taking an active part in the struggle to heave off the coils of his first marriage.

If falling in love was the first step, the King's second step was his recourse to Leviticus. This explicitly stated that what he had done in marrying Catherine was against the law of God: 'And if a man shall take his brother's wife, it is an unclean thing'. The penalty was also spelt out explicitly: 'they shall be childless'. The importance of Leviticus was that it chimed, immediately and absolutely, with the King's resentment on the subject of his marriage to Catherine – newly aroused by his relationship with Anne. God had punished him by not giving him what he wanted – a son – so that he, Henry, must have somehow transgressed. The dictates of the King's conscience and the dictates of the King's desire thus happily joined together. Both told him to get rid of Queen Catherine.

Unfortunately Queen Catherine was equally certain in her own conviction that she had been lawfully married to King Henry. Her marriage to Prince Arthur had not been consummated; she had been the virgin bride of Henry VIII; she was now his wife of many years' standing (and the mother of his only legitimate child). Through all the gyrations of popes, ecclesiastical lawyers, churchmen, nobles, politicians in London, in Spain, in Paris, in Bruges, in Brussels, at Rome, every conceivable argument would be offered for the validity or otherwise of this marriage, some of the greatest subtlety, others patently time-serving. In contrast, the positions of the two people who had originally been (or not been) married were at bottom extremely simple. But these two positions were basically opposed to each other.

The King's third step was to set in motion the process that would actually lead to a divorce. In May 1527 Cardinal Wolsey, by virtue of his authority as papal legate, set up an official examination – *inquisito ex officio* – into the validity of the King's marriage. This was a form of examination by which the accused person could be summoned on grounds of 'public infamy' and a judge could impose a sentence. Wolsey, however, set up the examination in secret, without Queen Catherine being informed; this was not in accordance with procedure. In any case what Wolsey learned from this preliminary investigation convinced him that the King's case was not going to be quite so easy as the lovelorn monarch may have supposed.

The King's own conviction that his marriage had been against the law of God was all very well: but there were complications. First, there was the matter of the text of Leviticus, which had in fact referred to lack of children rather than lack of sons. (King Henry allowed himself to be erroneously convinced that the word had been wrongly translated from the Greek into the Latin of the Bible then commonly used.) Even more damaging was a second biblical text in Deuteronomy (25: 5-7), which explicitly laid down 'the duty of an husband's brother' towards the latter's childless widow: he 'shall go unto her, and take her to him to wife'. This second text posed a great deal of difficulty to anyone relying on the argument that Henry's marriage to Catherine had been against the law of God – as defined by Leviticus – which no Pope had the power to dispense.

Under the circumstances, Wolsey, as an ecclesiastic and a supporter of papal authority, much preferred to concentrate on the dispensation granted on the occasion of Catherine's second marriage. Wolsey's argument left the power of the Pope to issue dispensations intact, but merely questioned whether one particular Pope – Julius II in 1503 – had managed to issue one particular dispensation correctly. Taking the King's case to Rome was fraught with difficulties. The imperial victory at Pavia in 1525 had been followed, in May 1527, by the sacking of Rome by a rabble of imperial troops and the imprisonment of the Pope, Clement VII. One solution might have been to get the whole body of English bishops to condemn the royal marriage as invalid. Here, however, Wolsey – and the King – found themselves up against another stumbling block in the shape of another immovable conscience. John Fisher, Bishop of Rochester, holy, learned and highly respected, insisted that the marriage had been valid.

Queen Catherine soon got to hear the humiliating and painful news of this secret enquiry: the imperial ambassador was tipped off by an informer and alerted her. The Queen's immediate reaction was to write off to her nephew the Emperor to seek his help. She wanted him to remonstrate with the erring

Henry on the one hand, and get the Pope to take up her case in Rome on the other. Thus another polarity between the King and the Queen was present virtually from the start of the 'great matter'. The King was understandably anxious that proceedings should take place in his own country – by virtue of Wolsey's legatine authority or by some other means. The Queen, equally understandably, preferred the prospect of Rome where she expected a fairer hearing.

Like Wolsey, the Queen grasped the importance of the 1503 dispensation. If there was a weakness in the structure of her second marriage to be exploited, it lay in the nature of this dispensation which had referred against her will to her first marriage as having been *'forsitan'* (perhaps) consummated. A non-consummated marriage, however, required a different kind of dispensation, that of 'public honesty': that is, despite the lack of sexual union, the couple had been publicly supposed to be married and that fact had to be acknowledged by the issuing of a dispensation. This apparently had not been asked for.

It was on 22 June that the King himself first communicated to his wife his 'scruples' concerning their marriage of nearly twenty years. There was certainly no reference to Anne Boleyn here, only to his conscience. He chose to accost Catherine 'in her closet'; one imagines that he must have dreaded such an interview, and perhaps hoped that the cosy domestic setting would somehow palliate the blow. If so, he was to be disappointed. The Queen became overwhelmed with 'great grief' and burst into floods of tears. Henry's intention was probably to persuade Queen Catherine to withdraw from the court voluntarily, expecting her to be as shocked as he had been by this theological bombshell. But he had mistaken his woman, not for the last time in what became the tragedy of Henry VIII and Catherine of Aragon. She now became 'very stiff and obstinate', affirming that Prince Arthur 'did never know her carnally'. The King and herself were man and wife and always had been. He might send her away but she would never go of her own accord. Furthermore, 'she desired counsel', from

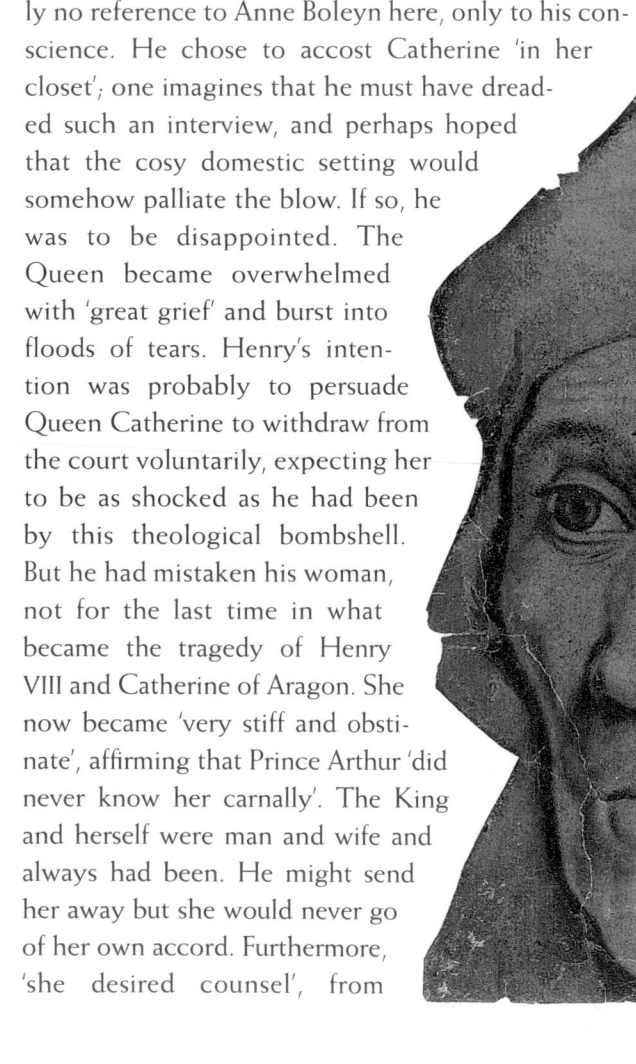

John Fisher, Bishop of Rochester, one of the most formidable opponents of the King's plan to get rid of Catherine of Aragon. Painting after Holbein.

By the summer of 1528 in general the King's letters to Anne Boleyn have a more settled tone: they are the letters of a lover, but one who is confident that 'the time for which I have waited so long', when he will be transformed into a husband, is approaching; he can thus contain his passion. In July he had been working so hard on his book *A Glasse of the Truthe* which argued for his marriage to Catherine being against the law of God – four whole hours on one day alone – that his head ached. His conclusion to this letter gives a glimpse at least of the physical course taken by Henry's dalliance with Anne: 'wishing myself (specially an evening) in my sweetheart's arms, whose pretty ducks [breasts] I trust shortly to kiss.'

Long afterwards it would be declared that Anne Boleyn had been the enemy of Wolsey, since he put an end to her romance with Lord Percy. But the evidence of Anne's own letters to Wolsey of this summer of 1528 is very much against this. In mid-June, for instance, she wrote: 'I do know the great pains and troubles that you have taken for me, both day and night, is never like to be recompenced on my part, but alonely . . in loving you, next unto the King's grace, above all creatures living.' Both Anne and Henry did have a great deal to thank Wolsey for. The Pope had been induced to grant a secret decretal commission which appointed Wolsey and another papal legate, Cardinal Campeggio, as joint inquisitors of the King's marriage. Although this was not the full public decretal commission of Wolsey's hopes – it was for the King's eyes only – it was a promising start. The Spanish ambassador Mendoza heard that preparations were being made for a royal wedding: 'Both the King and his lady, I am assured, look upon their future marriage as certain, as if that of the Queen had actually been dissolved.'

At Campeggio's first meeting with Henry VIII, the King had, not surprisingly, rejected the papal suggestion that Clement VII should grant a fresh dispensation for his marriage to Catherine. A newly valid marriage to Catherine was not the way the King's mind tended. But a voluntary withdrawal of the pious Queen into a nunnery was a new idea – a different matter altogether. Without the active opposition of the Queen, the question of a divorce would take on a new connotation. So with the permission of the King, Cardinal Campeggio, accompanied by Wolsey paid a series of three visits to the Queen to put this idea to her. At first she met this reasonable proposition – as it seemed to the two men before her – with 'irritation'. But then she 'grew calm' and answered Campeggio 'with great composure'. Queen Catherine, too, like King Henry, was not afraid to refer to conscience. She told the papal legate that she herself entertained no scruple at all about her marriage, 'but considered herself the true and legitimate wife of the King, her husband'. In other words, the Pope's proposal was 'inadmissible'.

One of the most peculiar elements in the triple relationship of Henry, Catherine and Anne – at least to modern sensibilities – was the way that the routine of the court rolled placidly on. There is even some doubt as to when conjugal relations between the King and Queen stopped. Certainly the King continued to dine in the Queen's chambers, when it suited him, as before. According to the French ambassador, however, in the autumn of 1528 he also continued to spend the night with her: 'till this hour, they have only had one bed and one table'. This official appearance of unity is confirmed by Hall's *Chronicle,* which states that at this period the King 'dined and resorted to the Queen as he was accustomed'.

Did the King also continue to make love to the Queen, out of royal habit? He was not after all, making love – fully – to Anne Boleyn. This continuance seems less likely. Hall denied it: 'but in no wise he would not [sic] come to her bed'. Campeggio also heard in late 1528 that the Queen 'had not had the use of his royal person for more than two years'. Then there was the question of the Queen's health: in January 1529 Wolsey reported that the King had resolved to abstain from lying with the Queen due to some diseases she had, 'pronounced incurable'. All this seems to add up to a cessation of physical intimacy between them around 1526.

Christmas 1528 was spent by Henry VIII and his 'Lady' at the palace of Greenwich; Queen Catherine was also there. But Anne Boleyn was by now lodged in 'a fine apartment close to that of the King'. Greater court, noted the French ambassador, was being paid to her every day 'than has been paid to the Queen for a long time'. As for Catherine, she was evidently depressed and downcast: she displayed 'no manner of countenance and made no great joy of nothing, her mind was so troubled'. If 1528 had not quite brought the successful resolution of his personal life that Henry VIII had confidently predicted, then surely 1529 would remedy the deficiency.

A late sixteenth-century view of Greenwich showing the palace. Henry VIII spent Christmas 1528 there with both Catherine of Aragon and Anne Boleyn.

SPLENDOUR AT COURT

PALATIVM REGIVM IN ANGLIÆ REG
Hoc est nusq

Effigiavit Georgius Hoefn

As memories of the Wars of the Roses receded, so the palaces and great houses of England came to be designed not for fortification but for comfort and display. Furniture, wall-hangings, tableware and jewels were all used to create a lavish setting for the courtiers who surrounded Henry VIII and his six Queens.

In 1538 Henry VIII razed the Surrey village of Ewell to build the palace of Nonsuch. Drawing by Hoefnagel, late sixteenth century.

Left: Brown calf binding executed for a presentation copy of a narrative of the campaigns of the Emperor Charles V in 1544, bearing the initials HR and the royal arms between medallions of Plato and Dido; at top and bottom is an inscription addressed to Henry VIII.

Left: The Howard Grace Cup, 1525-6. Ivory-covered bowl with silver-gilt mounts, set with garnets and pearls. Said to have been bequeathed to Catherine of Aragon

Left: Facsimilie of a rare piece of wallpaper found in the Master's Lodge of Christ's College Cambridge. Dated c. 1509.

Left: Holbein's design for a pendant incorporates an intricate monogram.

Right: Pendant, c.1540-60, resembling designs by Holbein. Note the similarity to the pendant in Holbein's portrait of Jane Seymour (p.131).

Above: The Malmesbury Cup. A silver-gilt standing cup, c. 1529.

Following pages: The Triumph of Bacchus from a series entitled The Triumph of the Gods woven for Whitehall Palace in the early 1540s.

Left and right: Detail from The family of Henry VIII *by an unknown artist, c. 1545. The setting is the King's lodgings at Whitehall showing part of Princess Mary's lodging. The view through the archway on the left shows the privy garden with low rails and beasts on poles, the roofs of the tennis courts can be seen through the archway on the right.*

Henry VIII's scissors, decorated with his coat of arms.

A tennis ball excavated from Whitehall Palace. Henry VIII played tennis from an early age and the Venetian ambassador Giustinian claimed that it was 'the prettiest thing in the world to seem him play; his fair skin glowing through a shirt of finest texture.'

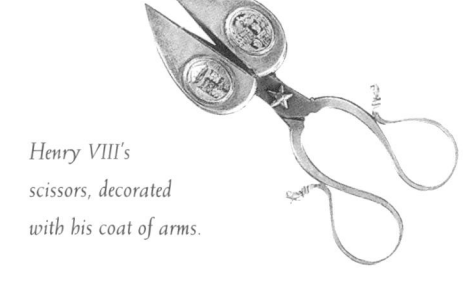

Below: When the King moved from one palace to another, several of the locks would be transferred too. The King had his own locksmith, Henry Romains, who travelled around with the court ensuring that the locks were correctly installed.

CHAPTER 5

Hail Anna!

THE TRIBUNAL PRESIDED over by Campeggio and Wolsey opened at the end of May 1529 in the Parliament Chamber of Blackfriars. A rapprochement between the Pope and the Emperor meant that in fact the two legates had divergent interests: Campeggio needed to deliver a verdict that would not upset the long-term policies of the papacy, whereas Wolsey needed, more simply, to deliver a verdict in favour of the dissolution of the King's marriage. He must be the King's good servant – not the Pope's. The tribunal met against a background of general uneasiness, of which 'Lutheran' resentment at papal authority was one small part. A more pressing cause for unease was the attitude of Queen Catherine. On 6 March she had asked the Pope to transfer her case to the Curia in Rome and six weeks later the Emperor also petitioned the Pope to the same effect. It was not absolutely certain, therefore, whether Catherine would obey the summons to the tribunal, and if she did, how she would conduct herself. Would she accept its authority?

Only fragmentary accounts survive of the tribunal's proceedings – it lasted for nearly two months – and these are sometimes contradictory in their details. Anxiety about the line the Queen would take was hardly allayed by an interview she had with Campeggio on 16 June. Queen Catherine 'very solemnly' swore that Prince Arthur had not consummated their marriage on their wedding night or on any other occasion: 'that from the embraces of her first husband she entered this marriage as a virgin and an immaculate woman'. She also formally requested before the notaries that the case should be tried in Rome. Two days later she made another solemn protest which included a complete denial of the tribunal's authority to try her case; furthermore her appearance before it should in no way be construed as accepting its authority nor as prejudicing her right to take her case to Rome. In return, the legates asked her to appear before them again in three days' time in order to learn their decision.

So on Monday 21 June the scene immortalized by Shakespeare took place, when Queen Catherine pleaded with King Henry for her future – in the name of their past. At the time a large crowd of spectators witnessed the scene which

had certainly never been paralleled. Although both King and Queen were seated on chairs under regal canopies of gold brocade – the Queen's slightly lower
than that of the King – they seem, from the course of subsequent events, to
have been somewhat divided from each other by these spectators. The King
spoke first, at least according to the Venetian ambassador, who wrote his report
the next day. His main theme was 'a certain scrupulosity that pricked my conscience', and he brought up all over again the manner in which his doubts had
allegedly been raised. He even repeated his assertion made at Bridewell the previous November that he would willingly take the Queen back as his wife, if the
marriage was found to be valid after all: although such an assertion must by
now have sounded utterly hypocritical.

Queen Catherine then spoke. According to the French ambassador she first
made an appeal. The King replied along the expected lines – how it was the
great love he bore her which had prevented him acting before now, how it was
his dearest wish to have the marriage declared valid, and how his desire to keep
the case from going to Rome was entirely due to his fear of the Emperor's
influence there. (This last argument at least was sincere.) But it was what happened after this which left the deepest impression on the eyewitnesses, from
the gouty Cardinal Campeggio, straining to understand what was being said in
English, to Wolsey's gentleman-usher, Cavendish, whose recollections would
provide the inspiration for Shakespeare.

Unexpectedly, the Queen left her seat and threading her way through the
spectators reached the King's chair. There she flung herself down at his feet. As
Cardinal Campeggio related it, the King immediately raised her up. At which
the Queen once more knelt in supplication before him. This left the King with
nothing to do but raise her up once more – and listen to her passionate out-
pourings. Her plea remains the ultimate expression of loss by a rejected first
wife, who had made her husband's life her own and whose only crime had been
to grow old before he did.

'Sir,' she began, 'I beseech you for all the love that hath been between us, let
me have justice and right, take of me some pity and compassion, for I am a poor
woman, and a stranger, born out of your dominion. I have here no friend and
much less indifferent counsel. I flee to you, as to the head of justice within this
realm. . . ' Catherine went on: 'I take God and all the world to witness that I
have been to you a true, humble and obedient wife, ever comfortable to your
will and pleasure, being always well pleased and contented with all things
wherein you had any delight or dalliance . . . I loved all those whom ye loved,
only for your sake, whether I had cause or no, and whether they were my
friends or enemies.'

Like King Henry, but with, one imagines, more conviction, the Queen was
even prepared to be 'put away' if any just cause of law was found against her:
'either of dishonesty [i.e. public honesty] or any other impediment.' She
touched also on their shared tragedy: 'By me ye have had divers children,

*Henry VIII in
truculent middle
age. The King's pose,
legs astride, is an
adaptation of a classic
Renaissance formula
that stemmed from
Donatello's St
George. Portrait
after Holbein.*

although it hath pleased God to call them from this world'. But it was her challenge on the subject of her virginity which was the most devastating point made to the man before whom she knelt: 'And when ye had me at first, I take God to my judge, I was a true maid, without touch of man. And whether this be true or no, I put it to your conscience.' The King did not answer – as he never had (and never would) publicly give her the lie on this intimate but crucial issue. When she had finished Queen Catherine rose up, swept her husband a low curtsy, and leaning on the arm of her gentleman-usher moved slowly out of the court. She resolutely refused to appear before the tribunal again.

In the Queen's absence – fortunately for her sensibilities – evidence about that wedding night with Prince Arthur at Baynard's Castle, now twenty-eight years ago, was supplied by various courtiers. The King's cousin, Thomas Grey Marquess of Dorset, had been present when Prince Arthur was escorted to the nuptial bed where 'the lady Catherine' lay under the coverlet 'as is the manner of queens' in that situation. Dorset was sure that the prince 'used the princess as his wife' since Arthur had been 'of a good and sanguine complexion'. The deposition of Sir Anthony Willoughby was more colourful. By virtue of his father's position as steward of the King's household, he was present both when Prince Arthur was taken to bed and when he emerged from the chamber in the morning. At this point the prince exclaimed: 'Willoughby, bring me a cup of ale, for I have been this night in the midst of Spain.' Later the prince said openly: 'Masters, it is a good pastime to have a wife.' This kind of story was a good deal more to the popular taste than the earnest deposition of the Bishop of Ely which followed: the Bishop had grave doubts about the consummation, since the Queen had so often told him on the testimony of her conscience that she had not been 'carnally known' by Arthur.

What is one to make of this evidence, of which the sexual boasting of a teenage boy, remembered over a long passage of time but mysteriously never before given currency, is the most vivid? The Spanish ambassador would in the future garner quite different testimonies to the effect that Prince Arthur had been impotent. These, if true, do not necessarily rule out the boy making his pathetic boasts; but the truth, as this ambassador would point out two years later, was that non-consummation was impossible to prove for certain nearly thirty years later in the case of a woman who had been for twenty years married to another man. The best course was to rely on the Queen's known character: that she was 'so virtuous, devout and holy, so truthful and God-fearing' that she would not lie. This (coupled with King Henry's tortuous attitude to the subject) still remains the best proof.

The Queen's defence was now being actively mounted with the help of her counsellors, including those in imperial Flanders, in terms of appeals to Rome. The Regent of the Netherlands, the Archduchess Margaret, sent her own appeal: she was of course the Queen's former sister-in-law and had long been her friend. But the important link between them was that both were aunts of

the Emperor Charles V. In June 1529 the imperialists routed the French at Landriano: the Peace of Cambrai followed. It was further helpful to Queen Catherine's cause at Rome that the rapprochement between Emperor and Pope had continued. Under the circumstances, it was difficult for Clement VII not to transfer the Queen's case to Rome as she requested. In any case Clement VII was disposed to believe that any fault in the dispensation was purely technical and could be righted since the intention to provide a proper dispensation had evidently been there. In mid-July therefore the Pope agreed to the official transfer of the case.

This was a death blow to the King's hopes of a summer divorce; 23 June was the last day on which the tribunal sat. King Henry himself was present to hear Campeggio declare that the case was too important to be decided without consultation with the Curia at Rome, unfortunately now on its long summer holiday. Campeggio therefore prorogued the tribunal until October. But in any case the night before he and his fellow legate Wolsey had heard that the Pope intended to transfer the case. King Henry was still no nearer getting free from his wife.

There was one manifest consequence of the whole process of the tribunal – and its failure. In the autumn Wolsey fell from power. In late September Queen Catherine informed the new Spanish ambassador 'in a very low tone' that there was no need to present his credentials to Wolsey, for his affairs at present were 'much embroiled'. Many contemporaries, including Cavendish, attributed the Cardinal's disgrace to the influence of Anne Boleyn who, they maintained, had never forgiven Wolsey for his high-handed removal of her eligible lover, Lord Percy. But this was a pleasantly easy piece of misogyny compared with the more onerous task of blaming the King. As Queen Catherine found it less painful to think of the divorce as Wolsey's project, so Wolsey himself may have found it easier to accuse the woman than face the man's ingratitude. Showing the fair side of his Janus face, King Henry parted from his servant on the most affable terms, giving no hint of his intentions. The sovereign was visiting Grafton in the course of his autumn progress; now he was on horseback in the courtyard ready to ride out. The previous evening Cavendish had watched the King motion to the Cardinal to replace his cap – a marked sign of favour. The King clattered away; and never saw Wolsey again.

Wolsey's fall was swift. A series of brutal coups stripped him of his powers, beginning with the Attorney-general on 9 October who charged him with praemunire, that is, exercising his powers of papal legate in the King's realm, thus derogating the King's lawful authority. He was dismissed as Lord Chancellor (Sir Thomas More replaced him) and sentenced to imprisonment. His fortune was stripped from him and all his goods taken 'into the King's hands'. Wolsey died a year later, on 29 November 1530, on his way to London for trial, having been arrested for high treason three weeks earlier. Thomas Boleyn promptly gave a large banquet, including an entertainment which depicted the Cardinal going down to hell.

The autumn of 1529 which saw the disappearance from court of Wolsey, also marked the arrival of a new ally for Queen Catherine. Eustace Chapuys, the incoming Spanish ambassador, would be posted in England for the next sixteen years; his reports back to Spain are therefore an extraordinarily important source. Chapuys was a doctor of canon law and a former ecclesiastical judge in Geneva. He would fully justify the Emperor's description of him to the Queen as 'a very trusty person and sure to take up your defence with all fidelity and diligence'. He was certainly well-equipped to steer her through the morass of debate and conflict that followed the advocation of the tribunal. Somebody – probably Thomas Cranmer, then a relatively unknown ecclesiastic but with

Portrait of Thomas Cranmer by Gerlach Flicke.

connections to the Boleyn family – had had the idea of transferring the argument from that of law to the realm of theology. This was to be done by appealing to theological scholars at universities throughout Europe that they should give their opinions.

Chapuys also understood the need for tact and charm in diplomacy, particularly where monarchs of tricky temperament were concerned. During his first interview with the King, Henry observed how awkward it was for both of them – Catherine as well as himself – not to be able to remarry, before going on to praise his own restraint. 'Other princes might not have been so kind'; nobody would have hindered him from adopting such measures, 'which I have not taken and never will'. Was he talking of the forcible removal of the Queen to a nunnery? It was left sinisterly vague. At this point Chapuys noticed a phenomenon upon which the French ambassador, du Bellay, had remarked a year previously. As he reflected on the wrongs done to him (and his own goodness in putting up with them), the King's demeanour suddenly changed into something 'so different from the mildness and composure of his former speech'.

The stalemate over the divorce meant that the King and Queen still continued, in a manner of speaking, to live together. The enforced formal relationship did not bring out the best in either of them. Queen Catherine persistently taxed the King on the subject of her virginity at the time of their marriage, which had now become an obsession with her. The Queen could not see that this was now irrelevant. The King had made up his mind that their marriage was against the law of God, and she, by reiterating her complaints, was simply driving him mad with irritation. It was certainly not a good plan to irritate King Henry VIII, particularly as the years advanced, since behind irritation lay a colder fury, and out of that would be bred cruelty, which was somehow justified in his mind by the original irritation.

In 1529 a court dinner to celebrate St Andrew's Day, 30 November, gave Queen Catherine an opening, as she saw it, to upbraid the King for never supping with her privately; as a result, she declared dramatically, she was suffering the pains of purgatory on earth. The ensuing argument ended with the King rushing from the room to seek consolation from his pretty sweetheart. Anne Boleyn, however, was in no mood to play that particular role. So the King found himself caught between a nagging wife and a nagging mistress. In her turn Anne Boleyn snapped at King Henry: 'Did I not tell you that whenever you disputed with the Queen, she was sure to have the upper hand?' Then from anger Anne turned to tears: one day the King would go back to the Queen and abandon her: 'I have been waiting long and might in the meanwhile have contracted some advantageous marriage, out of which I might have had issue, which is the greatest consolation in this world, but alas! Farewell to my time and youth spent to no purpose at all'. There was at least an exciting spice to Anne Boleyn's sharp tongue – courtiers noted that the King and his Lady were always particularly amorous after a row.

The evidence of Anne Boleyn's fiery temper, accompanied by some equally combustible words, is sufficiently widespread for it not to be dismissed as mere fabrication. Nor is such a tempestuous nature altogether to her discredit (although in the long term it might not prove wise). There is something splendidly fearless about the way she laid about her with her tongue, often going a great deal further than would be prudent, even for the most beautiful and beloved Mistress in the world. By the beginning of 1531 Anne was described as being so confident that she was 'brave qu'une lion'. She told one of Queen Catherine's ladies-in-waiting that she wished all the Spaniards were at the bottom of the sea. When the lady reproved her, Anne went further: 'she cared not for the Queen, nor any of her family [household].' She would rather see Catherine hanged 'than have to confess she was her Queen and mistress'. The lady-in-waiting was duly appalled, but then women as a whole did not warm to Anne Boleyn; she either could not, or never cared to, build up the nexus of female friendships that Queen Catherine had established.

Some of her explosions must have been provoked, directly or indirectly, by the continued unpopularity of the King's projected new marriage among his subjects. In August 1530 the Venetian ambassador thought that the people would actually rebel if King Henry married Anne Boleyn. This reaction was not purely snobbery, although of course it played a part: the people wanted a royal princess to look up to, rather than 'Nan Bullen'; especially since their particular royal princess had made herself so beloved. Beyond that, however, was the fact that Anne Boleyn stood for something in the popular imagination that absolutely everybody distrusted, at least in principle: what Cavendish called 'pernicious and inordinate carnal love'. She was 'the King's whore'.

But at court Anne's status was increasingly that of a future consort. At the ball to celebrate Christmas 1529 she was given precedence in the seating not only over the Duchess of Norfolk, but also over the King's sister, Mary Duchess of Suffolk, which angered both these ladies. Shortly before this her father had been created Earl of Wiltshire and had also finally received the family earldom of Ormonde. From 1529 onwards Anne Boleyn featured heavily in the expenses of the Privy Purse: yards of purple velvet in December to the tune of £180, at the orders of the King; the next year it was lengths of crimson satin, furs to trim her dresses, and fine linen for 'shirts' (smocks) to wear under them and at night. There were payments for the garnishing of Anne Boleyn's desk with gold while the expenses of her bows and arrows and hunting gloves, and payments to Anne for her 'playing money' (at backgammon, shovel-board, dice or cards) provide in themselves a picture of the life the lovers led together: pleasure-loving and apparently carefree, indoors and out.

The Lady Anne's insecurity and the gnawing jealousy of Queen Catherine which it brought did have one unlooked-for consequence. This was the development of a new centre for King and government in London, later to be known as Whitehall. York Place was one of Wolsey's palaces which was forfeit to the

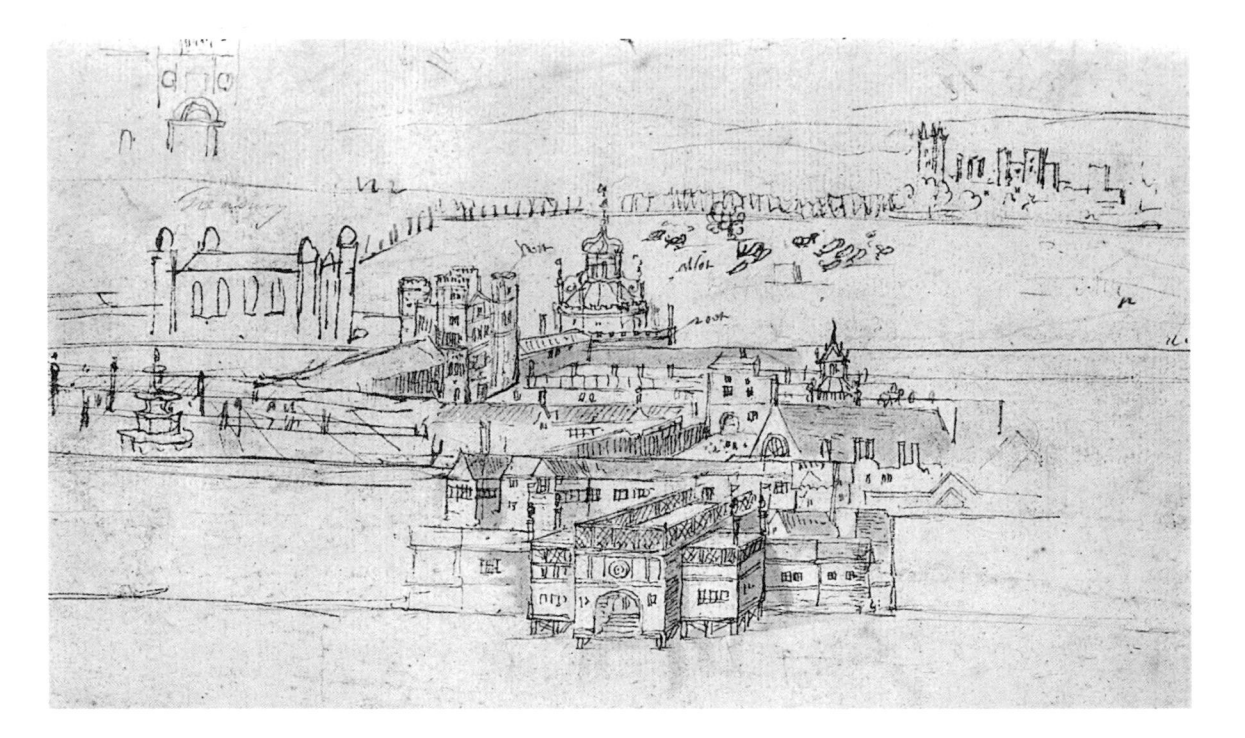

King at the cardinal's fall. Soon afterwards King Henry brought his sweetheart on a secret visit to gloat over the rich tapestries and plate with which the Cardinal had graced his magnificent life-style. The Lady quickly appreciated that this new royal residence would have one immense advantage: unlike other palaces, as for example Greenwich, it would not contain a series of apartments traditionally accorded to the Queen, which it was very difficult to prevent her occupying as she chose. At Whitehall there was to be no provision made for this awkward *ménage à trois*.

Meanwhile the King's appeal to the universities of Europe, the brilliant expedient on which he prided himself, produced in fact an unsurprising result. Most scholars found for their political masters; although in Italy scholars remained divided, despite large sums dispensed by Cranmer and others in bribing them to support the divorce. But the University of Paris produced a positive verdict (for divorce), since François I now viewed the whole affair approvingly as a useful way of making trouble between Henry VIII and Charles V. Spanish universities were negative. The majority opinion in Oxford and Cambridge favoured the King. In other words the stalemate was not relieved.

Practically speaking, even the King and Queen were in a kind of bizarre agreement that the Pope must make up his mind about the validity or otherwise of their marriage. But the King of England was also beginning to consider a more radical solution which would make no use of the Pope's authority. A papal blessing upon Henry's second union was still the most convenient answer – because such a union would not then be called in question – and he had after all accepted papal authority freely for the dispensation relating to Anne Boleyn.

But given that this blessing was being tiresomely withheld, did he really need to acknowledge sovereignty to Rome in such matters? Of course the theory of the royal supremacy did not spring from the King's head, fully armed, like the goddess Athena at her birth. The parliament, first convened on 3 November 1529, which was destined in seven years to carry through a religious revolution, started with very different objectives.

Thomas More, the new Lord Chancellor, was personally bent on trying to eradicate Lutheranism, whereas the rising star in the King's service, Thomas Cromwell, saw things from the financial angle. For the King's inadequate finances currently presented yet another frustrating problem. Cromwell, who had previously worked for Wolsey, was assiduous and intelligent. He had been

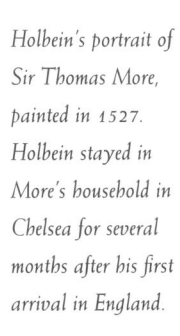

Holbein's portrait of Sir Thomas More, painted in 1527. Holbein stayed in More's household in Chelsea for several months after his first arrival in England.

Thomas Cromwell, after Holbein. The original is now lost and this portrait is known only through copies of which this one in the Frick Collection New York is the best preserved. The letter on the table is inscribed: 'To our trusty and right and well beloved Councillor Thomas Cromwell...'

in the past both an attorney and a merchant, and even a money-lender. Cromwell saw a way of solving the King's financial difficulties and bringing the clergy into submission by threatening them with a charge of praemunire – the charge of paying allegiance to Rome to the detriment of their allegiance to the King. This charge had brought down Wolsey. In January 1531 the clergy in convocation understood perfectly well what the penalty might be. They voted the King £100,000 to cover possible complicity with Wolsey. They also accepted that the King had a new title: 'Supreme Head of the Church and Clergy of England'. Even though Archbishop Warham added the words 'so far as the law of Christ allows' (which, if taken seriously, destroyed the whole concept of the title) and Bishop Fisher protested vigorously, it was undeniably a step away from Rome.

William Warham, Archbishop of Canterbury, 1504 to 1532, was one of the first people to sit for Holbein after his arrival in England.

King Henry saw Queen Catherine for the last time in July 1531. Unlike his behaviour towards Wolsey, he did not bid her an affable – if false – farewell. After twenty-two years of marriage there was no farewell at all. He merely rode off at dawn from Windsor to go hunting at Woodstock with the Lady Anne, leaving the unhappy Queen to find out from others that he had gone. But then the King did not necessarily plan this to be a final parting; he did not necessarily plan anything at all other than a carefree hunting expedition from which the Queen was excluded. It was easier that way. Then, when Catherine wrote him a polite letter – she was generally allowed to ask after his health before he departed – exasperation at her nagging could be allowed free rein.

'Tell the Queen', he shouted at her messenger, 'that I do not want any of her goodbyes.' He did not care whether she asked after his health or not, since she had caused him no end of trouble, refusing all the reasonable requests of his Privy Council. He wanted 'no more of her messages'. From his own point of view the exasperation of King Henry was perfectly understandable: why was Catherine so obstinate when submission would bring her, and all around her, so many benefits? As for the common people, who dared to call out to the King, 'Back to your wife!', they were enough to drive anyone to frenzy (was ever a man so tried for following his own conscience?).

When the court at Rome, appointed to try Queen Catherine's suit, had opened in June (only to be adjourned to October), there were protests from the King's lawyers that he could not be summoned to appear outside of his own realm. The King himself expressed his angry contempt to the papal nuncio in England: he would never agree to the Pope 'being judge in that affair' (the divorce), and as for the Pope's threat of excommunication, 'I shall not mind it, for I care not a fig for all his excommunications.' Let the Pope do what he liked in Rome: 'I will do here what I think best.'

This was the background to the King's precipitate dawn departure from Windsor. The wrangling – via messengers and letters – which followed merely convinced him that a move which had probably been spontaneous when it was made should be transformed into something more permanent. Orders came that Queen Catherine was to remove, with her household, to one of Wolsey's former residences, The More, near Rickmansworth in Hertfordshire. It was an innovatory move rather than a punitive one, in practical terms at least. Although The More was now showing signs of neglect, not so long ago it had been rated as even finer than Hampton Court, thanks to the Cardinal's embell-ishments. Nor was the Queen denied the large household to which her status had accustomed her. It was mental anguish that chiefly troubled her, as she signed her letters 'from The More, separated from my husband, without ever having offended him, Katharina, the unhappy Queen'.

From The More Queen Catherine was taken to Bishop's Hatfield, the palace of the bishop of Ely, and at some point had a sojourn in Hertford Castle; then in the spring of 1533 she was moved to Ampthill in Bedfordshire. This was an impressive castle, with four or five stone towers and a gatehouse. There for two years Queen Catherine was kept in seclusion while King Henry attempted to accustom his court to the idea that the Lady Anne would shortly and inevitably become his true wife.

Meanwhile religious reform and the concept of the King's supremacy had acquired a momentum of its own. In March 1532 a bill for an Act of Conditional Restraint of Annates was introduced into parliament. Hitherto the Pope had received the 'annates' or 'first fruits' of a see after the appointment of a new bishop: that is, its revenues for one year. By the terms of the act the Pope would in future only receive five per cent and if, as a result, he refused to consecrate a bishop, then the consecration would take place without papal consent. But the act was not to be put into force until the King so ordered: Henry now had a useful lever to use against the Pope who would hardly wish to be deprived of this income. A few days earlier, the so-called Supplication Against the Ordinaries had emerged (prompted by Cromwell). This was a list of complaints against the church, shared by many English people, from the 'Lutheran' Boleyns to much humbler persons whose lives were bedevilled by the frequent need to pay ecclesiastical fees and tithes or the clergy's unfair use of the weapon of excommunication. The death of Warham in August provided a further opportunity for the King to pursue his policies, unimpeded by clerical objections, by appointing Thomas Cranmer as the new Archbishop of Canterbury. Cranmer's credentials included not only a manifest desire to serve the King, but also an intimate association with the Boleyn family. He had probably once been the Boleyn chaplain and may well have lived under the family's roof for a period of about fifteen months.

Henry's impending royal visit to France and the prospect of a new and amenable archbishop (marriage could surely not long be deferred), enabled King Henry to take a further bold step in his public presentation of the Lady Anne. The French visit, envisaged as a minor version of the Field of Cloth of Gold, with the French King at Boulogne and the English King on his own ground at Calais, had become a pet project. King Henry wanted King François' support to counteract the Emperor's hostility, and, if possible, to overawe the Pope. On the seesaw principle, it was believed that King François viewed King Henry's proposed new marriage with approval, since it was condemned by Charles V. The French ambassador in England, Jean du Bellay, enjoyed a warm relationship not only with King Henry, but also with the Lady Anne who had given him numerous presents, including hunting clothes, and a hat, a special horn and a greyhound.

It was du Bellay who had the delicate task of getting King François actually to request the presence of Madame Anne at the impending celebrations so that he could both see her and entertain her. Nothing would give his brother King greater pleasure, wrote du Bellay, than if this should seem to be King François' own idea, and after all two such gallant sovereigns would not wish to be together 'without company of ladies'. The task was delicate, not only because of Madame Anne's status but also because the new Queen of France was the niece of Queen Catherine and had no intention of receiving the woman who was supplanting her aunt.

Meanwhile in England, King Henry took steps to make it clear that whatever the political prudery of the French, the Lady Anne was now his wife in all but name. Indeed, her existing name was to be glorified to fit her new station. On 1 September 1532 she was formally created the Marquess of Pembroke; the expenses of the Privy Purse for that month included payments for her ceremonial robes of silk trimmed with fur. The English people, especially the women, might indulge in 'hooting and hissing' when they saw the royal Mistress out

The clock supposedly given to Anne Boleyn by Henry VIII. On the weights the letters H and A are engraved, together with lovers' knots and their respective mottos, 'Dieu et Mon Droit' and 'The Most Happi'.

hunting, but in Calais the new Lady Marquess was to be accorded every honour. And that was what counted. She was even to wear the royal jewels, handed over reluctantly by Queen Catherine on the King's order.

The fraternal visit between the Kings fell into two parts. First King Henry and a large suite arrived in Boulogne on 21 October to be entertained for four days on French territory. The official report of the two Kings' first encounter since 1520 described 'the lovingest meeting that ever was seen'. But King Henry's suite did not include the Lady Marquess of Pembroke. Anne's turn would come during the subsequent four days spent in Calais: from 25 to 29 October. Here she blossomed: she was treated as the first lady of the English court and as such opened the dancing with the French King. The Lady Marquess also led the masking after supper, accompanied by several ladies of the court, all gorgeously apparelled in cloth of gold and crimson satin, knit with laces of gold, with visors over their faces.

It has been suggested that it was in Calais in the autumn of 1532 that King Henry, after nearly six years, finally transformed his newly ennobled Mistress into his lover, in the full sense of the word. An alternative theory has the Lady Anne receiving her title of Marquess at the beginning of September as a reward for giving way, but the title is so clearly linked to the French expedition, where the King wanted Anne to have a proper rank of her own, that this seems less plausible. The truth can never be known for sure. One can only say with certainty that Henry VIII made love to Anne – fully – some time before the end of 1532. Neither Anne nor the King had any desire to produce a son whose status was arguably extra-marital – no better than that of the young Duke of Richmond. Now at last, in a newly favourable atmosphere, vigilance could be relaxed. This was the real difference; King and putative Queen could set about conceiving that son and heir, the need for whom was the original *raison d'être* of their relationship, however much the fact had been lost in the mists of romantic declaration on the one hand and conscience-ridden self-justification on the other.

Around the end of the first week of December 1532 Anne Boleyn did become pregnant (this is to assume a nine months' gestation for the baby born the following September). In early January she must have suspected – hoped – as much. Thus as the month wore on, the question of marriage assumed a new urgency. Since royal marriages were then small private affairs there was nothing unconventional about a quick, secret ceremony taking place. 'About St Paul's Day' – 25 January 1533 – the King and the Lady Marquess were married at last.

The news was kept officially secret for the time being, although by the middle of February the Lady Marquess was finding it irresistible not to flaunt her pregnant state. But the secrecy had some point to it, quite apart from the fact that the Lady was not yet four months pregnant. The truth was that the King, although remarried, was not yet divorced. So an Act in Restraint of Appeals was quickly passed by a reconvened parliament on 3 February which would enable the matter to be settled in the King's own country, on the grounds that, as the act stated, 'this realm of England is an empire'.

There was a kind of crazy logic to the undivorced King's second marriage. If the original marriage to Catherine had never been valid, then he was still a bachelor, as Anne was a spinster. On the other hand the need for Anne's child to be unquestionably legitimate in the eyes of his subjects meant that this logic was not entirely pursued. In any case 'public honesty' demanded the dissolution

The divorce petition from Henry VIII to Pope Clement VII requesting an annulment of his marriage to Catherine of Aragon.

of his marriage to Catherine — to whom he had long been married in the estimation of the world and who had borne him children. A divorce procedure was still needed. It was planned to take place as discreetly as possible, in the little market town of Dunstable, in Bedfordshire, not far from Ampthill where the Queen was currently lodged.

At the beginning of April — when Anne was almost exactly four months pregnant — the news was made public, although the actual date of the wedding was

Design for a triumphal arch for Anne Boleyn's coronation procession, 1533; probably by Holbein.

tactfully fudged. On 9 April a deputation came to break the news to Queen Catherine. The Queen was told that the man she still regarded as her own husband had been married to Anne Boleyn for two months (since Chapuys had suspected Anne was pregnant in February, the Queen probably knew about that too). She was now to be treated as the Princess Dowager — the title she had borne thirty years earlier as Prince Arthur's widow. Naturally Queen Catherine refused to appear in Dunstable. Nor did the King attend; he was busy preparing for the coronation of Anne Boleyn.

If King Henry's remarriage did at least have a kind of logic to it, no such palliating excuse can be found for the behaviour and language of Archbishop Cranmer in the divorce court. Here was a man who was very shortly to crown the King's pregnant new wife in London – as he well knew – and yet he actually threatened to excommunicate King Henry if he did not 'put away' Queen Catherine. 'Did you not in fact laugh yourself', wrote Reginald Pole to Cranmer many years later, 'when you made a pretence of all this severity and threatened the King in this way?' But Cranmer had nothing to laugh about at the time; on the contrary, he was extremely wary about his language throughout the proceedings since by judging the King himself it was just possible he would encroach on the new doctrine of the royal supremacy. In short, Cranmer's main desire was, in his own words, not to deprive the King of 'his trust in me'. On 23 May the Archbishop gave his judgement that the marriage of Henry VIII and Catherine of Aragon was invalid. From Dunstable, archbishop Cranmer scurried back to London to place the crown on the head of Anne Boleyn exactly one week later.

The coronation of Queen Anne on 1 June 1533, when she was nearly six months pregnant, represented her apotheosis. This was true not only because, with hindsight, one can see that it was indeed the high point of her glamorous, adventurous and ultimately ill-fated life, but also because it was intended to be an apotheosis at the time. The coronation of a queen was a solemn and symbolic act, with a significance quite beyond that of mere marriage to a king. Not every queen was crowned. Those who were 'royally anointed' – a part of the coronation ceremony – were aware of the special sanctity which this conferred. On the day of the Dunstable judgement, Queen Catherine based her refusal to be relegated to the status of Princess Dowager on the fact that she was 'a crowned and anointed Queen'.

To prepare for the ceremony, Queen Anne came first from Greenwich to the Tower of London by water, as was customary. She was 'apparelled in rich cloth of gold' and escorted by fifty 'great barges, comely be seen', belonging to the various guilds of the city. According to one eyewitness nothing was to be seen for four miles but 'barges and boats all draped with awnings and carpeted, which gave pleasure to behold'. There had been some controversy about the arrangements. Queen Anne had insisted on using the royal barge of her predecessor, with its badges stripped off and replaced with her own, for her journey up river, although there were plenty of other barges fit for the purpose. Nor were the celebrations of the City an unalloyed success. Norfolk earlier questioned whether the City clergy should even be invited to attend since they were in a difficult and critical mood. Then it was customary for the dignitaries of the City to present the new Queen with a substantial financial gift; on this occasion the aldermen went round in person to collect the contributions in order to inhibit refusal.

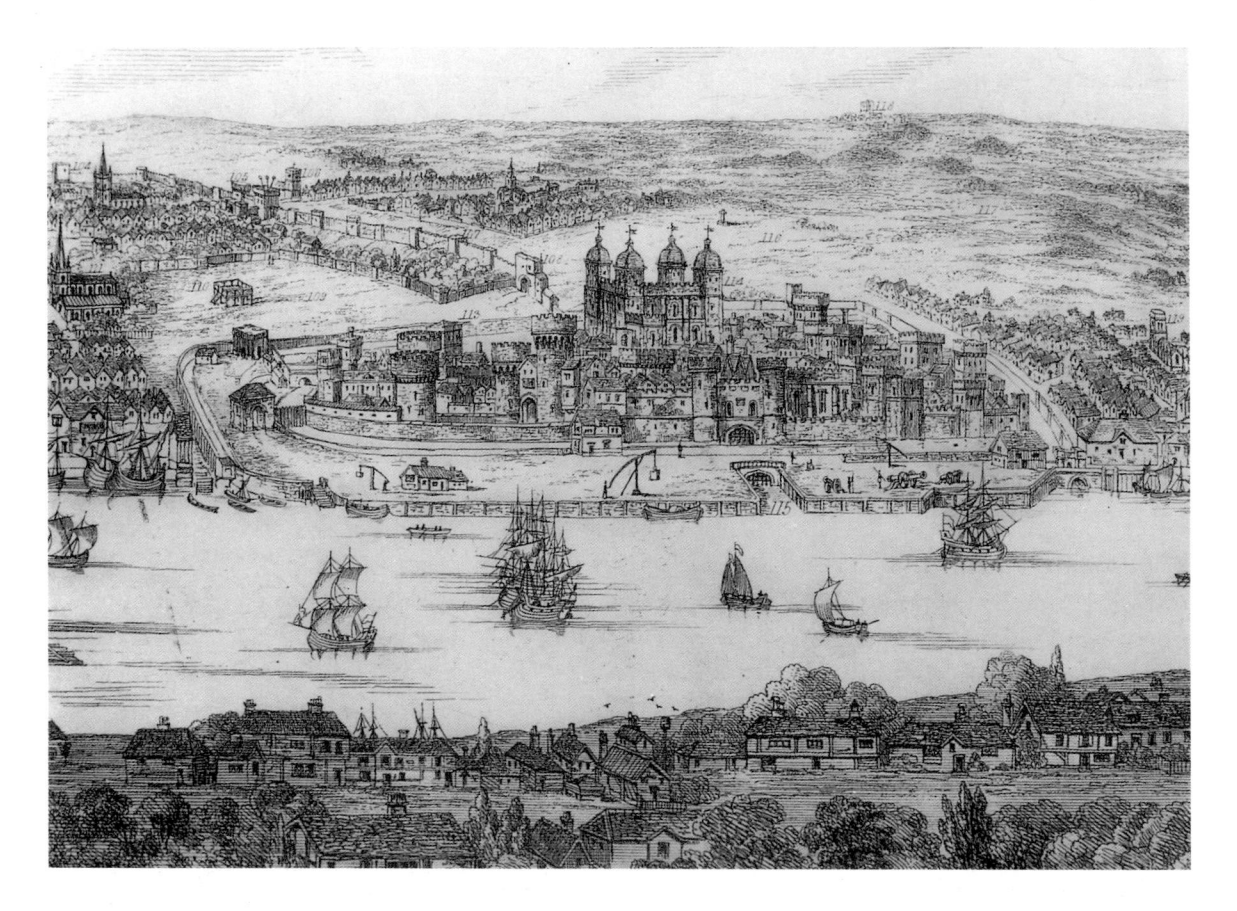

A mid-sixteenth-century view of the Tower of London by Wyngaerde.

Not a hint of this appeared, of course, in the elaborate pageantry of the procession on 31 May. Queen Anne's garb was a mixture of the virginal and the resplendent. Her long black hair 'hung down' her back like a bride's and she carried fresh flowers. But her dress of crimson brocade was encrusted with precious stones, while round her neck she wore 'a string of pearls larger than chick peas' and a large jewel 'made up of diamonds of evidently great value.' A robe of royal purple velvet surmounted it all. At eight o'clock the next morning, Queen Anne Boleyn, accompanied by noble ladies 'in their robes of estate' and all the peers of the realm in 'Parliament robes', proceeded to Westminster Abbey, where she received her crown from the Archbishop of Canterbury, Thomas Cranmer. 'Great jousts' followed the next day; everything was as it used to be – except that the King himself did not joust. All in all, Henry VIII could feel well pleased. The religious service in the abbey had not reflected the momentous break with Rome which had recently taken place: why should it? The King was conservative in his own piety, seeing no particular merit in 'reformed' rituals for their own sake. As to the royal supremacy, surely he was merely restoring the church to its ancient practices …

In a bull of 11 July 1533 Pope Clement VII declared Cranmer's judgement at Dunstable void, and ordered Henry to put away Anne, adding that any child of theirs would be illegitimate; he also excommunicated the King, although the operation of the excommunication was suspended. None of this materially assisted Queen Catherine. Only the Emperor could do that now, with troops, and he was not disposed to do so. He would by his influence prevent the Pope from reaching an accommodation with the English King (thus preventing one kind of solution for his aunt, who as a loyal daughter of the church would have had to bow to a papal decision in favour of divorce), but he would not bring about the other kind of solution in her favour. Thus Queen Catherine was stuck in a kind of unhappy limbo.

After all this there were now some indications at court to encourage Catherine and her supporters that all was not well between the King and the new Queen. For many years King Henry had been accustomed to treat the pregnancy of his wife as a period when a man could be forgiven a mild flirtation, gallantries that went perhaps a little too far ... He did not see that Queen Anne Boleyn should take exception to a pattern of behaviour that Queen Catherine of Aragon had so admirably tolerated. The ladies-in-waiting who surrounded the new Queen were just as pretty, just as tempting, as those who had attended Queen Catherine.

But there were crucial differences. First, the stakes were now much higher.

Buckden Palace in Huntingdonshire, the chief residence of the bishops of Lincoln, where Catherine of Aragon was moved in 1533.

There was at least a possibility that the King might abandon his wife for love of another, since he had done so once. Thus his passions, fleeting or otherwise, incurred even closer attention from the court. Secondly, this theoretical possibility inevitably stirred up the new Queen. She was already prone to fits of jealousy which (unlike Queen Catherine) she made no attempt to control. The King dealt with his tempestuous wife's protests in some sharp exchanges. There was much 'coldness and grumbling' between them. When Queen Anne made use of 'certain words' which he greatly disliked, he told her that she must shut her eyes and endure as those who were better than herself had done. He added, even more unpleasantly, that she ought to know that he could at any time 'lower her as much as he had raised her'.

Yet one should not see this grumbling as more significant than it appeared at the time. On another level, King Henry's happiness impressed observers, a by-product of the pregnancy in which he rejoiced. Such masculine pride was natural. After fourteen years the King had demonstrated himself once more to be 'a man like other men', a phrase he had used to Chapuys – three times over – in April. The child was after all certain to be a boy. Everyone knew that. Astrologers predicted it. So did the King's physicians. Preparations for a celebratory tournament were begun, and for the actual birth 'one of the most magnificent and gorgeous beds that could be thought of' was brought out of the King's treasure room; it had originally come from France as part of the ransom for a captured nobleman. The names proposed were Henry or Edward.

The announcement of the birth of Princess Elizabeth in 1533. The document had been drawn up in anticipation of a prince and an extra 's' was inserted after 'prince' to accommodate a princess.

According to custom, Queen Anne took to her chamber in advance, to await the birth, retiring from public view on 26 August, about two weeks before the baby was actually born. About three o'clock in the afternoon of 7 September 1533 Queen Anne Boleyn was delivered of a fine healthy child. But it was a girl, a princess: Elizabeth for the King's mother, not Henry for himself, nor Edward for his grandfather and a long line of male sovereigns stretching behind them.

116

CHAPTER 6

The Most Happy?

THE CHRISTENING OF this unexpected princess was a somewhat low-key affair: for instance the splendid joust planned in honour of a prince was immediately cancelled. Anne demanded a special 'triumphal cloth' which her predecessor Queen Catherine had brought with her from Spain for the purpose of baptisms. Predictably Catherine refused. 'God forbid', she shuddered, that she should give any 'help, assistance or favour' either directly or indirectly, in 'a case so horrible as this'. Yet low-key as the christening might be, the old order was finished, the old Queen set aside and the elder princess no longer heiress-presumptive to her father, a position she had occupied since her birth in 1516.

The royal herald hammered home Mary's change in status when he proclaimed the new-born Princess Elizabeth as the King's first 'legitimate' child. Before the birth of the new princess considerable caution had been exercised in handling Princess Mary. Queen Anne might ƒbe well advanced in pregnancy, but no one knew better than the King and his advisers how great were the perils of childbirth and how frail the life of infants could be. It was only in November 1533 that Mary's own household was dissolved and she was placed in the household of the infant Elizabeth, to whom she was officially inferior. Throughout this period, Mary's marriageability remained a factor: at seventeen-and-a-half in the summer of 1533, she was already older than her mother had been at the first of her weddings. Abroad Princess Mary's prestige remained high. Of Mary, after all, it could be said, as it was once said of her mother, that she was descended 'from great kings'. She was not only the daughter of the King of England, she was also the cousin of the Emperor. With Queen Catherine out of the picture, diplomatically speaking, Princess Mary came into stronger focus.

At home, there was also the intriguing question of King Henry's attitude to his daughter. Undoubtedly he was still very fond of her; he was an affectionate man, happy to dote upon his children – so long as they did not cross his will – and Princess Mary in youth had been a charming, submissive little girl, his 'pearl', as Henry once described her. Mary's own adoration of the powerful central figure in her life, her father, had been all any patriarch could have wished. The vulgar threats said to have been made by Queen Anne towards her – 'she would make of the princess a maid in her household … or marry her to some varlet' – were obviously rooted in jealousy of this paternal affection, potentially so dangerous to Anne's own position.

Now Queen Anne had produced her own heir for the King. In September 1533 everything was changed. Or was it? It is at this point that the complication of the new royal baby's inconvenient gender comes into play. The bold words of the royal herald concerning Elizabeth as the King's first 'legitimate' child glossed over the awkward fact that the King now had two daughters. It was already arguable which one was legitimate: if the divorce and subsequent remarriage was not accepted as valid, then it was actually Elizabeth who was the bastard. What was unarguable was that Mary was the elder, so that if both princesses, by some sleight of hand, were held to be legitimate (as the provisions of canon law would have allowed), then Mary's claims to succeed her father were still superior.

Thus the need for a male heir remained as urgent as ever; in fact it could be argued that the involuntarily threatening presence of poor Princess Mary made it even more important for Queen Anne to produce a son than it had been for Queen Catherine. A portrait medal struck in 1534 bears the motto round its rim: 'A.R. The Moost Happi', but it was difficult to see how this happiness could be complete

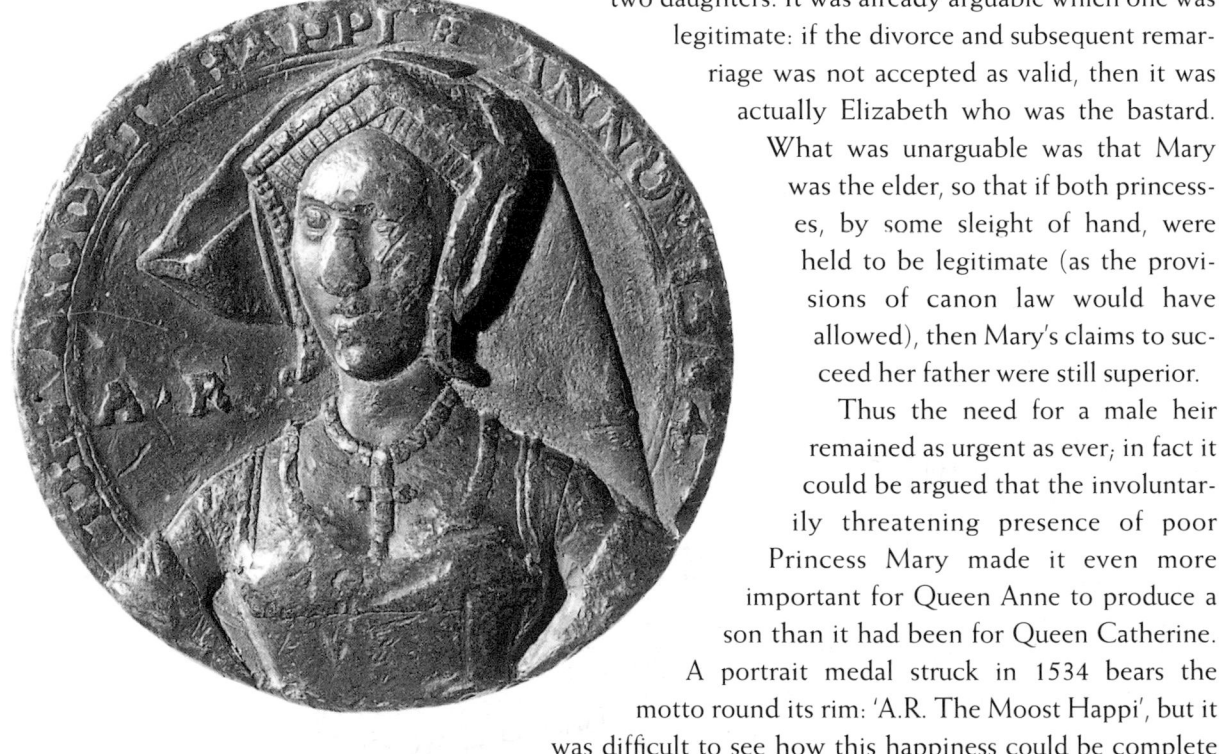

The 1534 medal of Anne Boleyn inscribed with her motto 'The Moost Happi'.

with a mere daughter. Ironically enough, not only Anne's but Mary's position might have been better had Elizabeth turned out to be that longed-for prince. Mary would then have represented no real threat: for all her relationship to the Emperor, her supporters would have had to acknowledge the tacit supremacy of a male heir. Mary could then have enjoyed a more placid existence as an English princess, for whom a suitable marriage – to one of the French princes, if not James of Scotland – would be found. As it was, Mary had to endure a campaign of cruelty from which she would not be rescued for many years with debilitating effects not only on her health but on her character.

Since this responsibility to provide a son was of course considered to be the Queen's, it must have been with an extraordinary sense of relief that around the turn of the year Anne Boleyn did indeed find that she was pregnant. On 28 January 1534 King Henry triumphantly told Chapuys that he would soon be a father again. During the spring work was done on the royal nurseries at Eltham Palace 'against the coming of the prince'. If we suppose Queen Anne to be roughly four months pregnant at the time the work was commissioned – the average period thought necessary for a pregnancy to be an established fact – then she had conceived in November, that is, some two months after the birth of Elizabeth. This timing was perfectly possible since like other royal or aristocratic ladies, Queen Anne did not breastfeed her baby (which might have inhibited conception).

For that matter Queen Anne did not care for her child in anything like the modern sense, since it was thought commensurate with the rank of a princess that the baby Elizabeth should have her own household. This makes Queen Anne's relationship with her little daughter peculiarly difficult to establish during the fleeting years in which she was alive to enjoy it. We know that Princess Elizabeth, having been moved to the care of Lady Bryan, was weaned from her wet nurse at the age of thirteen months. But the order came from the King, and the formality of its language – 'with the assent of the Queen's grace' – attests to

The hammerbeam roof built by Edward IV at Eltham Palace. In 1534 work was carried out in the royal nurseries there in anticipation of the birth of the expected prince.

a way of life in which ceremonial emphasizing the child's rank was a prime consideration.

During the spring of 1534 tumultuous events were taking place in England as the King and Cromwell pursued their remaking of the ecclesiastial structure of the country. Knowledge of his wife's pregnancy meant that the King had a satisfying emotional basis to it all: the plan intended for England and himself was surely working. As he told Chapuys at the end of February, Princess Elizabeth would not be his heir for very long, since he expected the Queen to give birth to a son 'very soon'. King Henry was certainly able to brush off the fact that in May 1534, even as the royal nursery was being prepared once again for Anne Boleyn's child, the Pope finally found for Queen Catherine. At long last he declared that her marriage to King Henry had been valid all along.

But like his bull against the King the previous July, the Pope's action availed Queen Catherine little. Who was to enforce her rights? The Emperor was fully occupied trying to handle his own dominions. King François, with his eyes on a European situation which he intended to manipulate to his advantage, had no wish to interfere in England. Clement VII died in November and the following year, when the new Pope Paul III suggested that the French King might carry out the sentence against King Henry by force of arms, King François' reaction was to propose a marriage for Princess Mary with one of his sons, the Duc d'Angoulême – not quite the same thing.

In England a tide of legislation was now being enacted. From the point of view of the country at large, the Act of Supremacy was the most momentous change. The powers claimed for the King under this act, as head of the church of England, stretched as far as the definition of faith itself. In future the King of England was to enjoy not only 'the style and title' of Supreme Head of the Church, but all the prerogatives 'to the said dignity of supreme head of the same church belonging and apertaining'. But from the point of view of Queen Anne, Queen Catherine and Princess Mary, the Act of Succession produced the more immediately revolutionary effect. Above all the oath of support for this act that was now required from individuals put partisans of the old order in an extremely difficult position.

The Act of Succession formally declared the validity of the marriage of King Henry and Queen Anne, together with the right of their lawful issue to succeed. Even now, however, Princess Mary was not specifically named as illegitimate. This may have been a precaution against the infant Princess Elizabeth's death or, equally practically, to avoid harming Mary's prospects in the marriage market. The value of a King's 'natural daughter' was, after all, a good deal less. Yet the title 'Princess' had effectively been taken from Mary, and in future she was not supposed to be addressed as such any more than her mother should now be greeted as Queen, but as 'Lady Mary'..

When Queen Catherine was brought the oath to swear in May 1534 she responded by passionately reciting all her familiar arguments regarding the divorce. But Catherine's Spanish servants had to swear – or leave. Some of her servants did leave rather than, in effect, perjure themselves, including Bastian, the Burgundian lackey who had served her for seventeen years. 'Now it pains me to be forced to leave so good a mistress', he told her as he knelt before her to say goodbye, and Queen Catherine wept. But Queen Catherine's servants were small fry. As for her personal safety, whatever Chapuys' oft-expressed fears, it can never have been the intention of the King to harm her. To put the situation at its most cynical, her health was already, by January 1534, giving rise to

The Bell Tower where Sir Thomas More was imprisoned in the Tower of London.

concern: the King told the French ambassador that she was 'dropsical and could not live long'. Mary refused to swear the oath, encouraged by her mother.

But the Act of Succession placed others in a more perilous position. Refusing to swear the oath which supported it carried a penalty of life imprisonment. Any person who could be shown to have gone further and denied that the King was head of the church would suffer death. Such a refusal sought to deprive the King of his title – and that was now treason. These clauses trapped a series of individuals, as well as whole religious communities, who declined to swear the oath. Over the next years there were those, most famously Thomas More and Bishop Fisher, who would perish by the axe as a result.

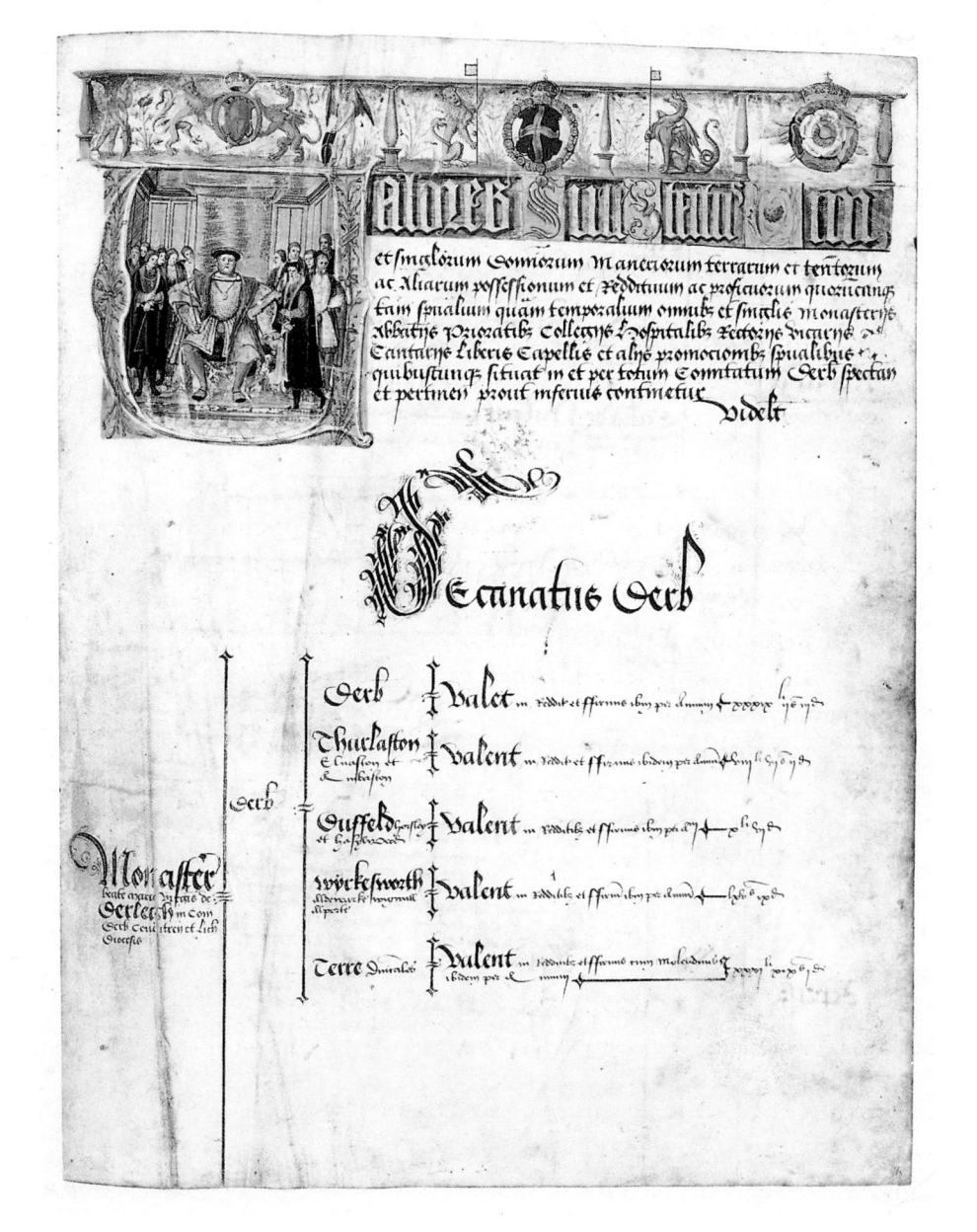

Title page of the Valor Ecclesiasticus, *the valuation of church property in England and Wales – benefices and bishoprics as well as monasteries and colleges – prepared in 1535 by Cromwell's commissioners. It was often referred to as 'the King's Book'.*

Meanwhile King Henry was preoccupied elsewhere. 'What a great expense it was for the King to continue his buildings in so many places at once': thus Thomas Cromwell in 1534 saluted, somewhat nervously, the explosion of refurbishment, reconstruction and new construction by Henry VIII which commenced in the years of his marriage to Anne Boleyn. It was as though the King, having made himself master in his own house, metaphorically speaking, was determined to hammer the point home publicly by adding enormously to the number of his actual houses. There is indeed something positively manic about his acquisitiveness and extravagance. By the 1520s, Fmost of the castles in the south of England were in his hands. The dissolution of great abbeys, priories and other institutions – bringing the King a further eleven palaces – provided other rich opportunities.

The intertwined initials of Henry and Anne Boleyn also survive in the roof of Anne Boleyn's gateway at Hampton Court, bearing mute witness to the brief but splendid era of 'Anne the Quene'.

There is something appropriately symbolic about the badges and initials of his new wife, represented in glass, stone and painted wood, which would decorate these new palaces – as well as replacing those of Queen Catherine in the old ones. For Queen Anne stood for the new order, not only because her personal tastes in religion had always tended towards reform. Her very presence by the King's side, jewelled and elegant, indicated that the King had taken on the fight to make of England and its church an 'empire', subject to no authority but his own – and had won.

Painting by Holbein of a court servant. The official wears the royal initials H(enricus) R(ex) on his jacket.

In other ways, her love of music, for example, Queen Anne was an appropriate consort for a Renaissance sovereign. One of her music books survives, consisting of thirty-nine Latin motets and five French *chansons* of the Franco-Flemish school. It has been suggested that this book was compiled for the Queen by a young musician called Mark Smeaton, a member of the King's chamber for the last four or five years, and a friend of her brother George Viscount Rochford. Such a youth, a talented virginalist and organist and a 'deft dancer', was typical of the kind of company the Queen, with her artistic tastes, enjoyed.

Dancing, of course, continued to take place. In 1533 Sir Edward Baynton, Queen Anne's vice-chamberlain, commented that there were 'never more pastimes' including specifically dancing, in the Queen's chamber. The fact that William Latymer, in his *Cronickille* of Anne Boleyn's life (published in the reign of her daughter), would paint a picture of danceless austerity merely shows how hagiography develops. Latymer had been chaplain to Queen Anne and is thus in many respects a most important source; later he became chaplain to Queen Elizabeth and Clerk of her Closet, with the delicate problem of handling the question of her mother's fate. His response was to stress all the most pious aspects of Queen Anne's character, blotting out the rest. But both sides could co-exist. Unlike Latymer, we can easily accept that a love of the arts, pleasure itself, is compatible with an interest in religion.

Latymer bears eloquent testimony to Queen Anne's patronage of evangelicals and her admittance of them to the ranks of chaplains. To take only one example, a known radical in religious matters, Nicholas Shaxton, appointed her almoner in 1533, became Bishop of Salisbury in 1535. (Queen Anne lent him £200 to pay his 'first fruits' to the King.) Her influence should not be exaggerated: certain evangelicals were executed as heretics during her time, but the evidence of her household, combined with that of ecclesiastical appointments, shows that there was a real connection for those of reformist tendencies between the Queen's favour and preferment.

On one subject, however, Queen Anne's scriptural 'disputations' in the presence of the King, Latymer does provide a valuable sidelight. At some point

Henry VIII decided that he did not like arguing with women – and thus women who chose to argue. It was far from being an exceptional view in the early sixteenth century for a man, let alone a monarch; on the one hand biblical texts enjoined silence on the part of the female; on the other hand it was generally agreed that, despite this prohibition most women had undesirably prattling tongues, possibly inspired by the Evil One himself. Nevertheless Henry VIII's exceptional dislike of disputatious women – or those who appeared to him to fall into this category – which he would evince in his later years, deserves further explanation.

At the beginning, the young Anne Boleyn's flashing, witty repartees had excited the King, and even her sulks had ended in amorous reconciliation. These ups and downs had their own pattern but they were very different from the kind of scene outlined by Latymer in his biography. Here Queen Anne never dined with the King 'without some argument of Scripture thoroughly debated'. Her chamberlain, Lord Borough, and her vice-chamberlain, Sir Edward Baynton, would take part. According to Latymer King Henry took 'such pleasure' in all this that 'diverse and sundry times he would not only hear them but sometime would argue and reason himself.' But perhaps his underlying feeling had been rather different. The King would specifically order his future wives to avoid argument. It seems likely therefore that female disputation became associated in his mind not so much with the sex in general, but with vanished, disgraced, contentious Queen Anne.

Latymer's picture of the pious Queen was completed by the strict morality which she enjoined on the young women who attended her. Given that she herself had waited on Queen Catherine and that she now had a girl called Jane Seymour in her chamber, one can either interpret this attitude as distasteful hypocrisy or practical vigilance. Certainly vigilance was justified, for the King was straying again. One of the girls in the Queen's chamber who was ticked off for frivolity was a certain Mistress Margaret (or Madge) Shelton. She was 'the concubine's first cousin', as Chapuys put it, since her mother, Lady Shelton, was sister to Sir Thomas Boleyn. Madge Shelton must have been extremely appealing; a few years

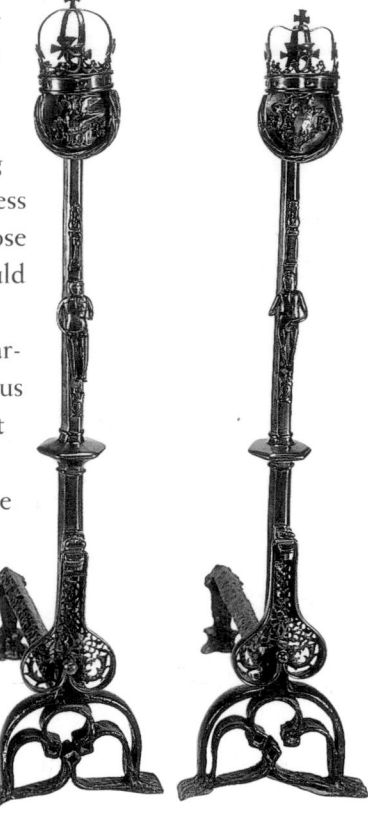

A pair of cast-iron and steel firedogs in the Great Hall at Knole, with the cipher of Henry VIII, the initials HR and the falcon of Anne Boleyn.

Left: Books in beautiful bindings and illuminated manuscripts survive as testimony to Anne Boleyn's interest in literature. This is her Book of Hours, *printed, and with hand-coloured miniatures and coloured initials.*

later when the noted beauty Duchess Christina of Milan was being investigated as a possible royal bride, it was declared in the Duchess' favour that she 'resembleth much one Mistress Shelton', late of the Queen's chamber, with dimples – 'pits' in her cheeks, 'very gentle of countenance' and 'soft of speech'.

Madge Shelton was not only attractive, she was also spirited and flirtatious:

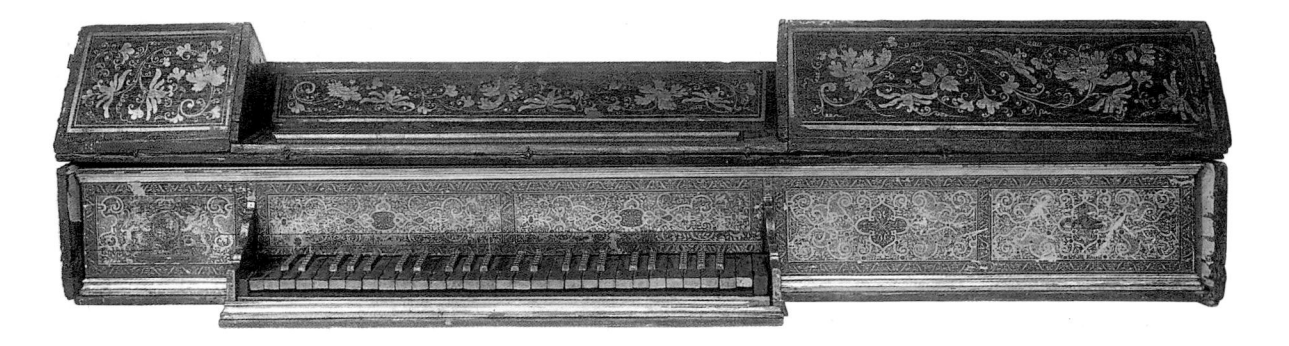

Anne Boleyn shared the King's love of music. These virginals reputedly belonged to her and are decorated with the Boleyn arms.

the type of the cheerful Bessie Blount, perhaps, that had always amused the King. From Anne's point of view, however, she was the kind of girl – oh horrors! – who wrote 'idle poesies' in her devotional reading. A defaced book came to light. Once the culprit was discovered, Queen Anne 'wonderfully rebuked her'. Human nature being what it is, it is surely not implausible to connect this incident with the King's dalliance with Mistress Shelton, dated by Chapuys from February 1533 onwards. Her enjoyment of royal favours seems to have lasted for about six months, for later in 1535 the King took another of his fancies, this time to Jane Seymour.

All this was worrying for Queen Anne – how could it not be, considering the circumstances of her own rise to power? – but it was not necessarily disastrous. It was in 1535 that Chapuys wrote to his master that Queen Anne was as powerful as ever: 'the King dares not contradict her'. The sexual magnetism she had once had for the King might be waning; at the age of thirty-five the dark gypsy looks, which had once been so striking, might be fading. Nevertheless her 'craft' in Chapuys' phrase, remained; and King Henry, much as he disliked being argued with by women, had no objection to being managed by them – provided they did it gracefully and gently.

But Queen Anne's real weapon was what it had always been: her ability to provide a male heir. In this context, therefore, the failure of the pregnancy of 1534 was a sharp blow. The most likely end of it was a stillbirth, probably a month or so early, since the Queen had not retired to her chamber. Such mishaps were never the subject of official communiqués. From the autumn of 1534 onwards Queen Anne sought her salvation in a third pregnancy. Almost certainly by this time she was having to cope with the problem of her husband's periodic impotence; not a fortunate combination of circumstances. The King had assured his parliament at the beginning of the 1530s that he was not proposing to marry Anne Boleyn out of any kind of self-indulgent passion: 'for I am,' he said, 'forty-one years old, at which age the lust of man is not so quick as in lusty youth.' Illness in the vital area may have contributed to the problem. The King had bladder trouble in 1528 and himself recommended a cure for a tumour of the testicles.

As to Queen Anne's reaction to the King's marital performance, a bitter remark she was said to have made to her sister-in-law Jane Rochford would be quoted against her later: the King could not satisfy a woman, she exclaimed: in this vital respect he had neither 'vertu' (skill) nor 'puissance' (virility). Queen Anne was never one to mince her words. Here was someone who was expected by the world to get pregnant, and who was getting blamed for a failure that was not of her own making.

Queen Catherine was by now at Kimbolton Castle, near Huntingdon. Built sixty years earlier by the widow of the lst Duke of Buckingham, it was now in a state of great decay. Queen Catherine had not wanted to be taken there. Nonetheless she comforted her servants at this latest development, adding that she trusted in the mercy of God that he would turn the heart of her dear husband 'so that he may see the error into which he has fallen.' Not every outside contact was eliminated: Queen Catherine's two Spanish physicians, first Dr Fernando Vittoria and later Dr Miguel da Sá not only looked after her health, but were able to correspond with Chapuys. But her maintenance was cut; having lived all her life in royal style she now had a manner of living which was more like that of the nun she had once refused to become.

All this could be endured. The true hardship for Catherine lay in the refusal to give her any chance to see her daughter, even when Mary was ill. Henry VIII's disgust at the unwillingness of either woman to bow her neck in submission had found its most effective form of expression. He pretended to believe that Catherine was 'so haughty in spirit' that she might take the opportunity of raising a number of men and making war 'as boldly as her mother, Isabella, had done'. This was fantasy. The reality was the cruelty of a thwarted man, visited on an ageing sick woman. For throughout the autumn of 1535, Queen Catherine's condition deteriorated. Finally on 31 December Cromwell was informed that 'the Princess Dowager' was 'in great danger of life'. Her doctor believed that even if she were to recover for a short while, the end could not long be delayed.

At court however, the traditional New Year's celebrations were joyous, particularly on the part of Queen Anne. It was not so much the mortal sickness of her predecessor that moved her with delight, but the fact that she was once more unquestionably pregnant: approaching three months at the turn of the year. In spite of her husband's 'amours', and his growing fancy for the demure Jane Seymour, Queen Anne had again conceived a child.

The doctor who had predicted that if Queen Catherine recovered it would not be for long, turned out to be right. She did rally at the beginning of 1536, long enough to receive the faithful ambassador Chapuys who came rushing down to Kimbolton, as did her old friend and lady-in-waiting Maria de Salinas Lady Willoughby. Mary was still far away. Catherine had not seen her for over two years; there was no mercy from the King in that direction.

The Queen was not strong enough to write a last letter to the King: the text was dictated to one of her ladies. At the last she remained concerned for his spiritual welfare: 'My most dear Lord, King and husband, the hour of my death approaching ... I cannot choose, but out of love I bear you, advise you of your soul's health which you ought to prefer before all considerations of the world or flesh whatsoever. For which yet you have cast me into many calamities, and yourself into many troubles.' If the tone was wifely, who can blame her for this? Then she commended 'Mary our daughter' to the King, beseeching him to be a good father to her. The fate of her remaining maids – 'they being but three' – and their need for their marriage portions concerned her and she wanted all her servants to have a year's pay beyond their due. These anxious requests were characteristic of Catherine of Aragon: under English law, as a married woman she could not make a will, but she was allowed to leave a list of 'supplications'. But it is her final words to King Henry VIII which are the most affecting: 'Lastly, I make this vow, that mine eyes desire you above all things. Farewell.'

The rally was brief. On the evening of 6 January the Queen had a relapse. Maria de Salinas had remained behind when Chapuys returned to London and it was she who now held her mistress. At nightfall, the Queen could still manage to comb her own hair and tie it back – that 'abundant' hair which had once been her greatest beauty – without the help of her maids. But as the night hours passed, she asked her doctor to tell her the truth. He replied with candour: 'Madam, you must die'. Still, scrupulous to the last, she refused to have Mass said for her before dawn (the earliest hour permitted by the rules of the Catholic church). Finally in that dark mid-winter season dawn did come and the Queen did receive the sacrament. Accepting it, she asked God's pardon for 'the King her husband, for the wrong he had done her.' Yet she lingered. It was two o'clock in the afternoon before she died.

Almost immediately the rumours that King Henry had poisoned her began to spread. That was inevitable, given that much of the imperialist correspondence during her last years had been taken up with fears for her safety. But the charge is ludicrous; not simply because God was likely to carry off Catherine soon enough without any extra help. There is also the question of the character of Henry VIII. He regarded poison with moral repugnance: it was alien to him. The axe and rope, wielded in public, not secret poison were the weapons of his authority against those who defied the royal will, preceded if possible by the culprits' profound repentance at having crossed or betrayed him.

At first sight it is equally fanciful – if more romantic – to suggest that Queen Catherine died of a broken heart. The link between grief and mortal disease is after all indefinable. And yet, oddly enough, the autopsy performed on her body by the castle's chandler (one of his official duties) did reveal a large round black growth on her heart which was itself 'completely black and hideous'. He found all the other internal organs perfectly healthy. In fact a late nineteenth-century specialist pointed out that Queen Catherine died of a form of cancer – melanotic sarcoma – then quite impossible for her physician to diagnose; the tumour on her heart was almost certainly secondary, the chandler having missed the primary growth.

King Henry VIII, according to popular legend, did not find the news particularly painful. He was said to have dressed himself in yellow – the colour of rejoicing – with a white feather in his hat (although Lord Herbert of Cherbury, in a seventeenth-century biography, wrote that the King wept at Catherine's last letter: both stories may of course have been true). Other sources attributed the tasteless yellow to Anne Boleyn, so that perhaps the royal couple radiated their 'joy and delight' in matching costumes. Almost immediately royal avarice took over. Catherine's favourite Franciscan convent was not to receive her robes: the King decided that its members had quite enough already. Nor were they to tend to her funeral. As for burial in St Paul's, that would cost more 'than was either requisite or needful'. The King also refused to comply with his former wife's other bequests of clothes and property until he had seen 'what the robes and furs were like'.

The tomb of Catherine of Aragon in Peterborough Cathedral. In January 1986, the four hundred and fiftieth anniversary of her burial, a new tablet was erected in her memory:

'A QUEEN CHERISHED BY THE ENGLISH PEOPLE FOR HER LOYALTY, PIETY, COURAGE AND COMPASSION'.

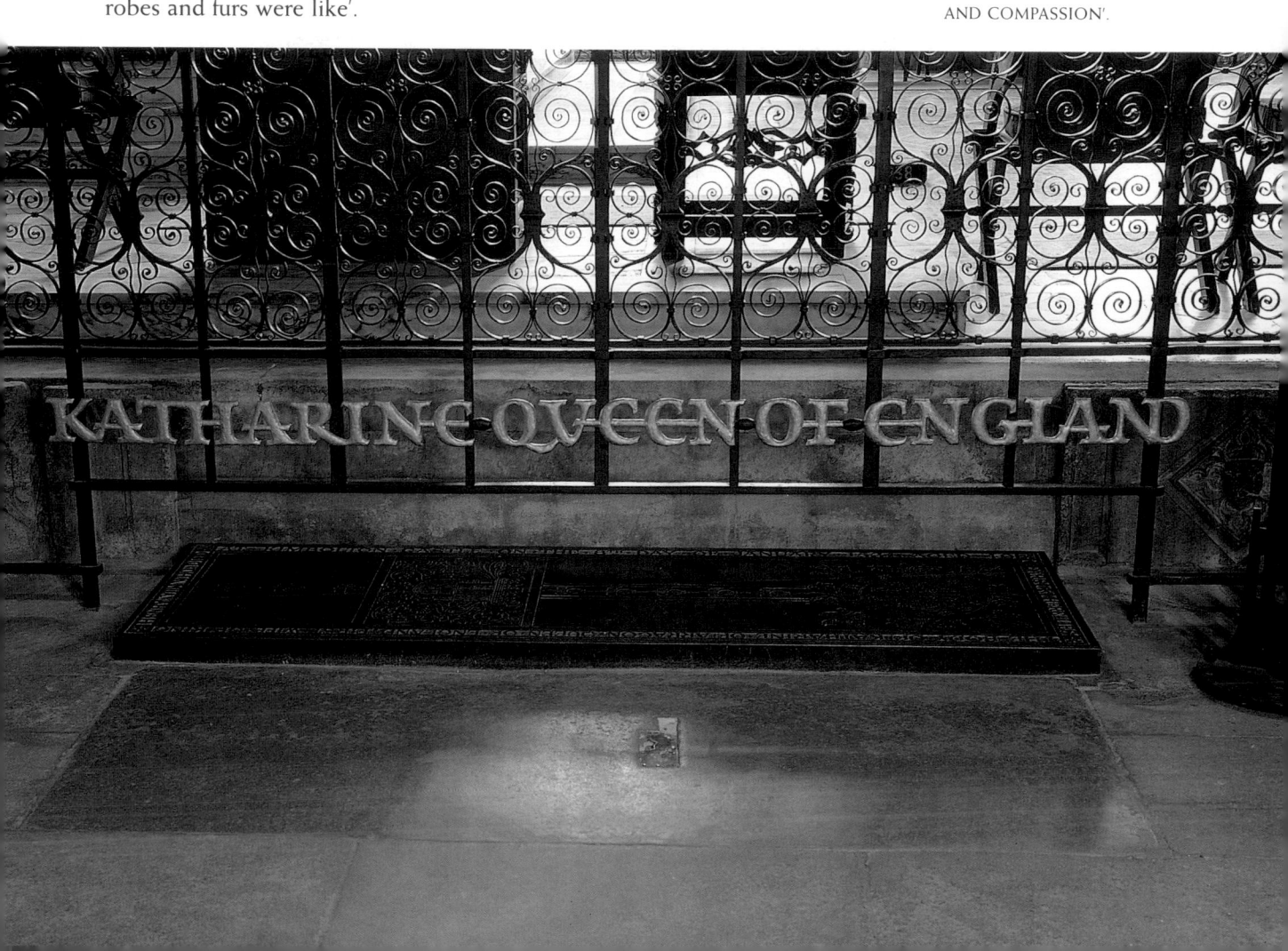

The King's eventual choice of burial place for Catherine – three weeks after her death – was the ancient and beautiful Peterborough Cathedral, about twenty miles from Kimbolton Castle. Obviously the funeral procession would attract less attention here than on its way to St Paul's (as well as costing less money); even so, the country people thronged the route to see the coffin of their 'good Queen Catherine' as it passed. The funeral itself was stately, though Chapuys expressed indignation about the position chosen for her burial: in the north-west transept of the cathedral, 'far removed from the high altar and much less honourable than that of certain bishops buried there'.

The removal of her rival should have ushered in the happiest period of Queen Anne's life. Instead it brought about her downfall. As Chapuys commented drily, the marriage of 'the Concubine' had not become 'more valid and legitimate' as a result of Queen Catherine's death. Henry VIII was now, by strict Catholic standards, a widower, since his only wife in the eyes of the church had died. Any monarch who was a widower – particularly one without a male heir – quickly regarded himself as not only free but bound to marry again. Of course by other standards – that of the new English church of which he was head – the King was far from being free. His fancy for Jane Seymour might be intensifying, but his second wife was pregnant, and that event for which the nation hoped – the birth of his son – apparently set in motion once more.

But it was not to be. At the end of January Queen Anne miscarried. It was 'a man child', something over three months old. According to a contemporary account Queen Anne was hysterical with disappointment – and no doubt apprehension. The King had had a recent serious fall at jousting. The Queen burst out that this dreadful shock had caused the mishap, so great was her love for him. The plea and the excuse fell equally on deaf ears. The King was supposed to have remarked 'with much ill grace' that when the Queen had risen from her bed of sickness, 'I will come and speak with you'. But a more ominous part of the same story concerned the King's exclamation: 'I see God will not give me male children.' Most sinister of all was his own explanation for this: he had been bewitched by Anne Boleyn. It was the ultimate denial of his own personal responsibility.

The King's relationship with Jane Seymour now took on fresh significance. A passion which might under other circumstances have been enjoyable but transitory, became the focus for universal speculation. Chapuys indeed heard that it was news of the presents the King had recently given to 'Mistress Seymour' which had brought on Queen Anne's mishap. A story of a later date had Queen Anne finding Mistress Seymour actually sitting on her husband's lap. There was said to have been 'much scratching and by-blows between the Queen and her maid'. However, there is no contemporary evidence for such robust incidents.

The character of Jane Seymour as it emerges in 1536 is on the contrary chaste, verging on the prudish. The Seymours were a family of respectable and even ancient antecedents in an age when such things were important. Sir John

Portrait of Jane Seymour by Holbein. It was Jane's sweet nature rather than her beauty that attracted the King in 1535. He probably first started to be attracted to her when he stayed with the Seymour family for a week at Wolf Hall in Wiltshire.

Seymour, father of Jane, was born in about 1474, had been knighted by Henry VII in 1497 and went on to enjoy royal favour throughout the next reign. Like Sir Thomas Boleyn, he accompanied Henry VIII on his French campaign of 1513, was present at the Field of Cloth of Gold, attended at Canterbury to meet Charles V and by 1532 had become a Gentleman of the Bedchamber. It was a career that lacked startling distinction but one which brought him close to the monarch throughout his adult life. But there was something outstanding about him, or at least about his immediate family. Sir John came of a family of eight children; then his own wife gave birth to ten children – six sons and four daughters. Jane was the fifth child but oldest girl. All this was auspicious for his daughter, including the number of males conceived, at a time when women's ability to bear children was often judged by their family record. It was however from her mother, Margery Wentworth – once again echoing the pattern of Anne Boleyn – that Jane Seymour derived that qualifying dash of royal blood so important to a woman viewed as possible breeding stock. Margery Wentworth was descended from Edward III, via her great-great-grandmother Elizabeth Mortimer, Lady Hotspur, which meant that Jane and Henry VIII were fifth cousins.

Apart from her presumed fertility, what else did Jane Seymour, now in her mid-twenties (the age incidentally at which Anne Boleyn had attracted the King's attention), have to offer? It seems likely that the charm of her character outweighed the charm of her appearance: Chapuys described her as 'of middle stature and no great beauty'. Her most distinctive aspect was her famously 'pure white' complexion. Holbein gives her a long nose and firm mouth, with the lips slightly compressed, although her face has a pleasing oval shape, with the high forehead then admired and set off by the headdresses of the time. Altogether, if Anne Boleyn conveys the fascination of the new, there is a dignified but slightly stolid look to Jane Seymour, appropriately reminiscent of English mediaeval consorts.

But the predominant impression given by her portrait at the hands of a master of artistic realism is of a woman of calm good sense. And contemporaries all commented on Jane Seymour's intelligence; in this she was clearly more like her cautious brother Edward than her dashing brother Tom. She was also naturally sweet-natured (no angry words or tantrums here) and virtuous – her virtue was another topic on which there was general agreement. Her survival as a lady-in-waiting to two Queens at the Tudor court still with a spotless reputation may indeed be seen as a testament to both Jane Seymour's salient characteristics – virtue and common good sense.

We cannot be quite sure when the project to substitute Jane Seymour for Anne Bolyn was hatched among Anne's political enemies (and the enemies of her family). Obviously nothing could be fully fledged while Queen Anne was pregnant but after her miscarriage events moved extremely fast, suggesting that news of the royal pregnancy had temporarily interrupted plots already laid.

After all, the court can only have heard of this pregnancy a few weeks before it terminated, if then. For half of 1534 and virtually the whole of 1535, as Queen Anne desperately tried to work her magic on the resentful body of her husband, she would have been regarded by courtiers as possibly incapable of conceiving a further child.

At least her accounts show that Queen Anne had the bravado to keep up her royal state – and her royal spending. Orange tawny silk was ordered for one nightgown (a loose *robe de chambre*, not a nightdress), and lengths of fine ribbon for rolling up her long hair. Payments for the adorning of her 'great bed' – gold fringe of Venice and tassels of Florence gold – have however a particular poignancy, since it is unlikely that King Henry now cared to visit it. Meanwhile, the anti-Boleyn faction at court advanced the cause of Jane Seymour to have her own richly ornamented great bed, which in this case the King would share. This faction had come to include not only grandees like

Sir Nicholas Carew, the Master of the Horse and a near contemporary of Henry VIII, who spent most of his adult life at court. Portrait by Holbein.

Lord Montague, heading the half-royal Pole family, and the Exeters, but some important members of the royal household network, jealous of the Boleyns, such as King Henry's longtime companion and contemporary Sir Nicholas Carew, Master of the Horse.

To the intricacies of English politics and in-fighting were now added international pressures. If there was to be an accord between Spain and England – as the English diplomatic weather vane turned once again away from France – then the Emperor had to swallow the insult to Spain posed by the treatment of his aunt. The death of Queen Catherine, followed by heavy hints that 'the Concubine' herself might be replaced, produced a generally benevolent atmosphere for this. In this context a crucial conversation took place between Chapuys and Thomas Cromwell on 31 March when Chapuys delivered the important message that the price of the Emperor's friendship was not in fact Henry VIII's submission to Rome, but getting rid of 'the Concubine'; nor were the rights of Princess Mary going to prove an obstacle. This was the third step in the destruction of Anne Boleyn, the death of Queen Catherine and her own miscarriage constituting the first and second.

Meanwhile the King's infatuation for Jane Seymour was deepening. A week or so before the Chapuys interview, King Henry had had the unpleasant task which sometimes falls to distinguished lovers, even monarchs, of explaining to his sweetheart that their relationship had not escaped satirical attention. Jane's brother Sir Edward Seymour had recently been made a member of his Privy Chamber by the King – an honour which could not fail to indicate the way the royal wind was blowing. To Jane, his 'dear friend and Mistress', the King counselled calm: 'Advertising you that there is a ballad made lately of great derision against us … I pray you pay no manner of regard to it.' But he sweetened the blow by enclosing a present of golden sovereigns, while promising that as soon as the author of this 'malignant writing' was discovered, he would be punished 'straitly'.

But Jane Seymour refused to accept his gift. Instead she flung herself on her knees and kissing the royal missive, begged the King (via his messenger) to remember that she was 'a gentlewoman of fair and honourable lineage without reproach'. 'If the King deigned to make her a present of money, she prayed that it might be when she made an honourable marriage.' Far from being put off, the King was still further enchanted. Such blushing reticence on the part of Mistress Seymour inflamed his ardour – an ardour popularly thought to be flagging these days, at least in physical terms.

A few weeks after this episode – on Easter Tuesday, 18 April 1535 – Sir Edward and Lady Seymour, chaperoning his sister, moved into the apartments at Greenwich hastily vacated by Thomas Cromwell. This was an official indication that Cromwell had decided to join with them at least for the purpose of getting rid of Anne Boleyn. (Conveniently enough the King could reach these rooms 'by certain galleries without being perceived'.) Cromwell would say later that this was the moment at which he realized that the presence of Anne as Queen threatened the safety of the kingdom – and his own as secretary. Certainly from now on Cromwell took the lead in what became open season for the destruction of Anne Boleyn.

Queen Anne was helpless. One can only feel sympathy for the desperate woman. After all, what crime had she actually committed (apart from not producing a son)? So she watched her future slip away from her amid the splendid rituals of the court: rituals which she of all people understood only too well how to interpret. On 23 April a ceremonial occasion offered the first outward sign of the inward revolution that was taking place. Sir Nicholas Carew was chosen as a new candidate for the Order of the Garter, instead of Queen Anne's brother, George Viscount Rochford, who had been widely expected to receive the honour. Everyone knew that Carew was 'counselling' Jane Seymour. Privately on 24 April, at the instigation of Cromwell, King Henry signed a crucial document This appointed Lord Chancellor Audley, some judges and a number of nobles, including incidentally both the Queen's uncle Norfolk and her father, to investigate certain unspecified activities which might result in charges of treason.

As a result, Mark Smeaton, the musician and 'deft dancer' in the King's chamber, was lured away from the court at Greenwich and arrested on Sunday 30 April. He was very possibly tortured. This was no nobleman, to be treated with circumspection, but a young man of humble origins. Smeaton had nothing to support him except his musical talent – the royal accounts show payments for his shirts, hose and shoes, and 'bonnets' since 1529 – that, and the fact that by general agreement he was 'a very handsome man'. Such a small frightened animal stood little chance against the power of the state. Mark Smeaton made a confession.

The action now moves back to Greenwich where May Day was being celebrated by the traditional tournament watched by both King and Queen. A feature of it was to be the joust between Lord Rochford and Sir Henry Norris, Keeper of the Privy Purse and the betrothed of the King's former fancy, Madge Shelton. Unexpectedly, the King received a message. Its contents can only be guessed, but whatever they were, they caused him to rise and leave the tournament, taking Norris with him. He did not give any explanation to his wife. Just as he had gone hunting from Windsor without saying goodbye to Queen Catherine, he now left Greenwich without bidding Queen Anne farewell. He never saw her again.

On his journey back to London, the King taxed Norris with certain revelations made by Smeaton; despite Norris' incredulous denials he was taken to the Tower of London. Even more chilling to those watching the tragedy unfold – and doing their earnest best not to become involved – was the arrest of Lord Rochford. If the Queen's brother was to be brought down, who could count themselves safe who had ever enjoyed her patronage, let alone her courtly favour? On Tuesday 2 May the Queen herself was arrested at Greenwich and taken before the commissioners who had held the investigation under her uncle Norfolk, to hear the accusations against her. These included not only adultery but incest (the penalty for which could be burning at the stake) and, most heinous of all, surely, conspiracy to murder the King. After this, Queen Anne was taken by water from Greenwich to the Tower.

Carved panels from the house of Sir William Kingston, Constable of the Tower of London.

When she arrived the Queen began screaming and was heard to cry out: 'I was received with greater ceremony last time I was here'. The Constable of the Tower, Sir William Kingston, a just and kindly man, tried to comfort her, assuring her that she would not be housed in a dungeon but in the lodging she had occupied before her coronation. She rewarded him by kneeling down and crying out, 'it is too good for me', then wept, then 'fell into a great laughing'. After this the Queen managed to pass through the court-gate, but then her strength appeared to give out. She sank to her knees. In front of her escort of lords, she prayed to God to help her 'as she was not guilty of her accusement'. Then she begged the assistance of the lords themselves: would they implore the King 'to be good unto her'?

PART III

JANE SEYMOUR

CHAPTER 7

A Good and Lawful Marriage

The Queen's House in the Tower of London was built in about 1530, possibly for Anne Boleyn. But she lived there only as a prisoner during the days before her execution.

THE TRIAL OF Queen Anne Boleyn was intended to have only one result: her death. In this respect it was completely different from the ordeal endured by Queen Catherine in 1529: then at least, at Blackfriars, there had been a genuine spirit of enquiry – or at any rate some genuine confusion – about the validity of her marriage to King Henry. But no one was in any doubt, either during the trial of Anne Boleyn's alleged lovers, or during her own, that a guilty verdict would be reached.

Why was it considered essential to dispose of Queen Anne so completely? The answer lies in the behaviour of her predecessor. Once upon a time the King and his advisors had envisaged a dignified withdrawal by Queen Catherine, possibly into a convent. Instead they had faced seven years of protest. Anne Boleyn was not going to be given the same opportunity. Dismissal with what was, in effect, another divorce would have saddled the King with yet another ex-wife, only a few months after he had been freed by death from the first one.

Very likely Cromwell did not even tell his master what he intended. There is a comparison to be made with the four knights who murdered Thomas à Becket in 1170; hearing Henry II cry out against 'this turbulent priest', they thought they knew the royal mind and acted accordingly. The King's disgust with his second wife was public property ever since those ominous royal rumblings about witchcraft and the like following her miscarriage. His conscience was once again uneasy and it was absolutely necessary for Henry VIII to feel that 'God and his conscience were on very good terms', as he had once assured Chapuys they were over the dissolution of his marriage to Catherine.

Queen Anne was probably housed in the so-called Royal Lodgings in the Inner Ward, to the south of the White Tower which she had occupied before her coronation, since this was what had been promised to her by Sir William Kingston. The terms of her confinement were not harsh; she was still to be treated as a queen. Nevertheless Queen Anne remained in a state of collapse. Her laughter in the old days had sometimes been a little too loud for the occasion, or not quite appropriate. Now she seems to have broken down completely, alternating between fits of weeping and fits of laughter, just as she had done when she arrived. Her sayings became wild and incoherent, more like ravings than the polished witty conversation with which she had once beguiled the King. Her words were however industriously noted down by her ladies whose instructions were to pass on everything the Queen said to the constable and so to Cromwell. Out of this fragile tissue, a solid tapestry of evidence was to be woven.

Even in her moments of sanity Queen Anne was badly frightened – and with good reason. She had no idea what the precise foundation for the charges laid against her might be. The notion that the Queen had conspired with Sir Henry Norris to 'imagine' the death of the King was ludicrously improbable – what would either of them gain from that? But the most outrageous charges can be the most difficult to combat, as experience of state trials, not only in the sixteenth but in the twentieth century, has demonstrated. Further courtiers – Sir Francis Weston and William Brereton – were arrested on grounds of being imprudently connected with the Queen. On 8 May Anne Boleyn's old admirer Sir Thomas Wyatt was taken in, although subsequently released. There was a dragnet out, instigated by Cromwell, to pull in anyone against whom scurrilous gossip and seamy revelation would add up to proof of treason with the Queen.

What was so frightening for the Queen was the sheer intimacy of the court positions of those who had been arrested. There was a constant history of close encounters with the four men – Smeaton, Norris, Weston and Brereton – who were put on trial first. How could there not be? And with close encounters went gallantries – the sort of romantic but unconsummated gallantries that the King had cheerfully permitted and which, following his lead, were part of the custom of a Renaissance court. In a sense, such involvements were a traditional way of passing the time during the endless court festivities, rather like jousting – except that during these bouts, men tilted gracefully against women and vice versa. Poetry, music and dance were woven into the fabric of such 'tournments', wistful amorous declarations perhaps, vows, sighs, but not sex – and certainly not something as specifically dangerous as sex with the King's wife.

For the trial of Smeaton, Norris, Weston and Brereton which took place in

Sir Thomas Wyatt.
Drawing by Holbein.

Westminster Hall on 12 May 1536, there is a contrast between the long list of charges read out at the time and the gossip purveyed then and ornamented later. The charges frequently have an absurd quality: for example the Queen is supposed to have committed adultery with Norris within weeks of the birth of Princess Elizabeth, at a time when she was still in seclusion at Greenwich. As for the gossip, none of it constitutes any kind of proof. But the stories, preserved in hostile biographies, do have a domestic flavour, as though some of these words might have been spoken in a different context, flirtatiously, even provocatively – but innocently.

So the handsome young musician Mark Smeaton was accused of being in love with the Queen, as well as receiving money from her. Perhaps Smeaton was in love with her. That was not in itself a crime. But there is certainly no evidence that the Queen had returned his love. Sir Francis Weston was also supposed to have made advances to the Queen a year earlier. Weston's flirtation with her first cousin, Madge Shelton, now betrothed to Sir Henry Norris, had annoyed the Queen and she apparently reproved him for it. Weston daringly excused himself by saying that he really came to the Queen's chamber to see quite another person – 'It is yourself'. But at this the Queen, 'defied him', that is to say, forbade him to advance further with his lance in this courtly joust.

The charges against Brereton were never made clear. But it is interesting that the most damning charge against Sir Henry Norris also touched upon the subject of Madge Shelton. It was proposed that his betrothal to Madge was hanging fire because of his passion for her mistress. The Queen was supposed to have made an extraordinarily reckless remark to Norris: 'you look to dead men's shoes, for if ought came to the King but good, you would look to have me.' Yet the kernel of such a story could have been any kind of light-hearted exchange, in which the one-off rivalry of the two first cousins, Anne Boleyn and Madge Shelton, may have been the real point. But the addition of that spicy detail about the death of the King brought with it the fatal tang of treason. By the rules of justice of the time, defending counsel were not permitted against charges of treason. All four men were condemned to die at Tyburn, with the extreme penalties of the law: to be cut down while alive, disembowelled, castrated and finally to have their limbs quartered.

On Monday 15 May the trial of Lord Rochford and Queen Anne took place in the Great Hall of the Tower of London. Chapuys estimated that 2,000 people attended the spectacle, for whom special stands were erected. The twenty-six peers who took part in the judgement were none of them strangers to the brother and sister, and some of them were closely connected. Their uncle, the Duke of Norfolk presided as High Steward. Lord Rochford's father-in-law, Lord Morley, took part. Even the Queen's youthful swain Lord Percy, Earl of Northumberland since the death of his father, was among the peers present, although he did plead sudden illness and left before the end of the proceedings.

The Queen was tried first. She arrived in a calm frame of mind. According to the herald Charles Wriothesley she gave 'wise and discreet answers to her accusers', excusing herself with her words so clearly 'as though she was not actually guilty'. But then the evidence presented was hardly of such a convincing nature as to bring about a volte-face and a confession. Queen Anne never admitted to any offence and the evidence against her was a patchwork of half-truths and outright lies. All this, however, is less cogent than the sheer psychological improbability of the Queen endangering her position by adultery, let alone attempting to destroy the one man on whose favour she was totally dependent – the King. The sexual fascination of Anne Boleyn, to which her

*Portrait after Holbein
of Thomas Howard,
3rd Duke of Norfolk
and uncle of both Anne
Boleyn and Katherine
Howard.*

career bears witness, was not founded on indiscriminate sharing of her favours, rather on her ability to manage herself – and her own attractions. Tantalizing mystery, even withdrawal, can after all exert as much fascination as sexual generosity, if not more.

The trial of Lord Rochford followed that of the Queen. Here the evidence against him of incest with his sister was little short of pathetic. Character assassination, which came much later, suggested that the Queen 'much wanting to have a manchild to succeed, and finding the King not to content her' used her brother (among others) to beget a child. That was of a very different order from evidence actually produced at the time. The worst that happened was some kind of allegation from Rochford's wife Jane about 'undue familiarity' between brother and sister. To this Rochford himself was supposed to have exclaimed bitterly to his judges: 'On the evidence of only one woman you are willing to believe this great evil of me'.

But the real purpose of the arraignment of Lord Rochford was to blacken the name of his sister to the point where her malevolent nature became an article of faith. On the one hand such a creature deserved to die; on the other, none of her own vicious charges was to be taken seriously. The question of the King's impotence, about which there was a good deal of private speculation – Chapuys thought it doubtful that Jane Seymour or anyone else would have a chance of conceiving a royal child – could be used neatly to get rid of the superfluous Queen Anne. It was now that the fatal words of Queen Anne to Lady Rochford were produced: *'que le Roy n'estait habile en cas de soy copuler avec femme, et qu'il n'avait ni vertu ni puissance'* (that the King was incapable of making love to his wife and he had neither skill nor virility). This was far more damaging than the nonsense talked about incest, because it was far more likely to be true. The motives of Jane Lady Rochford remain obscure: her father had been a devoted adherent of Queen Catherine, and she may have been intending to help the cause of Catherine's daughter Mary. Alternatively, and more simply, she may have hoped to remain on the winning side despite her husband's 'guilt'. At all events, the effect of such frightful words was to damn Queen Anne most efficiently.

The sentence, pronounced by Norfolk, was the same in both cases: the Queen and her brother were to be burnt or executed according to the wish of the King. Lord Rochford had denied that he was guilty, following the sentence, and Queen Anne did likewise. Thereafter they both formally admitted that they deserved punishment. This was in accordance with conventional procedure and provided a suitable frame of reference for asking for pardon, as well as, if appropriate, avoiding the forfeiture of property. Lord Rochford accepted the prospect of death with what has been described as 'oriental fatalism'; since the state had judged him guilty, then he could no longer be innocent. Mercy might be sought but it would not be found. Two days later, on 17 May, he and the other four condemned men were executed on Tower Hill, their sentences

142

commuted from the fearful penalties to be paid at Tyburn by the wish of the King. All five died with professions of loyalty on their lips, although only Smeaton asked for pardon for his 'misdoings'.

Queen Anne now lived in hourly expectation of her death. After the firm dignity of her conduct at her trial, she reverted to more erratic behaviour. She might be 'very merry' and eat 'a great dinner', or she might be in floods of tears. She veered between talk about retreating to a nunnery – 'and is in hope of life' – and discussing her own execution. The 'hangman of Calais' had been specially summoned since he was an expert with a sword. This was a favour to the victim, because her despatch was likely to be swift (the use of the axe could sometimes mean a hideously long-drawn-out affair). When the Queen learned this, she told Kingston that she had 'heard say the executioner was very good', which was just as well since she had 'a little neck'. Then she circled it with her hand – that 'ivory neck' once praised as her special beauty. All the time, according to Kingston she was 'laughing heartily'.

Queen Anne Boleyn was not in fact to die as a queen, that title for the sake of which she had kept the King in play for seven long years – and had incurred the hostility of nearly the whole country. Before the time came for her to die, a bizarre ritual had to take place: a second divorce was secured for the King. That is, Anne Boleyn's marriage to Henry VIII was pronounced to be invalid by Archbishop Cranmer. It is not known why this judicial farce was thought necessary. (The logic of it is another matter entirely: if Anne Boleyn had never been properly married to the King, she could hardly have committed adultery as his legal wife.)

The grounds which satisfied Cranmer that he could lawfully declare the King's marriage to Anne Boleyn invalid can also only be guessed. Possibly Anne confided to Cranmer that she had been not only precontracted to Lord Percy but also secretly married to him; alternatively that their relationship had been consummated following betrothal. In this Anne Boleyn may have been exaggerating in an attempt to save her life, or she may have been telling the truth – now that it was in her interest to be frank. The decree of nullity was dated 17 May 1536, and the official copy was signed on 10 June and subscribed by both houses of parliament on 28 June.

But by this time the former Queen Anne Boleyn was dead. They came for her early in the morning – about eight o'clock – on Friday 19 May. There had been some concern about the public nature of the erstwhile Queen's execution, based on worry about what she might say to the crowd in her farewell address. It was decided to hold the execution not on Tower Hill, where there was free public access, but on the green inside the Tower which was, as it happened, conveniently adjacent to a chapel. An added advantage of using this more private spot was the fact that the gates of the Tower were habitually locked at night, so that entry could be controlled.

In this way the gathering on Tower Green was comparatively small –

The plaque on the floor of the chapel of St Peter ad Vincula that marks the burial place of Anne Boleyn.

although it was in no sense a secret ceremony. Thomas Cromwell was there, to oversee the successful accomplishment of his plan, and Lord Chancellor Audley, accompanied by the herald Wriothesley. The Dukes of Norfolk and Suffolk were both there so was the sickly young Duke of Richmond whom Anne Boleyn was supposed to have tried to poison. Then there was the Lord Mayor of London and his sheriffs. After that came the inhabitants of the Tower, virtually a small town with its multiple dwellings.

Anne Boleyn wore a mantle of ermine over a loose gown of dark grey damask, trimmed with fur, and a crimson petticoat. She had a white linen coif holding up her hair beneath her headdress. She had promised to say 'nothing but what was good' when she begged for leave to address the people and she kept her word. She spoke simply and affectingly. 'Masters, I here humbly submit me to the law as the law hath judged me, and as for mine offences, I here accuse no man. God knoweth them; I remit them to God, beseeching him to have mercy on my soul.' Then she called on Jesus Christ to 'save my sovereign and master the King, the most godly, noble and gentle Prince that is, and long to reign over you'.

Anne Boleyn now knelt down. Her ladies removed her headdress, leaving the white coif to hold up her thick black hair away from her long neck. One of her

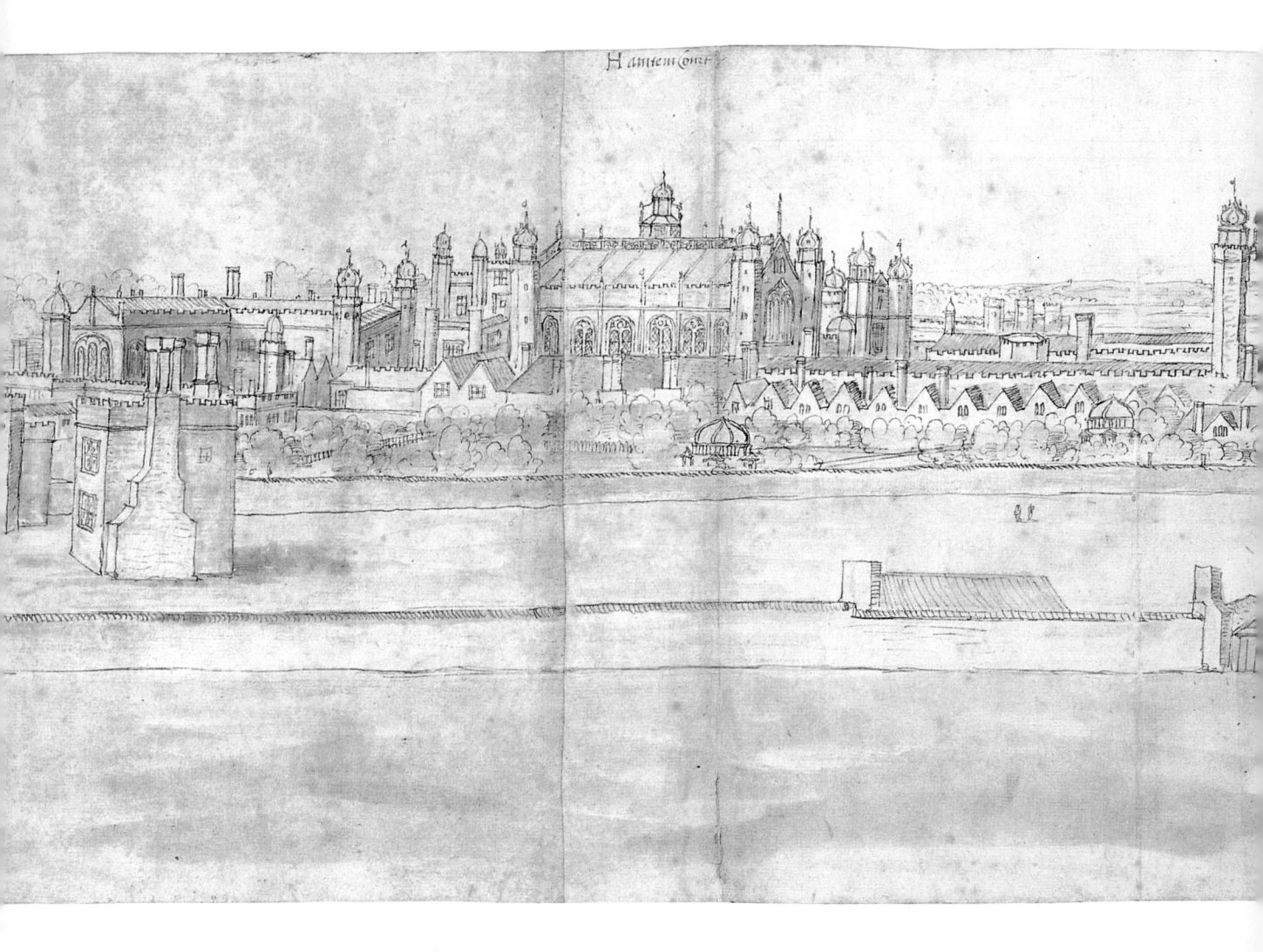

Hampton Court Palace from the north by Wyngaerde. The main buildings are in the centre with the tiltyard, enclosed by a wall, in the centre foreground. Anne Boleyn had taken an active part in the rebuilding programme after this palace passed from Wolsey to the King.

ladies put a blindfold round her eyes. She said: 'To Jesu Christ, I commend my soul'. To watchers it then seemed that 'suddenly the hangman smote off her head at a stroke', with his sword which appeared by magic, unnoticed by any-one. In fact the famous 'sword of Calais' had been concealed in the straw sur-rounding the block. In order to get Anne to position her head correctly, and stop her looking instinctively backwards, the hangman had called 'Bring me the sword' to someone standing on the steps nearby. Anne Boleyn turned her head; the deed was done.

The secret betrothal of Henry VIII and Jane Seymour took place at Hampton Court early in the morning of 20 May, twenty-four hours after his previous wife's execution. It was thought prudent to secure a dispensation for the mar-riage between a couple 'in the third and and third degrees of affinity', that is either of second cousins, or those who stood to each other as second cousins, through some sexual relationship. (Since the King and Jane Seymour were actually fifth cousins, it has been supposed that one of the King's mistresses must have been second cousin to Jane Seymour.) Archbishop Cranmer, ever industrious in his master's cause, signed this dispensation on 19 May, the date of the former Queen's death.

On 30 May the marriage between the King and Jane Seymour took place, quickly and quietly, in 'the Queen's closet' at Whitehall. It was of course a 'Queen's closet' which had been so named for the previous consort. Under the circumstances it was fortunate that Anne Boleyn's heraldic leopard proved easy to transform into Jane Seymour's heraldic panther 'by new making of the heads and tails'. All the same, badges of the previous incumbents were sometimes overlooked and lingered like awkward memories of the past – unless they were interpreted as grim reminders of the instability of the present. However, such

Jane Seymour's coat of arms outside the Chapel Royal, Hampton Court.

was the ostentation of the King's new-found happiness – a 'good and lawful' marriage at last! surely no one deserved it more – that stability, rather than instability, seemed the order of the day.

The King showed off his new bride, using the traditional Whitsun festivities of the City to introduce 'Jane the Quene' to his subjects. On the eve of their wedding, they walked together to the Mercers Hall to watch the setting of the City Watch with its torch-lit procession of 2,000 men and hundreds of constables in scarlet cloaks as well as morris dancers and elaborate tableaux. The celebrations went on in harmony with the great summer feasts of the church. There was another magnificent procession to celebrate the feast of Corpus

A piece of stained glass, believed to have come from Nonsuch Palace, depicting a shield with royal arms impaling Seymour, in reference to Henry's marriage to Jane Seymour in 1536.

Christi on 15 June. This time the King and Queen rode to Westminster Abbey, the King first, the Queen with her ladies following. Fourteen days later, the Feast of St Peter was marked by a pageant on the Thames, a joust at Whitehall – watched by the King and Queen – and a triple wedding of young lordlings and ladies, scions of the families of de Vere, Neville and Manners. The King appeared masked, surrounded by elegant attendants and wearing richly embroidered 'Turkish' garments. It was all quite like the old days, except that the general surprise when 'the King put off his visor and showed himself' must have been even more difficult to maintain. For the King was rapidly becoming enormously fat.

There were no more tributes to King Henry's 'angelic appearance'. Holbein shows him in a picture probably painted to celebrate his third marriage as having a face already enlarged to spade shape, a tight little mouth, tiny eyes and a beard vainly attempting to conceal the loss of a chin. A hat hides the head which had become 'bald like Caesar's'; the beringed fingers are chubby, to put it at its kindest. With his great height and commensurate girth the King was on his way to becoming, in physical terms at least, the most formidable prince in Europe, as he had once been the handsomest. There is however no indication – at this point – that his weight increase caused him any mortification. King Henry was extremely happy during the summer of 1536 and one of the things that brought about this happiness was the conciliatory, affectionate character of his third wife. He had made the right choice. Everything Queen Jane did seemed to confirm that.

Her treatment of her step-daughter Mary was especially sensitive. Queen Jane was generally credited with having caused the King to 'reinstate' his elder daughter. How much was she in fact responsible? In one way it is difficult to evaluate the Queen's precise influence. One can hardly believe that the new insecure Queen would have single-handedly secured a reversal of policy against her husband's real wishes. On the other hand, Queen Jane's quasi-maternal desire to reconcile father and daughter was obviously quite genuine. Maybe the real importance of her intervention on behalf of her step-daughter was in the pleasing light it cast on her character in the eyes of her husband: she had shown herself in the most womanly light as one prepared to plead on behalf of the helpless. Such a Queen – such a wife – who was always on the lookout for the good of others, was not such a bad thing to have.

As regards the rehabilitated Mary, from now on 'kind and affectionate behaviour' was to be the order of the day. On 6 July the King and Queen spent the day visiting her at Hunsdon. Queen Jane took the opportunity to present a 'very fine' diamond ring, and the King a cheque for 1,000 crowns, with instructions that Mary should ask for anything else she wanted. The royal accounts bear witness to a constant stream of gifts exchanged between Queen Jane and her 'most humble and obedient daughter and handmaid'. There were all manner of things, not only rich jewels, but intimate little luxuries: touching smaller

150

presents included fresh cucumbers sent from Mary to the Queen and further presents to Queen Jane's gardener at Hampton Court. What Mary needed was happiness; now it seemed that under the benevolent auspices of Jane Seymour she stood a chance of finding it.

As for King Henry, he would look back on Jane Seymour as the wife with whom he had been uniquely happy; forgetting perhaps those early years with Catherine of Aragon, the charming young Spanish princess so eager to please him. Queen Jane's state was to be commensurate with his esteem, the speedy matrimonial turnover of May making it particularly important to emphasize her high position. Thus the chamberlain to the new Queen was to be the King's cousin, sharing Plantagenet blood, Thomas Manners Earl of Rutland whereas Lord Borough, Anne Boleyn's chamberlain at her coronation, had been a peer of a mere four years' standing. Wonderful jewels were fashioned for the new Queen, with H and I (for the Latin Ioanna) replacing the previous Hs and As, much as the leopards had given way to the panthers.

The court of Queen Jane, if it was to be splendid, was also to be decorous. The Queen was, for example, strict about the dress of her ladies. The contemporary desire to install a young woman in the Queen's household was unaffected by the change of mistresses there; indeed, it could be argued that a place at a court where already two ladies-in-waiting had risen to the rank of royal consort was likely to be more advantageous than ever. But under Queen Jane there was to be uniformity of dress: Lady Sussex had just managed to infiltrate Lady Lisle's daughter Anne Basset when a message came from the Queen that Mistress Anne's 'French apparel' would not be suitable. It was probably not irrelevant that Mistress Anne would be described a few years later as 'a pretty young creature' who had caught the King's eye. Queen Jane's love of gardening, a thoroughly English taste to which the royal accounts attest, puts her in a more sympathetic

Opposite: Holbein's magnificent portrait of Henry VIII. This is the only oil painting of Henry VIII accepted as the work of Holbein and done from life.

A turret at Hunsdon House in Hertfordshire. Henry VIII bought this house in 1525 and Prince Edward spent much of his boyhood there.

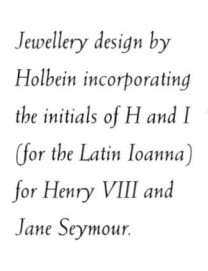

*Jewellery design by
Holbein incorporating
the initials of H and I
(for the Latin Ioanna)
for Henry VIII and
Jane Seymour.*

light; she had a celebrated gardener at Hampton Court called Chapman. Equally a passion for eating red-deer buck and quails – which, at 12d for six dozen, were ordered repeatedly from Calais – points to the earthy woman within the kindly but staid figure painted by 'Hance' (Holbein).

The vexed subject of the succession had been temporarily settled in a satisfactory manner – to the King. A second Act of Succession, replacing that of 1534, was passed by parliament in June 1536 and gave the King extraordinarily wide powers. The future children of his latest marriage were, naturally, to be the heirs to the kingdom. Should however there be 'a lack of lawful heirs of your body', parliament empowered Henry VIII to 'give, dispose, appoint' the crown 'to such person or persons … as shall please your Highness'. The King himself was to nominate the councillors who were to rule the kingdom, should he be succeeded by a minor. The implication of the 1536 Act was that Elizabeth, as well as Mary, was now illegitimate. But the relative positions of the two girls at this point were very different. With Mary's rehabilitation, the question of her marriage (she was now twenty) naturally loomed again; with that came the further question of her precise status. Given her grand connections there was some talk of her being recognized as her father's heiress-presumptive. But Elizabeth, with no connections worth mentioning, for the time being simply shared in her mother's disgrace.

In effect the King now had both his daughters perfectly under his control. He could, if he wished, at any time ask parliament to remove the stain of bastardy, and he could even, if he wished, allow Mary, as the elder, the coveted position of heiress-presumptive. Under the circumstances the King, prompted by Queen Jane, was prepared to be extremely affable to his daughters. Thus 'Madame Marie' was said by the French ambassador to be 'first [at court] after the Queen' in October 1536 and given the honour of presenting the napkin for washing to the King and Queen at the end of the state banquet. As for Elizabeth, the King was described as being 'very affectionate' towards his little 'Madame Ysabeau': the verdict of the court was that 'he loves her very much'. And for all his refusal to grant his 'natural' children proper status, it was notable that the King allowed them to take precedence over their lawfully born cousins, the ladies Frances and Eleanor Brandon, children of his sister Mary who had died in 1533. When all was said and done, Mary and Elizabeth were still the daughters of 'so great a Prince' – himself.

Outside the court, however, there was a challenge to the royal will more difficult to control than a young woman or a little girl: rebellion in the north. The Pilgrimage of Grace, as the multiple northern risings came to be known, was in essence a huge popular demonstration of disgust. It was a disgust which contained many different elements. There was, for example, the gathering indignation of the great northern lords, who found their historic independence threatened by Cromwell's new central (and southern) organization. Then there were people who were simply oppressed by Cromwell's novel taxes and disliked

Blakbre. Burche.

Illustration from a Tudor pattern book of the early sixteenth century showing strawberry (incorrectly labelled 'blackberry') and birch with two sprays of birdseye.

the King's new 'low-born' counsellors in consequence. Above all there were those who deeply resented the religious changes imposed from the centre, hated Archbishop Cranmer, loathed the new Bible (no matter to which Queen it was dedicated) and wanted their old customs back – including their old feast days, now banned or discouraged. In particular the forcible dissolution of the monasteries, a highly visible operation affecting the whole structure of a community, provided a focus for such widespread discontent. But the King was quite cut off from such feelings. He had never visited the north and from his point of view the dissolution provided a welcome way of refilling his coffers.

The French ambassador heard that, at the beginning of 'the insurrection', Queen Jane had thrown herself on her knees before her husband and 'begged him to restore the abbeys'. But the King had not got rid of Anne Boleyn and married Jane Seymour to listen to these kinds of pleas. He told his wife to get up. 'He had often told her not to meddle with his affairs', he said, and made a pointed allusion to 'the late Queen'. As the French ambassador commented, that rebuke was enough to frighten a woman 'who is not very secure'. The incident provides confirmation of Queen Jane's own religious conservatism; she shared the feelings of the majority of her husband's subjects who preferred the old ways. In later years Jane Seymour would be regarded as a Protestant heroine, due to a false identification with other male members of her family who did become keen Protestants. But the evidence of her own time is quite clear: unlike Anne Boleyn she was not in any way 'Lutheran', but rather the reverse. Indeed Luther himself heard that the new Queen was 'an enemy of the gospel', as he put it.

Furthermore the gossip of ambassadors and others is backed up by the suggestion that Queen Jane did attempt to prevent the suppression of at least one religious house, the condemned Cistercian convent at Catesby. In fact Catesby did not escape suppression: it vanished before the end of 1536 for all Queen Jane's pleading. Feminine lectures and admonitions had always sat uneasily on the King, even when he was young, as Queen Catherine had known and Queen Anne may have known but ignored. Anne Boleyn was the last woman the King would permit to speak challengingly to him with impunity. If he was to be troubled in any way, then he could either hint or point to the fate of 'the late Queen'. Every Queen following the execution of Anne Boleyn was there on sufferance, with a dreadful penalty awaiting her if she failed the test, just as every Queen was in another sense on sufferance following the casting-off of Catherine of Aragon, with the lesser penalty of divorce to be feared if she failed to meet the King's requirements.

At the same time Queen Jane was not expected to be a complete cipher. One notes that the King's outburst referred to the fact that he had 'often' warned her against meddling; she had simply gone too far on this occasion and on a particularly sensitive matter. In May the following year a special envoy arrived from Charles V, charged with negotiating a suitable marriage for Mary – Don Luis, heir to the throne of Portugal and brother of Charles V's wife Isabella, was being suggested. Chapuys, on leaving the King, went on to present a warm letter addressed by the Emperor to the Queen. According to the ambassador, Queen Jane 'showed great pleasure, and said that she would always do her best to advance the Emperor's affairs and those of the Princess [Mary]'. She then

Cardinal Reginald Pole was descended from George Duke of Clarence
and thus represented the Yorkist line. Portrait by an unknown artist.

PARVVLE PATRISSA, PATRIÆ VIRTVTIS ET HÆRES
    ESTO, NIHIL MAIVS MAXIMVS ORBIS HABET.
GNATVM VIX POSSVNT COELVM ET NATVRA DEDISSE,
    HVIVS QVEM PATRIS, VICTVS HONORET HONOS.
ÆQVATO TANTVM, TANTI TV FACTA PARENTIS,
    VOTA HOMINVM, VIX QVO PROGREDIANTVR, HABENT
VINCITO, VICISTI. QVOT REGES PRISCVS ADORAT
    ORBIS, NEC TE QVI VINCERE POSSIT, ERIT.

Holbein's portrait of Prince Edward, aged
about two years old, holding a rattle.

156

told Chapuys that she had tried to persuade the King to abandon his old friend-ship with France and seek that of the Emperor 'that very night after supper.'

Whether Queen Jane was being strictly truthful in her assurances to Chapuys we cannot know for sure; she may have been merely exercising the fine old art of diplomatic flattery. What is clear is that Queen Jane regarded it as normal to discuss political matters with her husband six months after the King's rebuke. To be married to Henry VIII was to conduct an elaborate game of Grandmother's Footsteps – with the King as a gigantic Grandmother. There could be cautious advances but there must also be swift retreats at the sight of

Mother Jak, Prince Edward's nurse. Drawing by Holbein.

the terrifying royal frown. Queen Jane Seymour understood the rules of the game. Was she not bound to obey and serve?

And now, in the most vital way, she showed herself to be the perfect spouse. For early in January 1537 – oh wondrous event! – King Henry succeeded in getting his third wife pregnant. The Queen's condition was made known in March, although she must have been aware of it in late February when she stood as godmother to the son of her brother Edward and his second wife Anne Stanhope. The news of the 'quickening' of the Queen's child was celebrated on Trinity Sunday 27 May: that is when she was roughly four and a half months pregnant, working the date backwards from that of her baby's birth. Some of the expressions of delight were positively biblical: the Convocation of Oxford University, for instance, rejoiced that 'our most excellent lady and mistress Queen Jane, our noble and godly princess, King Henry the Eighth's wife, had conceived and is great with child, and upon Trinity Sunday … like one given of God, the child quickeneth in the mother's womb'.

As in the case of those many bygone royal pregnancies, now officially erased from the popular imagination, everyone knew that the coming baby would be a boy. The Queen took to her chamber in late September. By October the people were said to 'look daily for a Prince'. The King even had a Garter stall made ready for his son in St George's Chapel, Windsor. Once again there were astrologers on hand to assure Queen Jane quite positively that the King's instinct was correct. Then on the afternoon of 9 October the Queen went into labour. She lay in the recently refurbished royal apartments at Hampton Court, where Anne Boleyn's leopards had been turned into panthers, and her falcons replaced with phoenixes.

Her ordeal was not quickly over. After two days a solemn procession was mounted through the City to 'pray for the Queen that was then in labour of child'. Finally, at two o'clock in the morning of the next day, 12 October, the child was born. The prophets had got it right: it was a boy. The child was named Edward, for his great-grandfather, but more especially because it was the eve of the Feast of St Edward. King Henry is said to have wept as he took his baby son in his arms. It is a touching story and certainly believable: what better cause could Henry VIII, an emotional man, find for his tears? At the age of forty-six, he had achieved his dream. God had spoken and blessed him with an heir male, nearly thirty years after he had first embarked on matrimony.

The whole world, or so it seemed, went mad with joy. The *Te Deums*, the bonfires, the hogsheads flowing with wine in the direction of the ever-present poor to 'drink as long as they listed', the bells which sounded from morning till night from every church, the noise of the guns – 2,000 shot from the Tower – which drowned them, all this may be imagined. Then there were the ecstatic congratulations put forward by all parties, for not only 'every good English man', in the King's generous phase, felt himself involved in this wonderful result, but every good English woman. As the Dowager Marchioness of Dorset, exiled at Croydon owing to possible infection with the plague, explained: not only had it 'pleased God so to remember your Grace with a prince', but also 'us all, your poor subjects'.

The christening, on 15 October, was sumptuous. In the absence of the Marchioness of Dorset, Gertrude, Marchioness of Exeter carried the baby, assisted with her precious burden by her husband and the Duke of Suffolk. The train of his robe was borne up by the Earl of Arundel, Norfolk's son. Among the gentlemen of the Privy Chamber holding up the canopy over the baby's head was his uncle, Thomas Seymour. Edward Seymour, however, had a more weighty duty: he carried the Prince's four-year-old sister Elizabeth, on account of 'her tender age'. As for Mary, she acted as godmother to the child who had at last supplanted her – even in the eyes of her most devoted adherents – as the heir to the English throne. On 18 October the baby was proclaimed Prince of

Edward Seymour, Queen Jane's oldest brother. He received valuable grants of land as well as the title of Earl of Hertford on the same day that his nephew was proclaimed Prince of Wales.

Wales, Duke of Cornwall and Earl of Carnarvon. On the same day, the yet-further-enhanced prospects of the Seymour family were recognized. Edward Seymour Viscount Beauchamp was created Earl of Hertford. The King granted him lands worth over £600 a year – compared to the £450 a year he had inherited from his father. Thomas Seymour was knighted and would subsequently receive grants of Coggeshall in Essex and Romsey in Hampshire.

Only the sister who had made all this possible failed to flourish. At about the same time as her brothers' elevation, Queen Jane fell ill of puerperal fever. This 'child-bed fever', if it turned to septicaemia, was the great cause of maternal mortality before the nature of hygiene and the course of infection were properly understood. For a time she struggled, and on the afternoon of 23 October was reported to be slightly better, thanks to 'a natural laxe'. But the rally did not last. Septicaemia did set in and with it delirium. By eight o'clock on the morning of 24 October, the Queen, who had been 'very sic' all night, was failing; her confessor was sent for, and the sacrament of extreme unction prepared. Cromwell was informed that the King had intended to go on a hunting trip to Esher that day, but had put it off. Nevertheless he would go to Esher on the morrow: 'If she amend, he will go; and if she amend not, he told me this day, he could not find it in his heart to tarry'.

Queen Jane died before midnight on 24 October, just twelve days after the birth of her son. She was twenty-eight years old and had been Queen of England for less than eighteen months. The same churches which had celebrated the birth with such enthusiasm were now draped in black. Sad and solemn Masses for the repose of 'the soul of our most gracious Queen' replaced the jubilant *Te Deums*. As King Henry told the King of France who was congratulating him on the birth of his son: 'Divine Providence has mingled my joy with the bitterness of death of her who brought me this happiness.'

The burial of Queen Jane was planned for 12 November. Well before this date, the question of a new Queen had already been discussed. Cromwell in fact used a single letter to Lord William Howard, the English ambassador in France, to break the happy news of the prince's birth ('in good health and sucketh like a child of his puissance'), the tragic news of the Queen's death ('departed to God') and the interesting news that the King must once more be regarded as in need of a wife ('his Council have prevailed on him for the sake of the realm'). This does not mean that the King's grief was not sincere: 'Of none in the realm was it more heavily taken than of the King', wrote Edward Hall in his *Chronicle*, and that was surely true. His only rivals in mourning would have been his daughter Mary who became 'accrazed' with sorrow following the death of her beloved step-mother and of course the Queen's family, whose sadness must have been tinged with worldly disappointment.

On 12 November Queen Jane's hearse was taken in solemn procession to Windsor, borne on a chariot drawn by six horses, and accompanied by nobles and heralds with banners. 'The Lady Mary' had sufficiently recovered to play

the role of chief mourner, and rode at the head of the procession on a horse with black velvet trappings. The poor who watched the hearse pass were presented with alms; at Eton College the Provost and boys saluted it 'with caps and tapers in their hands'. The coffin was accordingly installed within St George's Chapel and the next day solemnly buried in a vault beneath the centre of the choir. A magnificent monument was now planned for the grave which the King intended to share in the fullness of time. The late Queen's jewels including beads, pomanders and 'tablets' were distributed among her step-daughters and ladies of the court (Mary was a principal beneficiary). Chains and brooches of gold went to the Queen's brothers. Queen Jane's jointure and dowry, however, went back into the King's hands.

How long would it be before the Council, if not the King, found another use for them? King Henry kept Christmas of 1537 at Greenwich in 'mourning apparel': he did not in fact leave off his black until the day after Candlemas, 3 February 1538. By this time Cromwell was directing a hunt on an international scale for a new woman to share the English King's marriage bed. John

The Whitehall mural showing Henry VII, Elizabeth of York, Henry VIII and Jane Seymour standing around a sarcophagus in a richly decorated Renaissance interior. The original wall-painting by Holbein was destroyed in the fire at Whitehall Palace in 1698 and this is a copy made for Charles II by Remigius van Leemput.

161

Hutton, ambassador in the Netherlands, was one of those ordered to draw up a list. He did so reluctantly: 'I have not much experience among ladies and therefore this commission to me is hard'. Those proposed ranged from a fourteen-year-old girl 'of a goodly stature' waiting on the French Queen, to the widow of the late Count of Egmont who was described as being over forty but not looking it. The presumed fertility of both ladies was extremely important ('goodly stature' was thought to indicate 'aptness to procreate children', and a continuing appearance of youth was another helpful sign). Prince Edward, pale

The moulded and decorated ceiling of the Wolsey closet in Hampton Court was added by Henry. The Prince of Wales feathers date it from after the birth of Edward VI in 1537.

like his mother, was not a particularly robust baby; and in any case experience showed that two sons was really the minimum needed to keep a monarch secure about his succession.

Hutton particularly commended the sixteen-year-old Duchess Christina of Milan: 'an excellent beauty', tall for her age, with 'a good personage of body'. The daughter of Christian II of Denmark and Charles V's sister Isabella, Christina had been married at thirteen to the Duke of Milan and widowed without children a year later. The King's excitement grew: would it be possible to get her portrait? And he would like to know more of the current crop of French princesses ... Hutton also mentioned a certain 'Anna of Cleves', daughter of the ruler of that country, a dukedom on the edges of France and the Netherlands whose main significance derived from its strategic position. But he added, 'I hear no great praise neither of her parentage nor her beauty'. Naturally the King felt no particular excitement on that score.

PART IV

ANNA OF CLEVES
&
KATHERINE HOWARD

CHAPTER 8

An Unendurable Bargain

THERE WERE THREE ways of looking at the quest for a new Queen of England. On a purely domestic level, the English court, having enjoyed the continuous presence of a consort since 1509, suddenly felt the lack of a Queen's household in which maids (and others more senior) could find remunerative places. Then there was the diplomatic angle. Cromwell saw in the quest a heaven-sent opportunity to forge some new European alliance. The moment was certainly propitious. Signs that the feuding between François I and Charles V might draw to an end brought the corresponding threat of English isolation. The aggressive policies of Pope Paul III towards England were likely to be encouraged by any Franco-Imperial truce. Under these circumstances, marriage – or at least marriage negotiations – with one side or the other would keep England in the game.

Thirdly there was King Henry's own need for a helpmate – and bedmate. Paradoxically, the King in his late forties, gross, no likely object of desire, was far more difficult to please than that handsome boy of 1509, ready to fall in love where policy directed, whom any girl might easily love in return. In the selection of a wife, as in so many other matters, Henry VIII had grown used to having his own way. He had chosen two out of his three wives himself, and for romantic reasons. This was unusual and set him apart from his contemporaries. It also shaped the King's assumptions about any new bride. In 1538 Henry VIII wanted – no, he expected – to be diverted, entertained and excited. It would be the responsibility of his wife to see that he felt like playing the cavalier and indulging in amorous gallantries. At the same time the King allowed his ambassadors to proceed in the time-honoured manner with the ritual inspection of suitable candidates, not seeing that there might be some innate contradiction between the demands of diplomacy and those of a romantic but deeply self-indulgent nature.

Unfortunately by now the King of England did not have an altogether savoury reputation as a husband. The execution of Queen Anne Boleyn had left a worrying impression and jokes about the King's marital career were already current as he sought a fourth wife. Even if the young Duchess Christina of Milan did not actually remark that if she had two necks, the King should have one of them, the wisecrack was a significant piece of contemporary myth-making. At first the basic choice for Henry VIII seemed to be the same as had faced his father when designing a marriage for his heir half a century before: France

Marguerite de Valois was one of the French princesses on Henry VIII's list of prospective brides after Jane Seymour's death. Holbein's portrait has not survived and this is a later sixteenth-century portrait of her, after François Clouet.

or Spain (now enlarged to the Empire). In 1538 France happened to be rich in princesses: there was the French King's daughter, fifteen-year-old Marguerite de Valois and several other possibilities. Of the French King's cousins, Marie de Guise was rumoured to be betrothed to James V of Scotland, but she had two younger sisters, Louise and Renée de Guise, and two further cousins were also available as possible candidates.

Phillip Hobbie Knight

There were two conventional methods of selecting an eligible princess. One was a personal inspection by a trusted envoy, either the ambassador on the spot or someone specifically entrusted with this delicate task. The other method was complementary: it consisted of commissioning a special portrait in order to check up on the diplomatic reports. In this way Hans Holbein, as King's painter, was in for a busy time in 1538. His first task was however to depict not a French princess but the most suitable candidate from the imperial side: the sixteen-year-old Duchess of Milan commended by John Hutton. She had many advantages. Quite apart from her all-important status as the niece of Charles V, there was the question of her dowry, what she would derive from the duchy of Milan; while with her sister she had further possible rights involving her father's Danish kingdom. But what the King really hankered after was an opportunity for a personal inspection at Calais.

His envoy Sir Thomas Wyatt was told his views on the subject: 'His Grace, prudently considering how that marriage is a bargain of such nature as must endure for the whole life of man, and a thing whereof the pleasure and quiet, or the displeasure and torment of the man's mind doth much depend.' Was it not common sense for the pair to meet? They could then, if necessary, without 'dishonour or further inconvenience' break off the alliance. But the imperial court was not disposed to ignore the conventions. So the King had to trust to portraiture – although in view of what was to come, one cannot help feeling sympathy for his prescient if clumsy attempts to trust only to the evidence of his own senses.

The imperial court despatched its own picture. But, by tradition, the enquiring country preferred to place its trust in its own artist. So before the first picture had been received, Holbein had already set off for Brussels with the King's special envoy Sir Philip Hoby. On 12 March the Duchess stood for Holbein from one o'clock to four o'clock in the afternoon. Despite the limitations of 'but three hours space', the English ambassador John Hutton was enthusiastic about the results and Holbein was back in London with his drawing by 18 March. King Henry was enraptured. Holbein's picture 'singularly pleased' him, confirming as it did the lively description of Christina, smiles, dimples and all, that he had already received.

The court had been a gloomy place since the death of Queen Jane. Now the King was reportedly 'in a much better humour than he ever was, making musicians play on their instruments all day long.' Chapuys also noted that there had been numerous masques: 'a sign that he proposes to marry again.' In her dark widow's dress, with her dignified air belied by a mischievous curling mouth, the Duchess looked as if she might combine the royal graciousness of Catherine of Aragon with the liveliness of the young Anne Boleyn. The King immediately commissioned a full-length portrait in oils from Holbein.

Negotiations for the King's union with this paragon were however maddeningly protracted. What was now envisaged was a double yoking of the King to

Drawing by Holbein of Philip Hoby who accompanied him on two trips to Europe in 1538 in order for Holbein to execute portraits of selected princesses for Henry VIII to inspect.

the Emperor's niece and his daughter Mary to the Emperor's brother-in-law Don Luis of Portugal. But the Spanish commissioners who had arrived in London in February to bring all this about were a disappointment: the King referred bitterly to their 'gay words' which concealed a lack of any real authority. As the usual wrangling went on about dowries and jointures, the King boasted of the future he could provide for his new family. Although he already had an heir, he intended to provide dukedoms for 'our younger sons': the titles of York, Gloucester and Somerset were mentioned. Yet by June, the arrival of such a string of baby dukes seemed as far away as ever. The King, his Council and his various envoys were beginning to make statements such as 'time lost cannot be recovered', which amounted to the obvious fact that the royal bridegroom was not getting any younger.

These languid imperialist overtures raise doubts as to whether the Emperor ever really intended the marriage to go through. It seems likely that the Emperor's true intention was to scupper the French negotiations, which were of course proceeding in parallel. In June Holbein and Hoby set off again to the Continent to paint Madame Marguerite, daughter of Francois I, and another princess, possibly Marie de Vendôme. The travellers were back again in

August, to capture the images of Renée and Louise de Guise at Joinville. After that it was on to Nancy to draw Anne of Lorraine. But Holbein had wasted his French journeys. Within two years one of these princesses would be dead, one in a nunnery and two married elsewhere. In any case the King's real desire – to 'honour the said Duchess' Christina by marriage – remained undiminished. He was, however, about to receive a singular and unwelcome check to his hopes, both personally and publicly.

On 17 June 1538 Charles V and King François I declared a ten-year truce at Nice, through the mediation of Pope Paul III. The feasting which followed was seen by the Pope as a celebration of Christian unity against the encroaching Turks. For Charles V it represented more an unpleasant necessity: a series of unsuccessful imperial campaigns, contrasted with French successes, all in the shadow of the Turkish threat to Italy, made such a peace essential to his security. For Henry VIII, however, the spectacle of his brother kings feasting together in a new amity symbolized the dangerous isolation of England. The marriage negotiations continued, but no one now really expected them to succeed.

The Pope's success in uniting France and Spain gave him the confidence to propose more public action. The bull of excommunication of 1535 had been issued but not executed. Now the Pope considered issuing a bull of deposition against King Henry; Cardinal Pole was sent as papal legate to Spain in order to encourage the Emperor to invade England and bring the country into the fold of the Catholic church once more. There was certainly little to comfort the Pope in the reports that he was receiving of religious affairs in England: shrines and cathedrals were being pillaged of their treasures; an emerald cross was taken from Winchester and three caskets of jewels from Chichester. Most painful of all was the news that the famous shrine of St Thomas à Becket at Canterbury Cathedral had been looted in September. On 17 December the Pope would proclaim that the bull of excommunication originally issued in 1535 should now be put into effect.

Meanwhile the mood of the King of England was increasingly paranoid. Given his hereditary preoccupation with the subject of the Tudor dynasty, it was hardly surprising that this paranoia took the form of a many-pronged attack on his cousins of royal blood: the Courtenay family headed by the Marquess of Exeter, and the Poles, headed by Lord Montague (see 'The Tudors and their Rivals' family tree). Despite the lack of proper evidence, both men were found guilty and executed on 9 December. Women and children came next: Gertrude, Marchioness of Exeter and her twelve-year-old son, Edward Courtenay, Earl of Devon, were taken to the Tower in November. Even Margaret Countess of Salisbury, now 'aged and feeble', was not spared. It is highly unlikely that the Countess was guilty of conspiracy. In religion she clung to the old ways, but that was hardly a crime in someone who, having been twelve years old at the Battle of Bosworth Field, was in fact a mediaeval survivor. Way beyond childbearing age, she constituted no threat to the King.

Opposite: Holbein's painting of the young widow Christina of Denmark, Duchess of Milan. She is supposed to have quipped that if she had two necks, the King of England might have one of them.

As her son Cardinal Pole wrote, the real crime of this 'most innocent woman' was to be 'allied to him in blood'. For the time being the Countess was kept under house arrest, and was transferred the following year to the Tower of London.

It was in this hysterical atmosphere of judicial deaths at home and fear of invasion from abroad that Cromwell decided to resurrect a matrimonial project for his master that had previously attracted little enthusiasm – the marriage to Lady Anna of Cleves. The duchy of Cleves belonged to the intricate world of the Lower Rhine: a maze of duchies, electorates and bishoprics at first sight far removed from the great game being played out elsewhere between mightier powers. There had been Counts of Cleves since the eleventh century; they were transformed into dukes at the beginning of the fifteenth century. Then in 1521 the marriage of Duke John III to Maria, heiress to the nearby duchies of

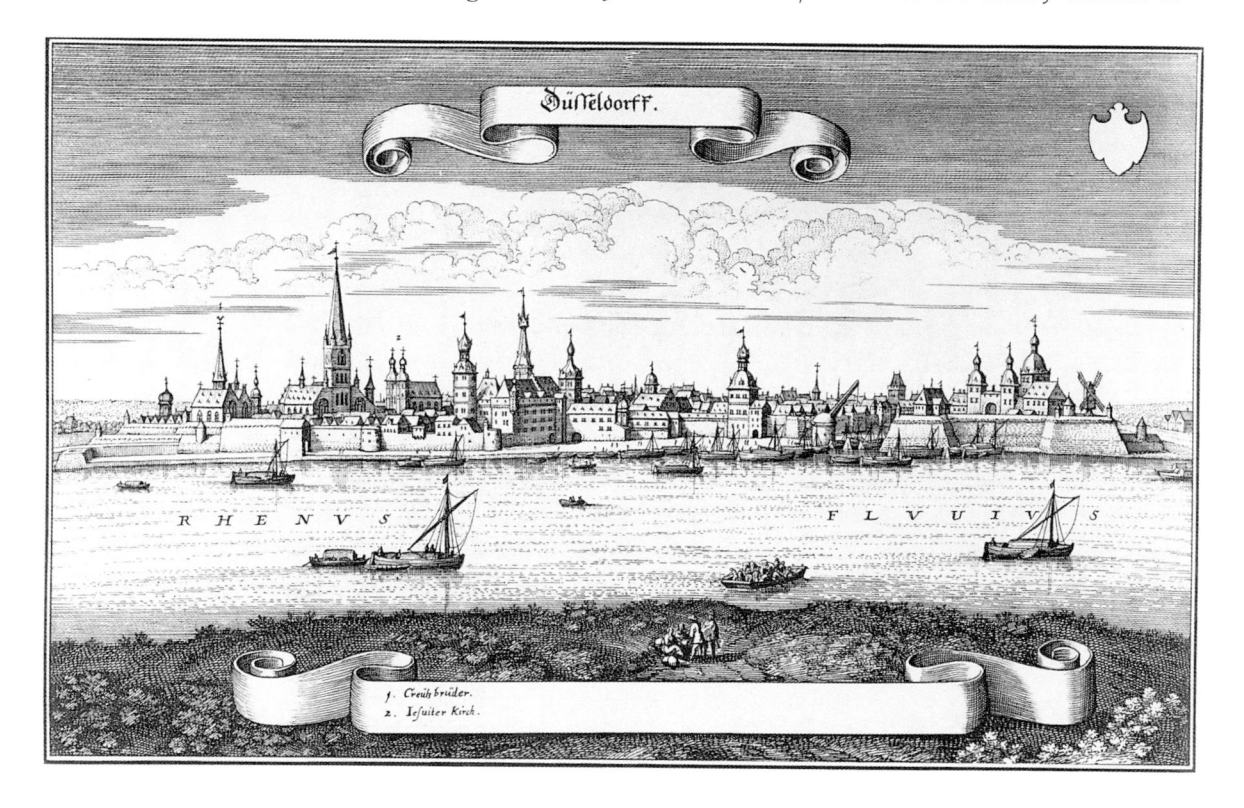

Düsseldorf, on the river Rhine. The marriage of Anna of Cleves' parents had brought together the duchies of Cleves, Mark, Jülich and Berg, with Düsseldorf as their capital.

Jülich and Berg, brought all these territories together, with Düsseldorf as their capital. Four children were born to the ducal couple. Anna, born in 1515, was the second, three years younger than Sybilla; after Anna, in 1516, came William; lastly Amelia, born in 1517. The next step in the territorial aggrandizement of Cleves came in the summer of 1538 when Duke John's heir William, was recognized by the inhabitants of Guelderland as their new Duke, taking his claim from his mother. The house of Cleves now looked like controlling a strategic portion of the Lower Rhineland – a development that was naturally most unwelcome to Charles V.

It was, however, the interplay of religion, territory and revolt which made Cleves not so much a provincial threat to Charles as a potentially exciting ally for England; this was what Cromwell had grasped. The autumn of 1530 had seen the foundation of a League of 'all Protestant princes and free cities'. The persistent Turkish menace, coupled with the danger that the League would join

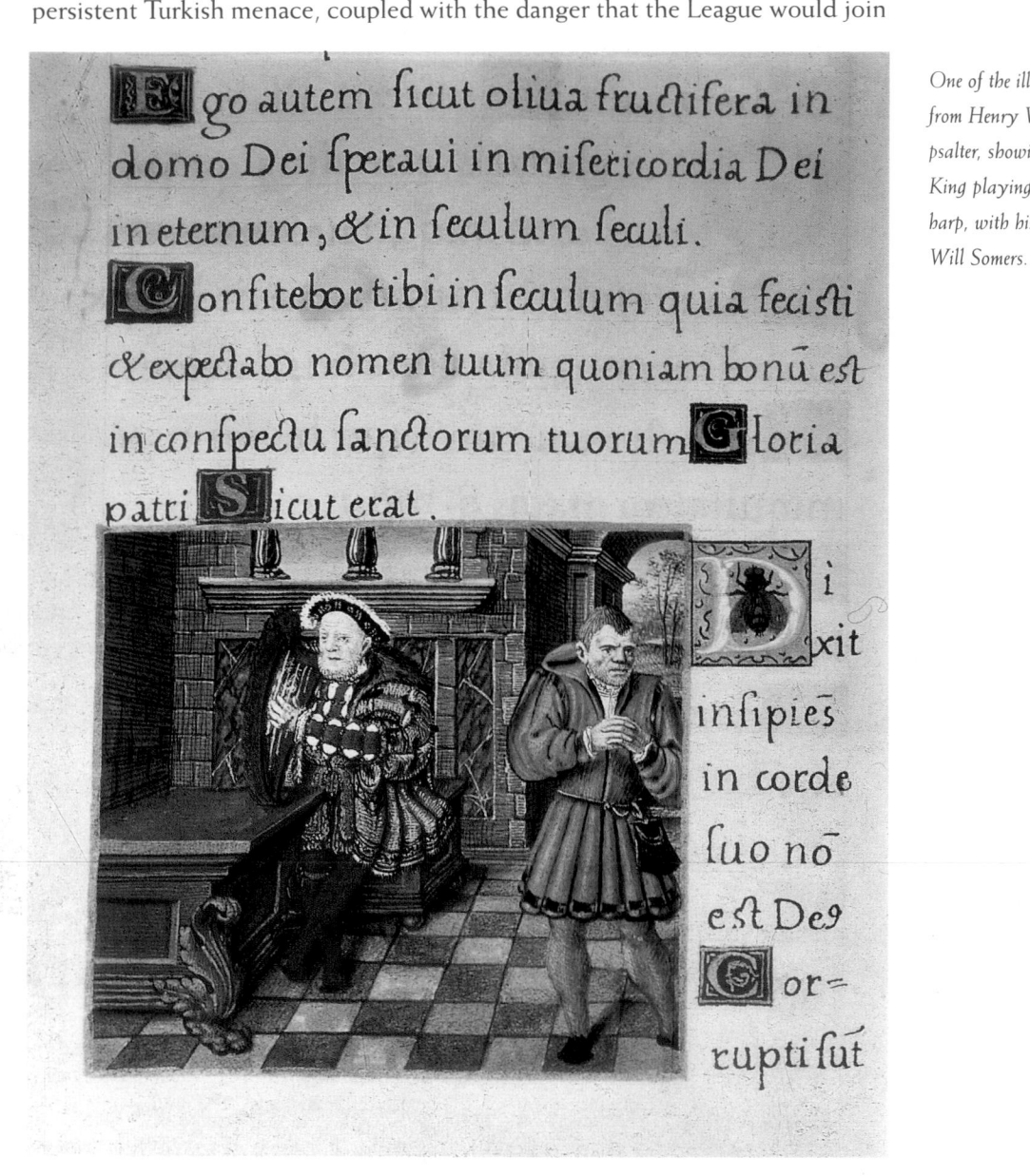

One of the illustrations from Henry VIII's psalter, showing the King playing a small harp, with his fool Will Somers.

with France, meant that the Emperor was not secure enough at this point to suppress it. But it is important to realize that not every Germanic princely house was Lutheran Protestant. The real influence at the Clevian court of Duke John III, a well-educated and cultivated man, was Erasmus, not Luther. Many of the chief men there were close associates as well as admirers of the

Dutch scholar and theologian. In many ways therefore the court of Cleves might seem to have provided the ideal background for raising an English Queen for the 1540s: fundamentally liberal, but serious-minded, theologically inclined, and profoundly Erasmian, as the court of Catherine of Aragon had once been.

Unfortunately Duchess Maria was no Isabella of Castile; nor were the exciting ideas of the Renaissance concerning the education of women (or at least princesses) allowed to hold sway here. Duchess Maria was herself a strict Catholic and not subject to the liberal, reforming notions of her father and husband. She certainly had strict ideas on the upbringing of her daughters – 'one that looketh very straitly to her children' who were never allowed 'far from her elbow'. Anna could not read or write in any language other than her own. This was the dialect called *deutsch*, or *dietsch*, known as Dutch to the English, who found it oddly grating on their ears.

The court of Cleves was another world from that of Renaissance Spain or England. It was true that its inhabitants were reputed to love a drink: 'good cheer'. But there was no evidence that Anna herself indulged. On the contrary, it was said of her that 'she occupieth her time mostly with her needle'. Of course a propensity for needlework was not in itself a disaster, remembering Catherine of Aragon's wifely determination to continue sewing her husband's shirts. It was just that the master of the English court had been accustomed to wives who could do all this and a great deal more. Above all music was of the greatest importance to him. A gifted musician himself, Henry VIII's love of song and dance was part of the air he breathed; he took it for granted that his consort would possess musical accomplishments.

But the Lady Anna of Cleves could not sing nor could she play on any instrument. Once again the contrast with previous consorts was vivid: in vain would be sought the graceful training of the young Catherine, the artistic talents of Anne Boleyn, to say nothing of Catherine's Latin studies and Anne Boleyn's fluent, witty French. At the age of twenty-three, shy, ignorant and humble, poor Anna of Cleves was ill-equipped for the contentious, sophisticated world which lay somewhat beyond her mother's elbow. She certainly did not possess the arts to enchant a corpulent testy husband, uncertain of his own virility, and nearly twenty-five years her senior.

In February 1539 Duke John died, leaving the Cleves-Guelderland territories now welded together in the control of his son, William. In the meantime the marriage negotiations ran merrily along, with good reports of the Lady Anna reaching Cromwell. The reception of the English envoys who came to inspect Anna and her sister Amelia was, it is true, slightly disconcerting. The 'daughters of Cleves' were produced, so wrapped up that they could see neither their figures nor their faces properly. When the envoys protested, the Chancellor of Cleves was indignant: 'Why?' he said, 'would you see them naked?' It was clearly a case of filling out descriptions with portraits. Pictures

were promised for England, and very possibly despatched. In the meantime Holbein, on England's behalf, was to be once again employed and, of course,

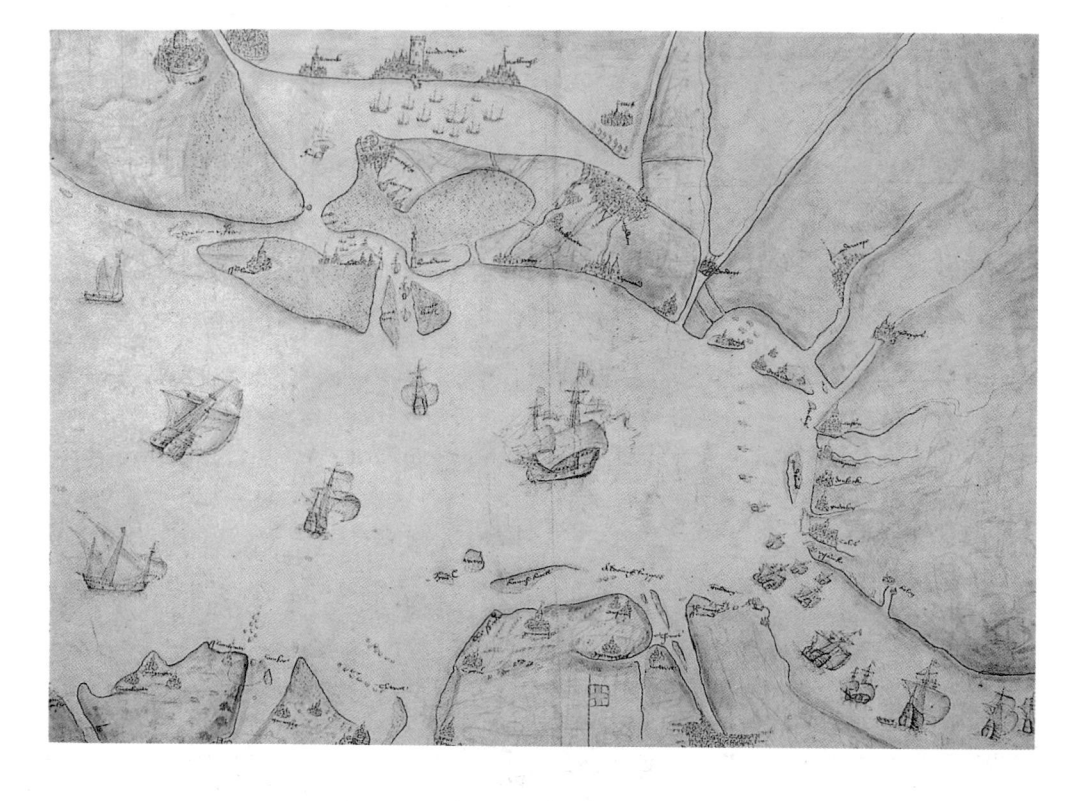

An ink and water-colour sketchmap, oriented to the east and showing the North Sea between England and the Netherlands. It was drawn in October 1539 to convince the ambassadors from Cleves of the viability of sending Anna of Cleves to London from Guelderland. The ambassadors were fearful of a long voyage in winter and by 25 October Henry had agreed she should embark from Calais.

expense apart, that was really the preferred option. So Holbein set out on his third mission in pursuit of his master's fourth marriage.

He arrived in August 1539, expenses already paid, including £13 6s 8d 'for the preparation of such things as he is appointed to carry with him'. It has been suggested that this meant that Holbein was put in the unusual position of painting on the spot (under the inspection of court officials), instead of making sketches, to be worked up into paintings later with the aid of his excellent memory. The result was certainly on parchment, mounted on canvas, which would have made transport of a proper painting easier. Whatever the stringency of Holbein's working conditions, Wotton, the English envoy, who knew the ladies concerned, found that the artist had 'expressed their images very lively'.

For all Cromwell's desire for an alliance with the Lutheran princes in Germany – in which category Cleves, with its connection to Saxony, counted – England itself had recently lurched away from any kind of Protestant extremism. In June 1539 parliament passed the so-called Act of the Six Articles, specifying for the first time that certain opinions constituted heresy (a matter hitherto left to the discretion of the ecclesiastical courts). Carried out ostensibly in the interests of moderation and uniformity, these were clear and savagely punitive measures of religious conservatism: denial of the real presence in the sacrament, for example, was to be punished by death by burning; those who denied the efficacy of private confession and private Masses were to be hanged; former priests and nuns who broke their vows of celibacy by marrying were also to be hanged unless they remedied their situation before the Act became law. Whether intended to defuse that Catholic crusade envisaged by the Pope or to placate a country still looking nostalgically to the old ways, the Six Articles certainly represented a blow to men of reforming zeal like Cranmer (who was obliged to put away his wife) and Cromwell.

Yet in terms of foreign policy the Cleves alliance continued to be seen as part of an offensive against the Emperor. If the passing of the Six Articles represented a reverse for Cromwell, such a German Protestant-oriented treaty would represent a positive gain for him. Holbein was back in England by the end of August; his works were shown to the King on his summer progress at Grafton. The King liked what he saw – or at any rate, since his reaction is not recorded, he did not dislike it. If the picture of Anna of Cleves did not make him call for musicians and masks as that of Christina of Milan had done, he was content for the details of the alliance to be hammered out. The marriage treaty, which had been brought over to England at the end of September, was signed on 4 October 1539.

Unfortunately it was not until 27 December that Anna of Cleves was able to make the crossing from Calais to Deal. By this time the King had been waiting at Greenwich for far too long – including the Christmas season – and the patience of this notoriously impatient man had worn thin. Furthermore – another factor in the story of Anna of Cleves – with the passing days his

The Gateway of St Augustine's Abbey in Canterbury where Anna of Cleves spent her first night in England.

imagination had begun to run riot. This was after all a new experience for him: the arrival of an innocent and unknown young bride. Anne Boleyn and Jane Seymour were two ladies familiar to him before marriage; as a boy he had grown up with Catherine of Aragon before he married her.

It was when Anna of Cleves reached Rochester where she was lodged in the Bishop's Palace that the King's thin patience snapped; alternatively his boyish

Sir Anthony Browne Knighte, etat' sua 25 afterwardes
Knighte of the garter, and m of the horse to K: h: 8 and E: 6·
and of there moste honorable privie Councell.

romantic nature – on which he prided himself – got the better of him. In order
to 'nourish love', as he told Cromwell, he decided to pay a visit to his affianced
bride the next day, New Year's Day. In true fairy-story fashion, the King proceeded to ride from Greenwich to Rochester, attended by some of the gentlemen of his Privy Chamber, all dressed alike in hooded 'cloaks of marble colour'

(that is, multi-coloured). On arrival, he sent Sir Anthony Browne, his Master of the Horse, up to the Lady's chamber to say that he had a New Year's gift to deliver to her.

Sir Anthony Browne said – afterwards – that from the moment he set eyes on the Lady Anna, he was immediately struck with dismay. Whether that was true or not, what was quite sure was that the Lady's next visitor, a certain anonymous gentleman in a multi-coloured cloak, was deeply disappointed by what he saw. The interview itself did nothing to assuage the royal feeling of being let down. Lady Anna, who was in truth probably bewildered (she spoke no English), gave the fatal impression of being bored. She had been watching the New Year's Day bull-baiting out of her window when these mysterious visitors began to appear. Beyond the common courtesies, she saw no reason to interrupt her spectator sport further. Suddenly – as it seemed to her – her unknown visitor embraced her. He showed her a token the King was supposed to have sent his betrothed for a New Year's gift. All this left the Lady Anna in her turn thoroughly 'abashed'. Her only recourse after a few words (in her grating *deutsch*) was to continue to look out of the window. The King was left to retire to another room, and assume the purple velvet coat of royalty, which left the attendant lords and gentlemen bowing deeply (they were well trained when to recognize and when not to recognize their master). Thus, more majestically garbed, the King returned to the Lady Anna. Reports vary as to what happened next. According to Wriothesley, the Lady Anna now 'humbled herself lowly', the King saluted her all over again, and so they 'talked lovingly together'. But this is probably the herald's tactful gloss on what had been a ludicrously misjudged scene on both sides. The important comment was that made by the King to Cromwell after he left. 'I like her not', said Henry VIII.

What did the King see, compared with what he had expected to see. Was there a deception and, if so, by whom? Let us take the actual appearance of Anna of Cleves first: for this we are fortunate in having a first-hand description, written only a few days later by the French ambassador, Charles de Marillac, who was not prejudiced in either direction, towards her beauty or her ugliness. Anna of Cleves looked about thirty, he wrote (she was in fact twenty-four), tall and thin, 'of middling beauty, with a determined and resolute countenance'. The Lady was not as handsome as people had affirmed she was, nor as young (he was of course wrong about that), but there was a 'steadiness of purpose in her face to counteract her want of beauty.' The 'daughter of Cleves' was solemn because she had not been trained to be anything else and the German fashions did little to charm in a court in love as ever with all things French. Henry VIII never actually 'swore they had brought over a Flanders mare to him'. (The story comes from Bishop Burnet at the end of the seventeenth century, with no contemporary reference to back it up.) But the story does sum up, as apocryphal stories often do, the profound cultural gap that existed between the courts of Cleves and England.

Sir Anthony Browne, the Master of the Horse, who was sent to deliver the King's New Year's gift to Anna of Cleves. Portrait by an unknown artist.

However Anna of Cleves was not beautiful, and those reports which declared that she was were egregious exaggerations in the interests of diplomats – to this extent, the envoys are the real culprits, not the painter. But was Anna of Cleves actually hideous? Holbein, painting her full-face, as was the custom, does not make her so to the modern eye, with her high forehead, wide-apart, heavy-lidded eyes and pointed chin. But it may be that in giving this frontal view, intended to prevent the concealment of defects, Holbein unintentionally minimized one of Anna's. Recent X-rays of another contemporary portrait have revealed a considerably longer nose underneath the paint. In Holbein's version Anna's nose is not short – but neither is it excessively long – no longer, for example,

Portrait of Anna of Cleves attributed to Bathel Bruyn the Elder. It is possible that this is one of the two paintings of Anna and her sister Amelia originally offered to the envoys of Henry VIII. The envoys were dissatisfied with them on the grounds that their high-necked bodices were too concealing.

A selection of jewellery designs by Holbein, incorporating the entwined initials of Henry VIII and Anna of Cleves.

than that of Jane Seymour. But a slightly bulbous nose may be one explanation for the King's disappointment. Another problem may have been Anna of Cleves' complexion. When the King roared at his courtiers that he had been misinformed – by them, amongst others, since they had seen her at Calais – the only explanation which could be stammered out was that her skin was indeed rather more 'brown' than had been expected.

Even allowing for all this, we are still left with something mysterious in the whole episode, and the sheer immediacy of the King's disappointment (followed by his indignation – which was, however, never directed at Holbein). The explanation must therefore lie in something equally mysterious: the nature of erotic attraction. The King had been expecting a lovely young bride, and the delay had merely contributed to his desire. He then saw someone who, to put it crudely, aroused in him no erotic excitement whatsoever.

179

And still more intimate embraces lay ahead, or were planned to do so.

In the royal apartments and elsewhere, the usual rites of passage were taking place: the initials of Jane Seymour were being altered to those of the future Queen Anna. Conveniently enough, in certain places medallions with the initials of H and A, left over from the regime of the last Queen – but one – could simply be enamelled. In the ceiling of the Chapel Royal at St James' Palace the heraldry, ciphers and mottoes of the King and the new Queen were accordingly joined together.

On Twelfth Night, 6 January 1540, the marriage took place between Henry VIII, a widower of forty-eight with three children, and Anna of Cleves, a foreign-born 'maid' half his age. Around the bride's 'marrying ring' ran the words 'God send me wel to kepe'. Afterwards the royal couple went on 'a procession'

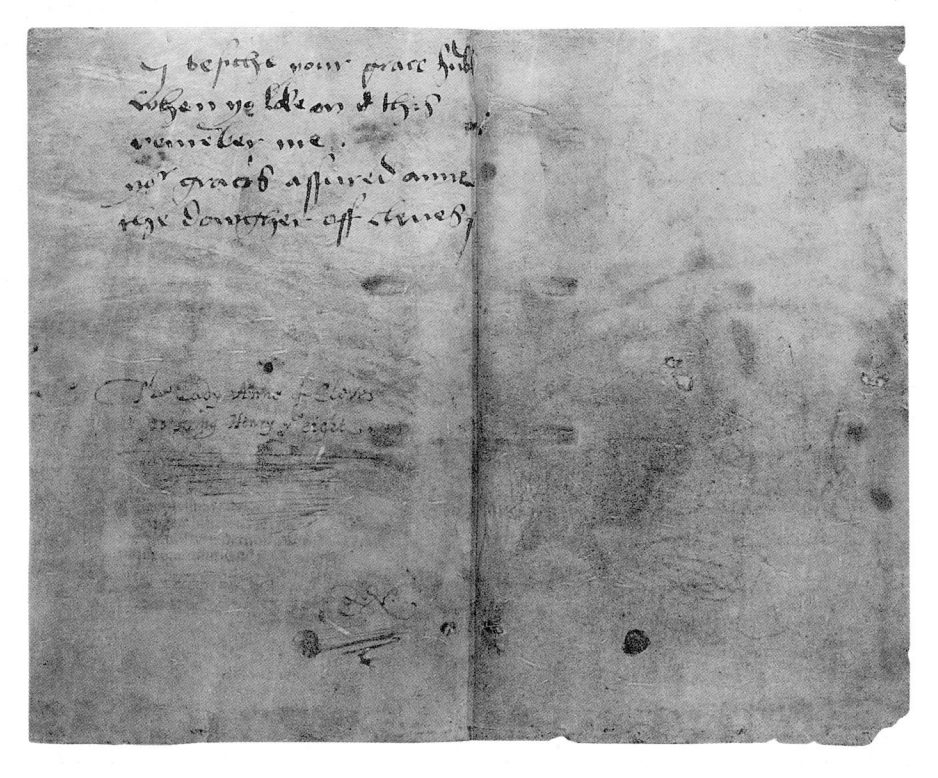

The dedication at the back of a Book of Hours, printed in Germany c. 1533, given by Anna of Cleves to Henry VIII.

together, the new Queen dressed in cloth of silver 'hanging' with jewels and 'being in her hair', that is, with her hair flowing loose to indicate her unmarried state. It was, wrote one observer, 'a goodly sight to behold'. But the King did not find it so – and he had already made that quite clear. In the days before the wedding, Henry remained in a mood of resentful despair. To Cromwell he cried out that if he had known what he now knew, the Lady Anna 'would never have come within the kingdom'. 'By way of lamentation', he added, 'What Remedy?' Cromwell replied, 'I know none', and added that he was 'very sorry therefore'.

In this crisis, it was still just possible that the King could be saved at the

eleventh hour. In 1527 there had been some question of a precontract between the Lady Anna and Francis of Lorraine; this had never been examined very thoroughly. Now the King's Council, 'much astonished and abashed' in their turn, were asked to investigate. The result was unsatisfactory: 'A revocation' had indeed been made, they found, and besides 'they were but spousals' (that is, *de futura*, or without the force of marriage). But no dispensation from the precontract was produced by Cleves. It is therefore one of the paradoxes of the marital career of Henry VIII that the marriage he entered with such reluctance may well have been invalid from the start.

In view of the King's manifest gloom, why did the ill-omened marriage ever go through? It was hardly a popular alliance in the country. Anna of Cleves was not a magnificent princess as Catherine of Aragon had been and her dowry was small since in his haste to bind the Duke of Cleves to him, King Henry had been uncharacteristically magnanimous. Furthermore Anna of Cleves was envisaged (inaccurately) as the kind of virulent Lutheran who would not come to England 'so long as one Abbey is standing'. King Henry's own explanation is probably the correct one. It was 'for fear of making a ruffle in the world: that is … to drive her Brother into the hands of the Emperor and the French King's hands'. This was no moment to upset Cromwell's carefully calculated foreign policy and lose the one ally – Cleves – who might cause the Emperor a great deal of trouble. So Henry VIII found himself in the

Oak panel carved with Tudor emblems from Abbey House at Waltham Abbey, granted on lease to Sir Anthony Denny. Sir Anthony was one of the members of the Privy Chamber to whom the King complained that he suspected Anna of Cleves' virginity.

unlikely role of sacrificial victim of his secretary's manoeuvres.

It was hardly surprising that the wedding night did not go well. If the King had entertained faint hopes of experiencing an access of lust – after all, his bride was quite 'seemly' – they were not fulfilled. When Cromwell rashly enquired the next day, 'How liked you the Queen?', the King replied succinctly: 'I liked her before not well, but now I like her much worse.' Naturally he was quick to blame the Lady rather than himself. Her body, not her beauty, was now the issue. He told Sir Anthony Denny, a member of his Privy Chamber, that his wife was not only 'not as she was reported, but had breasts so slack and other parts of body in such sort that [he] somewhat suspected her virginity'. The King's verdict was that 'he could never in her company be provoked and

Above and right:
Painted oak bedhead,
1539, with the initials
of Henry VIII (detail
right) and Anna of
Cleves. This is the only
surviving piece of
furniture that can be
certainly ascribed to
Henry VIII's court.

steered to know her carnally'. Cromwell was given the same message and the King imparted it privately to two of his doctors. There were various other testimonies, but they all added up to the same thing: the King was not able to consummate his marriage.

This unhappy state of affairs did not alter. The following month the King told Cromwell that even though he lay with his wife 'nightly', or every second night, yet she was still 'a Maid'. There was however no question of King Henry's own virility: he told Dr Butts that he had had two nocturnal ejaculations in the same period. No, the reason for his failure was that the King had now settled into 'mistrusting' his wife's virginity. This of course tells us more about King Henry than Queen Anna; the King's suspicion about her virginity certainly need not be taken seriously. It must simply be seen as part of the King's campaign to rid himself of his unwelcome new wife – at no blame to himself. But these charges remind us that a wedding night involves two sets of reactions. What did Queen Anna feel about these unsuccessful gropings and

STEEVEN   GARDNER

fumblings? And had she any realization that her own physical attributes were being blamed for this lack of success?

Fortunately for Queen Anna, she seems to have been wonderfully protected from humiliation by a complete ignorance of the facts of life. Her senior English ladies conducted a conversation with her on the subject some months later and suggested to the Queen that she was in fact still 'a maid'. In response

Queen Anna described the procedure which had succeeded the earlier, more energetic efforts. 'When he comes to bed', declared Anna, 'he kisses me and taketh me by the hand, and biddeth me, "goodnight sweet heart" and in the morning kisses me, and biddeth me, "Farewell darling". Is this not enough?' she enquired innocently. Such ignorance was not a universal condition. Most girls grew up with a good healthy knowledge of these matters. Furthermore, it was generally considered the duty of a mother to prepare her daughter for what to expect on her wedding night; otherwise, as St Bernardino of Siena had vividly expressed it in the previous century: 'it is like sending her to sea with no biscuit'. But Anna of Cleves was different. Her closeness to her mother's elbow had denied her a proper worldly education, since the strait-laced Duchess Maria evidently saw no need for what St Bernardino called 'biscuit'.

Yet, on the surface, all the turbulence of the spring of 1540 in England seemed to relate to religious matters, and their impact on politics, rather than to the King's personal life or diplomatic intrigue. The events of this period confused even those who lived through them, 'so shifting were political fortunes and so uncertain was the prospect of reform or reaction'. On the one hand Bishop Stephen Gardiner, the most prominent 'reactionary' prelate, attacked the reformers; he had recently returned to the Council having been ambassador in France for three years. On the other hand reformers such as Dr Robert Barnes, Thomas Garret and William Jerome fought back with energy. These three ended up in the Tower 'by the King's commandment': they would be executed on 30 July. Yet on the same day, equally, three priests, long-term supporters of Queen Catherine and of course the Pope, would also be put to death.

As for Cromwell, there were mixed signals here too. In April observers might legitimately have thought that his star was still in the ascendant: on 18 April he became Earl of Essex and Lord Great Chamberlain. But appearances were once again confused and deceptive. As spring turned to summer, the important star in the ascendant was not Cromwell's but that of the young girl who had first come to court to serve Queen Anna: Katherine Howard.

Bishop Stephen Gardiner, 'the most prominent reactionary prelate' who headed the 'Catholic' party in the King's Council in the last years of his reign.

Self-portrait, c. 1543, shortly before Holbein's death.

HANS HOLBEIN

The King's Painter

HANS HOLBEIN ARRIVED in England from Basle in 1526, with an introduction from Erasmus to Sir Thomas More. He began his career in England by painting portraits of More and his circle of friends. He returned briefly to Switzerland, but in 1530 he settled permanently in England, and he had attained the position of King's Painter by 1536. By the time he died in 1543 he had created one of the most remarkable pictorial records of a royal court ever made. His legacy included portraits of many of the leading figures of the age, a number of preparatory sketches and an exquisite group of portrait miniatures. Holbein also produced a rich variety of designs for books, furniture, fireplaces, tableware and jewellery.

Holbein's portrait of Robert Cheseman, Henry VIII's falconer.

Design for a fireplace attributed to Holbein, possibly for Bridewell.

Right: Sketches of dresses worn at court, c. 1540.

Within the painting: *Anno D˙ M CCCC XX VII*
Etatis Suæ XL IX

Sir Henry Guildford, Comptroller of the Household.
He is wearing the collar of a Knight of the Garter and
is holding his staff as Comptroller.

Opposite: An unidentified lady with a squirrel and a starling. An
outstanding example of Holbein's skill as a portrait painter.

Portrait of Nicholas Kratzer, Astronomer to Henry VIII, 1528.

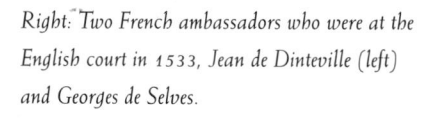

Right: Two French ambassadors who were at the English court in 1533, Jean de Dinteville (left) and Georges de Selves.

Design for the Jane Seymour gold cup, incorporating her motto 'Bound to obey and serve'.

CHAPTER 9

Old Man's Jewel

NO INDISPUTABLY AUTHENTIC picture of Katherine Howard survives, although there are two versions of a miniature by Holbein which may portray her, since the lady in question wears jewellery belonging to the deceased Queen Jane; there may also be a tantalizing glimpse of her, in profile, in a window of King's College Chapel Cambridge. The fact that she is the only one of Henry VIII's wives for whose appearance we must rely properly on contemporary descriptions, gives her career an appropriately evanescent quality. The same mistiness surrounds her date of birth. She was eighteen or nineteen when the King's roving eye first fell upon her; that is, roughly thirty years younger than he was. Despite his growing size, the King had evidently given up his desire for 'a big wife', for Katherine was not only small but diminutive. If King Henry was about thirty years older than Katherine, he must have been well over a foot taller. We need not speculate further about their respective weights. The French ambassador rated her beauty as only middling but he did praise her gracefulness, and he found much sweetness in her expression.

Even if Katherine Howard was not a beauty, she must have had considerable prettiness and obvious sex appeal since we know that she captivated the King instantly. It was tempting afterwards to see Katherine Howard planted as some kind of decoy duck to lure the ageing King and in a sense this was true. Time had not dimmed the lessons of the past. Thomas Boleyn had recently died but he died in dignity, having profited from the rise of his daughter but avoided the taint of her disgrace. The careers of the Seymour brothers, as uncles to Prince Edward, were evidently flourishing. The King's obvious disgust with Anna of Cleves made it clear that there was some kind of opportunity here. But in another sense the Howard family found themselves with a slightly unexpected candidate in little Katherine.

Here was no intelligent adult woman, wise in the ways of the world, as both Anne Boleyn and Jane Seymour had been. Katherine Howard was a child compared with these two, as well as being born a generation later. She was not

illiterate as is sometimes suggested: her ability to read and write (after a fashion) put her into a very small category of women, noble or otherwise. But being
literate did not mean that she was in any way educated; in this she was
absolutely typical of the girls of her time. Katherine Howard had been brought
up poor, despite the grandeur of her Howard lineage. Katherine's father and
Anne Boleyn's mother were brother and sister but their respective backgrounds
were very different.

Compared with the hard-working, ambitious Sir Thomas Boleyn, her father
Lord Edmund Howard was feckless and rather lazy, inhibited (as he saw it) by
his aristocratic birth from making the efforts suitable for those of a lesser
degree. His real importance for Katherine was to place her within a vast sprawl-
ing network of cousins. The Howards were amazingly prolific: Lord Edmund

*Holbein miniature,
probably of Katherine
Howard. The sitter is
wearing jewellery that
belonged to Queen Jane
Seymour.*

195

had twenty-two brothers and sisters, of whom nine lived long enough to marry. By 1527 he himself was responsible for ten children. Some of these he seems to have inherited: for his first wife and Katherine's mother, Jocasta Culpeper, was already the widow of Ralph Legh with Legh children when Lord Edmund married her in about 1515. As the wife of Lord Edmund Howard, Joyce gave birth to another six or seven children, before dying when her daughter Katherine was still quite young.

Katherine may have spent her childhood at the home of her maternal uncle. The significant moment in her life, however, was when she was taken into the household of her step-grandmother Agnes Duchess of Norfolk. The practice of sending girls (and boys) away from home to be raised elsewhere was widespread and was independent of family circumstances. It was a custom whose value obviously depended on the nature of the household concerned, the choice having nothing to do with moral values, and everything to do with the nobility of the household in question. In the case of Katherine Howard, the household of Agnes Dowager Duchess of Norfolk was the obvious selection, quite apart from the family relationship. The Duchess had certainly been a prominent figure at court for the last forty years. She had, for example, been attendant upon Catherine of Aragon at her wedding night to Prince Arthur in 1501; she was one of the godparents to Princess Mary in 1516; she bore the train of her step-granddaughter Queen Anne Boleyn at her coronation and a few months later acted as godmother to Princess Elizabeth.

Edward Prince of Wales, holding a pet monkey. Painting by Holbein.

Afterwards, vultures hovering round the carcass of Katherine Howard's reputation would suggest that Duchess Agnes had kept something closely approaching a high-class brothel, but the true comparison was to a high-class finishing school in which some quietly prospered and others more daringly looked round to exploit its opportunities (or were in their turn exploited). Certainly Duchess Agnes was considered to be a responsible figure, quite apart from her rank, to whom the care of the young could be safely entrusted, as the lists of those to whom she was made guardian demonstrates. But of course the comparison to a large school occurs once again when one considers the enormous size of the Duchess' household – over one hundred people at Lambeth – and the scandals which might take place as a result.

Katherine's first romance took place while she was still in the country, at the Duchess' house, Chesworth, in Sussex. A neighbour called Henry Mannox was hired to teach music there in 1536 and tried to seduce the fifteen-year-old girl in between the virginal and lute lessons, although if we are to believe Katherine's subsequent confession, full sex did not take place. Mannox himself also swore that he never knew her 'carnally'. No one seems to have taken this behaviour among young people particularly seriously; the trouble with Mannox was not his morals but the fact that, as a mere music teacher – he was no kind of match for Katherine, the Duke's niece.

Her next romance, with Francis Dereham, a gentleman-pensioner in the Duchess' Lambeth household, was much more serious. There is every reason to suppose that, unlike her relationship with Mannox, it was fully consummated. Since the couple were also in the habit of addressing each other as 'wife' and 'husband' one can go further and suggest that Katherine and Francis Dereham were actually precontracted to each other, their private vows reinforced by full sexual union. Certainly Mannox was jealous enough to warn the Duchess by means of an anonymous note left in her chapel pew. The Duchess discovered Katherine embracing Dereham and was 'much offended', hitting out – literally – at everyone in sight. But Dereham, if better born than Mannox, was still no great match, and Katherine appears to have cooled towards him, especially when she made the acquaintance of the gallant Thomas Culpeper in the King's Privy Chamber. Katherine's early feelings for Culpeper can only be gauged by her behaviour to him at a later date but it seems probable that she fell genuinely in love with him in the autumn of 1539. Then that momentous event took place which was liable to make her fortune – and to transform that of her family: the King fell in love with her.

It is this record of Katherine's past which makes it more likely that the Howard family made the most of their good luck when the King fell for her, rather than deliberately pushed her. She was not an ideal candidate for Queen. Katherine had not been wildly promiscuous – many girls of that time, if their private lives were exposed, would prove to have had similar experiences, especially when they expected to marry the man concerned. The real awkwardness lay in the fact that Katherine had been in some form precontracted to Dereham. Once the King declared his interest, all this was conveniently forgotten. The Norfolks could hardly be expected to point out the unsuitability of the King's choice, still less the stained feathers in the plumage of their little goose who had turned out to be a swan.

Instead Duchess Agnes coached Katherine on 'how to behave to the King'. The royal passion grew. The first official indication of the King's feelings was the granting of lands, confiscated from a felon, to Mistress Howard on 24 April 1540. In May she received twenty-three gifts of quilted sarcenet, paid for by the King. At some point around this time the King made love fully to his sweetheart. This can be deduced from the change in the King's treatment of Queen Anna. In late March he was still lamenting his situation while parliament duly confirmed Queen Anna's dower. But after Whitsun – in mid-May – the pace changed. The King felt an urgent need to get rid of Queen Anna, and the reason was surely that there was at least a possibility of Mistress Howard being pregnant. The May Day celebrations were to prove Queen Anna's last ceremonial appearance as royal consort.

This month also saw the formulation of questionnaires concerning the precise nature of an individual's faith – with emphasis on belief in the sacraments. It was this new concentration on heresy that enabled Norfolk and his allies to trap the recently ennobled Earl of Essex – Thomas Cromwell. On 10 June the King was apparently so convinced of Cromwell's lack of proper orthodoxy that he ordered his arrest. The magic spell that had for so long protected him – the confidence of the King – had been fatally weakened by the whole affair of the Cleves marriage. It was Norfolk's beguiling little niece who had now sexually rejuvenated the King where Cromwell's candidate, Anna of Cleves had failed. Cromwell was sentenced to death by an Act of Attainder; there was to be no

trial. Ironically enough it was a novel method of procedure that he himself had suggested for dealing with Margaret Countess of Salisbury who was, however, still languishing in the Tower. Cromwell was therefore to be the first person to die in this way, his crimes being high treason and heresy.

There was however one last service he was able to perform for the King: from the Tower he deposed all those conversations on the vexed subject of the King's fourth marriage, the wedding night and thereafter, which would be helpful to the King's case for nullity. The King had in effect two possible grounds for divorce. First here was the question of Anna of Cleves' precontract with

Thomas Cromwell, Earl of Essex wearing a magnificent enamelled gold chain and the George of the Order of the Garter. Miniature in a circular gold locket by Holbein.

Francis of Lorraine, although this might prove difficult to establish. Second there was the question of non-consummation, in itself the clearest cause of nullity by the rules of the church but inevitably difficult to establish, especially when a couple had indisputably shared a bedchamber all night on more than one occasion. Thus each of the arguments had its weakness. But by combining them – he had not been able to consummate the marriage because it was unlawful in the first place – the King was able to occupy that territory to which he was so partial in these situations, the moral high ground.

The next step was to secure the cooperation of Queen Anna herself. It would not help England if the Duke of Cleves was gratuitously turned into an enemy by the rejection of his sister. A great deal depended on how Anna of Cleves took the news of her dismissal; her agreement to the fact of non-consummation was especially important since, however much the King could lament and swear his impotence, his situation remained extremely complicated if his wife told another story.

So far as can be made out, Queen Anna had no inkling of the fate awaiting her. When she was transferred to Richmond on 24 June, on the excuse of the threat of plague, she had no reason not to enjoy life in the pleasant riverside palace. However the next day she received a rude awakening. A deputation came and informed her that the King had discovered their marriage to be invalid. It was a frightening situation. The knowledge that King Henry had had one unsatisfactory wife executed must surely have played its part in her submission. (Her brother the Duke of Cleves would say later that he was glad his sister had fared no worse.) For submit she did. The Queen 'made answer', wrote the commissioners, 'the effect of which tendeth to this, that she is content always with your Majesty'. Whether by luck – out of sheer terror – or by instinct – Anna of Cleves had managed to return that answer most likely to gratify the King. And she presented him, furthermore, with a deeply pleasing image: that of a submissive woman, accepting his will, his decisions in all things, casting herself on his mercy.

Under such circumstances Henry VIII had always shown himself capable of being generous. He was generous now to 'the daughter of Cleves'. Anna was to have precedence over all the ladies in England, except the Queen, the King's daughters by any future marriage, and his existing daughters. She was to receive a handsome settlement of manors and estates 'in divers counties'. All this was for her lifetime – provided she did not pass 'beyond the sea'; instead she was to be naturalized as the King's subject and lead a new, prosperous and happy life as the King's adopted 'good sister'. This condition was of course essential for damage limitation: the English could not have a disgruntled Lady Anna at liberty to stir up trouble abroad.

The various steps needful for the King's latest divorce were now set in motion. The obedient findings of the clergy were that there had both been a precontract *de praesenti*, insufficiently investigated, and that the union had not been consummated; furthermore the marriage was void because Henry had acted under duress – from Cromwell. On that basis, the King's latest 'great matter' was passed by convocation on 9 July and was approved by parliament four days later. So Anna of Cleves was formally removed from the position of Queen of England which she had occupied for six months and a few days.

On 28 July, the same day on which Thomas Cromwell was executed in the Tower of London, Henry VIII married his latest sweetheart. In her marriage vows, which the King already had good reason to believe that she would carry out, Katherine swore to be 'bonair and buxom in bed'. Henry VIII was besottedly in love with her. His constant public caresses led several observers to the conclusion that King Henry loved this particular wife more than he had 'the others'. Whatever the comparisons with the past, the King's passion certainly aroused general comment. Just as the King lavished affection on his young wife, he showered her with rich gifts. The girl who had been brought up as a poor relation to the grandees about her was now the recipient of a stream of magnificent jewels, gold beads decorated with black enamel, emeralds lozenged with gold, brooches, crosses, pomanders, clocks – whatever could be most splendidly encrusted in her honour. Naturally, the usual transformation scene had to take place, courtesy of Galyon Hone, the King's glazier, with badges removed, and new badges supplied. The status of Queen Katherine as consort was further underlined by the castles, lordships and manors granted to her, many of which had belonged to Jane Seymour or to Thomas Cromwell.

The motto Katherine chose to go with her emblem of the crowned rose was 'Non autre volonté que la sienne' ('No other wish but his'). This was certainly politic and likely to bring comfort to an elderly husband sexually entranced by his new young wife. But it was not necessarily insincere. Nor should one assume that Katherine Howard lacked any feelings for King Henry, just because he was much older than her, fat and sometimes sick, while she had already shown herself to be a flighty young thing with an eye for a handsome young man. As with Jane Seymour, the clue to Katherine Howard's wifely emotions lay in the office of King and the enormous, awed respect it evoked. The two young women were of totally different character; nevertheless they had both been brought up since birth to bow without question before the great royal sun which blazed at the centre of every courtier's life.

As Queen, Katherine now had new ways of enjoying herself: the exercise of patronage for example. By mid-November she was arguing with Archbishop Lee about the advowson, or right of presentation, of the archdeaconry of York. Members of her family were duly advanced. Katherine's brother Charles was placed in the Privy Chamber. The following year an interesting appointment was made in the Queen's own household, apparently at the instigation of Duchess Agnes. Francis Dereham, Katherine's erstwhile fiancé, to use the modern term, was made her secretary. With hindsight it was not a very wise appointment by those who surely wished to seal away the incriminating past;

on the other hand the intention may have been to shut Dereham's mouth with what was in effect a handsome bribe. When the appointment was made it caused no particular comment; it was simply part of the conventional pattern of a Queen's patronage in which friends as well as relatives naturally found a place at court.

The husband whose will she had vowed to make her own was, at this stage of his life, no desirable older man like his contemporary, the Duke of Suffolk (also with a new young wife), but rather close to an obese – if doting – monster. It is clear that King Henry suffered a violent increase in his weight – already vast enough – in the year 1540. Merry and lusty King Henry might be – especially following his summer marriage to Katherine – but with his 54-inch waist and 57-inch chest, measurements attested by his armour made in 1540, he can hardly be described as being in prime condition. The King's health was giving serious cause for concern. He had been a wonderfully healthy young man until the check of a jousting accident in 1524. But in the late 1520s he began to suffer from varicose ulcerations of his legs which in time became chronic. Gradually the inflamed veins became thrombosed, and the next stage was the cruelly painful swelling of the lower legs causing intermittent bouts of fever, a condition liable to cause rage and frustration in a far more moderately tempered man than Henry VIII. It was a vicious circle. Naturally the King's expanding weight did not help the condition of his legs; at the same time the condition of his legs frequently prevented him from taking exercise.

In December 1540 the King went on a special regime – inspired no doubt by his passion for Katherine. This 'new rule of living', as the French ambassador called it, specially designed to cure corpulence, meant that the King would rise between 5 and 6 am, hear Mass at 7, then ride till 10, which was his dinner hour. Regrettably, the new rule could not stave off a serious attack of fever in the spring of 1541. One of the ulcers kept open to maintain health suddenly closed, to the King's 'great alarm'. The danger was considered extreme and the King's temper matched the danger. At his own request, his young Queen was not among those who tended him. Understandably he did not want his fresh romantic relationship clouded with images of illness, swollen suppurating legs and so forth. Thus King Henry went at least ten or twelve days in March 1541 without seeing his wife. It seems likely that this was the period when Queen Katherine began to wonder whether she might not combine the substantial

BEATVS vir qui non abiit
in confilio impiorum, & in via
peccatorum non ftetit, & in cathedra pe=
ftilentiæ non fedit.

fquis qui bene

joys of being Queen of England with the more light-hearted pleasures of her previous existence.

One of the bizarre aspects of the court of King Henry and Queen Katherine must have been the visits of the King's 'good sister', the Lady Anna of Cleves. At New Year 1541, for example, the Lady Anna celebrated by flinging herself down on her knees before Queen Katherine, 'as if she herself were merely the most insignificant damsel'. At the banquet which followed it was noted that the Lady Anna looked as happily unconcerned 'as if there had been nothing between them' (herself and the King). Anna of Cleves, aged twenty-five, ended the evening dancing with Queen Katherine Howard, aged nineteen, while the old King stumped off to bed because his leg was hurting him.

Since King Henry always felt bonhomous towards those who bowed to his will, he was fully prepared to be on the best of terms with his ex-wife. Indeed so jolly were King Henry and Lady Anna together at the beginning of August that rumours began to spread that he was about to restore her to her previous position. This was nonsense but it does show how incomprehensible the putting aside of a princess with connections in favour of a chit of a girl, was to most outsiders. But there was good reason for all this cordiality. The Lady Anna was not a fool; she had been bewildered at first, but once she assessed the situation, she conducted herself not only with dignity but also with shrewdness. Here in England she now had an honourable position at court no rejected woman but the first lady after the Queen and the royal daughters. Like a rich widow (ever a favourable position for any woman untroubled by grief), she had a household, a large income and property. Not only were there a great many women who were far worse off but one might go further and argue that the Lady Anna of Cleves was, for the time being, one of the happiest women at the Tudor court.

Katherine Howard certainly faced a more challenging destiny. After he recovered from his illness the King decided to take her with him on a northern tour – possibly culminating in a northern coronation at York for the new Queen. In the popular imagination the crowning of Queen Katherine was linked with her production of a son. Rumours of her pregnancy at least indicate that a royal birth was believed to be a possibility. Although the King had not fathered a child for four years, during this time his then wife, Queen Jane, had been pregnant for nine months, he himself had been a widower for over a year, and he had then been trapped (his version) for six months in a physically impossible marriage. The procreation of 'a Duke of York' by the King was certainly not out of the question.

Yet at some point in the spring Queen Katherine renewed her involvement with Thomas Culpeper. Why did she do so? And why did Culpeper agree? Taking the Queen's point of view first, it seems right to seek an explanation in Katherine's fatal lightness of temperament rather than in some more Machiavellian intention. Katherine Howard was reckless, not devious. She was the sort of girl who lost her head easily over a man, a girl who agreed generally with what men suggested. It might be that Queen Katherine took up with Culpeper in order to provide the King with a healthy living (secretly bastard) child. But this is to misread both relationships – Katherine's with Culpeper, and Katherine's with the King. The one was intended to be a romantic dalliance – within certain limits: Katherine was, on her own admission, one who knew how to 'meddle with a man' without conceiving a child. The other was based on the duty of a consort to a husband of whom she stood in awe. If Katherine dallied with Culpeper to please herself, she in turn made it her business to please the King. Naïvely, she saw no harm in combining the two.

Culpeper's point of view was different. Here was the kind of young man all too easily thrown up by the Tudor court: ambitious, ruthlessly using his personal attractions to further his career. He was now in his late twenties, with charm an important part of his armoury. One might compare Culpeper to the young Charles Brandon, thirty years earlier, working his way up to wealth and a dukedom (of Suffolk) through royal favour. The difference was that in the early years of the reign the ambitious sought to be boon companions to the King. Now it was clearly more far-sighted to seek the favour of the Queen. There were rich pickings to be had there during the King's lifetime and then there was a question of what would happen next. Prince Edward was only three-and-a-half years old in 1541 and a Dowager Queen would have a strong position.

In April Queen Katherine wrote a love letter to Culpeper (the only one of her letters to survive). The first eighteen words, in another hand, are innocuous enough: 'Master Culpeper, I heartily recommend me unto you, praying you to send me word how that you do'. After that Katherine herself weighed in, clearly labouring over the spelling. Towards the end of the letter she writes: 'I would you were with me now that you might see what pain I take in writing to you'. But the passion is unmistakable, and comes across as clearly through the misshapen words as the King's love for her was signalled to his courtiers by his caresses. 'I heard that you were sick and never longed so much for anything as to see you', writes Katherine. 'It makes my heart die to think I cannot be always in your company.' The letter is signed – touchingly perhaps but how indiscreetly, 'Yours as long as life endures – Katheryn'.

When Katherine wrote this letter Culpeper had occupied an envied position

Katherine Howard's fateful love letter to Thomas Culpeper.

Margaret Pole, Countess of Salisbury, daughter of George Duke of
Clarence and mother of Cardinal Pole. Her execution in May 1540 was
the most repulsive piece of savagery ever carried out at the King's wish.

in the King's Privy Chamber for at least two years. In this capacity he too would go on the northern progress during the following summer. Henry VIII baptized this progress in blood. On the flimsy excuse of feared insurrection – the Tower was to be cleared of state prisoners – he ordered the execution of Margaret Countess of Salisbury, held there for the last two years. This can claim to be the most repulsive piece of savagery ever carried out at the King's wishes. Here was a woman he had long revered for her piety and decency, who had stood to him over the years almost as a mother figure. Now, on 27 May 1541, she was executed – the last and bloodiest death in the bloodstained history of the house of Clarence.

Freed from the fearsome danger presented by the continued existence of this old lady, King Henry set forth for the north with Queen Katherine. His political aims included not only the settlement – by his dominating presence – in northern England, where some of the old religious ways were obstinately retained, but also some kind of accommodation with his nephew, the King of Scots. The two Kings had never met, but perhaps King James, now nearly thirty, could be lured south. So the King of England – and the Queen – solemnly

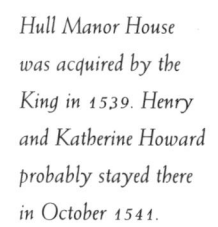

Hull Manor House was acquired by the King in 1539. Henry and Katherine Howard probably stayed there in October 1541.

progressed on from Grafton Regis to Lincoln and so to Pontefract and York. By the beginning of October the King had arrived at Hull, where he occupied himself with a favourite pursuit, inspecting and designing fortifications. From there the King and Queen travelled slowly south. On 1 November the royal entourage reached Hampton Court, and there the King made a solemn thanksgiving for the happiness which the Queen had brought him. It was to be his last moment of pure joy where Katherine was concerned.

When the crisis came it came very suddenly. To outsiders – like Chapuys – one moment Katherine was the beloved consort, the next moment her coffers and chests were sealed, Archbishop Cranmer had 'charge of everything', and the Queen herself was held apart (and incommunicado) from her husband. What brought this crisis about – so startling, so unexpected – was a visitation from the past in the shape of a tale told by one John Lascelles. He came to Cranmer with details related to him by his sister, Mary Hall, who was a chamberwoman to Dowager Duchess Agnes and had known Katherine at Lambeth. What Lascelles told Cranmer was enough to convince the horrified Archbishop of three things, all in their different ways extremely unpalatable. First, the young Queen's life before marriage had been far from irreproachable. Secondly she might well have been precontracted; although in a sense this condoned her behaviour, nevertheless it presented an immediate problem of the validity of her marriage to the King. Thirdly, he had to break the news to the King.

What inspired Lascelles to make these revelations? The most convincing explanation lies in the fears of Lascelles, and others, of further triumphs of the 'reactionary' religious party in England, due to the paramount influence of Katherine's uncle, the Duke of Norfolk. Lascelles' record shows him to have been a convinced reformer, one who had lamented the fall of Cromwell, and denounced Norfolk publicly.

On 2 November – All Souls' Day – at Hampton Court, during a Mass at which he was not the celebrant, the Archbishop slipped a paper bearing details of Lascelles' charges into the King's hand. At first the King seemed 'much perplexed'. He 'loved the Queen so tenderly' that for the moment he honestly believed the paper must be a forgery. For the time being, at any rate, the matter was to be kept utterly private.

It should be noted at this point that all Lascelles' revelations, and those subsequently related by Mary Hall, concerned Queen Katherine's behaviour before marriage. But of course details of what Katherine had been up to in the north (and elsewhere), while the King slept off his exhaustion at reviewing his fortifications, were ticking away like a time bomb. As with Katherine's behaviour before marriage, there had been witnesses – all too many. For the time being it was Dereham who was hauled off to the Tower, along with various waiting-women, and Dereham who was tortured. Culpeper was still 'merry a-hawking'. His merriment however was not to last long since, in the general flood of revelation which followed, Dereham himself took care to implicate Culpeper, hoping to save himself by stating (correctly enough) that Culpeper had followed him in the Queen's affections. So Culpeper too was arrested and tortured.

As the hideous truth emerged – this was no calumny, the Queen was not innocent – the King's 'perplexity' gave way to an orgy of self-pity. He blamed his Council – who else? – for 'this last mischief'. After that his mood turned to mighty anger in view of his Queen's ingratitude, the monstrous betrayal she had brought about. He called for a sword to go and slay her 'that he loved so much'. He vowed that all the pleasure 'that wicked woman' had had from her 'incontinency' (wantonness) should not equal the pain she should feel from torture. And finally 'he took to tears'. Some of his courtiers thought he had actually gone mad. But this reaction was hardly madness. The unbearable fact was that the King had been tricked in the first place to accept as a virgin one who was anything but that, and since then he had been cuckolded. He knew it and so did everybody else. His madness was the natural outrage of the tyrant who found there were areas of human behaviour that even tyranny could not regulate.

In the meantime Queen Katherine had to be brought to make a confession, and Cranmer was the man to do it. She collapsed completely when confronted. His account of his conversation with her makes pitiful reading; nor indeed was he himself unmoved. 'I found her in such lamentation and heaviness, as I never saw no creature, so that it would have pitied any man's heart in the world, to have looked upon her.' Her attendants talked to him of her wild and vehement moods; Cranmer himself mentioned 'frenzy'. Cranmer now conceived it to be his duty to extricate his master from his marriage with as much speed and decency as possible. It was not an experience he can have relished, particularly since the scandal over the dismissal of Anna of Cleves, murmured against by Protestants in Europe, had scarcely died down. But the Dereham precontract seemed momentarily heaven-sent to solve everyone's difficulties. The King's fifth marriage could be pronounced as having been invalid from the start and Katherine herself could simply be disgraced and put away, since her behaviour with Dereham was excused by the precontract.

As a result of what the Queen confessed to him, Cranmer felt he had enough evidence of a precontract, especially since 'carnal copulation following' reinforced a shaky betrothal and gave it proper force. One of the problems, however, now and later, was that the devastated Queen, her brains addled by sheer terror, kept failing to grasp the point that a precontract, if proved, was more likely to save her than condemn her. Instead she took refuge in excuses, which showed yet again how young and foolish she was, talking of Dereham's violence and his 'importunate forcement' of her. In any case it may have been that the King would not finally have allowed the excuse of the precontract to stand.

He never saw Queen Katherine again after her arrest on 12 November. As ever, he distanced himself physically from the crisis. On 5 November he left Hampton Court 'suddenly after dinner', without explanation and did not return until the Queen had been removed – on 14 November – to Syon. As the arrests and interrogations and revelations proceeded, distance scarcely lent enchantment to his contemplation of his wife's behaviour, nor that of his predecessor in her embraces, Dereham. Discovering the marriage to be invalid might have the effect of leaving the Queen alive – it would also, logically, absolve Dereham.

And the King continued to harbour a special resentment against Dereham, pre-sumably as the 'spoiler' of his bride, even greater than that against Culpeper, who was after all accused of the greater crime of adultery. But by accusing both Dereham (in his period as secretary to the Queen) and Culpeper of an adulter-ous liaison, treason could be invoked, and Dereham's death, as well as Culpeper's could satisfactorily follow. Another death would be that of Katherine. But here the King could simply take his stand on the law. Let justice be done.

Maids, waiting-women, gentlemen and other terrified informers were now pouring out their salacious stories of life after dark during that northern progress, quite apart from stories of Katherine's past. Torture was used on oth-ers: Robert Damport, for instance, a friend of Dereham, was stretched on the rack. Even if only half of what was now related was true – the introduction of torture makes it difficult to be certain about the absolute truth of every detail – then Queen Katherine had behaved with such wild folly since her marriage as to make the question of adultery a purely technical one.

Perhaps that was the answer. Perhaps the Queen had not – technically – committed adultery. She may have stopped somewhere just short of having full sex with Culpeper, using the most common contemporary method of birth control, *coitus interruptus*. Culpeper continued to deny full 'carnal knowledge' even under torture, and the Queen, in her various confessions, held to her inno-cence. (However she indubitably lied about the Dereham affair – he had not forced her – so not a great deal of reliance should be placed on the word of a shattered girl.)

The repeated confessions and reports of clandestine meetings between a man notorious for his gallantry and a woman who was already sexually awakened really do not admit of any other explanation than adultery. Queen Katherine can have been innocent of the charge only if the narrowest possible interpre-tation of the word is used. After all, what else did she do with Culpeper, out of her chamber two nights running and up the backstairs at Lincoln, until two o'clock in the morning? Remorselessly, the detailed stories piled up to confirm what Culpeper – and the Queen – admitted, a sequence of stolen rendezvous by night at places which included Greenwich, Lincoln, Pontefract and York.

Many of the charges involved the Queen's attendant, Jane Viscountess Rochford (she who had damned Anne Boleyn for an incestuous relationship with her husband). Lady Rochford attempted to paint herself the innocent bystander who had somehow been at the other end of the room where the Queen was meeting Culpeper without knowing what was going on. Katherine reversed the image and described a woman, like Eve, who had persistently tempted her with seductive notions of dalliance; while Culpeper took the line that Lady Rochford had 'provoked' him into a clandestine relationship with the Queen. The truth is impossible to establish but clearly Lady Rochford, Queen Katherine and Culpeper were all in their different ways involved up to the hilt in something that none of them should have countenanced for a moment.

The case of Dereham is rather different. There is no proof, or even likelihood, that he was intimate with the Queen following her marriage. That appointment to the secretaryship, however unwise, was more likely to have been intended to keep his mouth shut. Yet he would suffer torture and then, on 10 December, the full barbaric death accompanied by disembowelling and castration while still conscious, demanded by the law of treason. The King could have granted mercy from these extreme penalties at least. For Dereham he did not. He did choose to do so for Culpeper – who died on the same day, simply by having 'his head stricken off'.

Meanwhile at Syon arrangements for Queen Katherine's reception were punitive, although not excessively so. She was held in rooms 'furnished moderately' with only 'a mean number of servants' – yet there were to be rooms, not a cell, and there were to be servants, not jailers. As usual at the Tudor court, dress was the medium to convey the message. Sir Thomas Seymour was deputed to confiscate all the Queen's jewels and bring them to the King. She was to be allowed six of her favourite becoming French hoods – but they were to be edged with gold, not gems. Satin, damask and velvet kirtles were all permitted, so long as they too were not adorned with precious stones.

On 24 November Katherine Howard – whom the Council had formally demoted from the title of Queen two days earlier – was indicted for having led 'an abominable, base, carnal, voluptuous and vicious life' before marriage, maintaining however 'the outward appearance of chastity and honesty'. So she had led the King to love her and thus 'arrogantly coupled herself with him in marriage'. She had also concealed the contract she had had with Dereham 'to the peril of the King and of his children to be begotten by her' (who might have found themselves bastards). After marriage she had again shown Dereham 'notable favour', while inciting Culpeper to carnal intercourse.

In December a number of people were taken into the Tower: their crime was 'misprision of treason', that is advance knowledge that someone else intended to commit treason – in other words, concealing the secrets of Katherine's past. They included her step-grandmother, old Duchess Agnes and other Howard relatives. The Tower of London became so crowded that the royal apartments had to be pressed into use. But the head of the house, Thomas Howard Duke of Norfolk was not among the prisoners. The grovelling letter he sent to his sovereign referred – with what true anguish! – to 'mine ungracious mother-in-law' and above all to 'abominable deeds' done by two of his nieces. Norfolk referred to himself as 'prostrate at the King's feet'. And so he survived.

On 10 February Katherine too was transferred to the Tower. As she was taken to the small sealed barge which would convey her there, the truth hit home. Katherine struggled and had to be forced on board. When she arrived she wept and cried out and tormented herself 'miserably without ceasing'. Katherine had been brought to the Tower in response to the Act of Attainder which had been first read in the House of Lords on 21 January and had received the King's assent on 11 February. The following day Katherine was informed she was going to die and on 13 February members of the Privy Council came for her at

The site in the Tower of London where Katherine Howard followed her cousin Anne Boleyn to the block.

seven o' clock in the morning. According to the French ambassador, she was 'so weak that she could hardly speak', but confessed in a few words that she had merited a thousand deaths for so offending a King who had treated her so graciously. Katherine Howard was then executed on the same block and in the same place as her cousin Anne Boleyn not quite six years previously. It was then the turn of Jane Viscountess Rochford. Both bodies were taken to the nearby chapel of St Peter ad Vincula, where the body of Anne Boleyn also lay, and were there interred. At the time of her death Katherine Howard had been Queen of England for just over eighteen months, and may still not have reached her twenty-first birthday.

PART V

CATHERINE
PARR

CHAPTER 10

A Satisfactory Widow

CHAPUYS LIKENED THE King's grief after the fall of Katherine Howard to that of a woman crying more bitterly at the loss of her tenth husband than she had over the deaths of all the other nine put together: 'the reason being that she had never buried one of them without being sure of the next, but that after the tenth husband she had no one in view, hence her sorrow and her lamentations'. It was true that after five wives and thirty years of matrimony the King – for once – had no one in view. It was also correct that this was unlike any previous situation: King Henry had actually married Anne Boleyn before he divorced Catherine of Aragon, got rid of her to marry Jane Seymour within days, and equally rid himself of Anna of Cleves for a more-or-less instant wedding with Katherine Howard. Even the unexpected decease of Jane Seymour had found the Council discussing their master's matrimonial plans in the very letters abroad which broke the tragic news.

There was another more sinister difference. This stemmed from certain clauses in the act which had condemned Katherine Howard to death. Ostensibly intended 'to avoid doubts for the future', these clauses in fact had quite the contrary effect. Anyone who knew anything 'incontinent' (wanton) about the Queen now had to reveal it under pain of treason. Furthermore, if the King should propose marrying any woman 'whom they took to be a pure and clean maid' but was not, there were the same dire penalties. The deceitful woman herself would be guilty of high treason 'and all who knew it and did not reveal it were guilty of misprision of treason'. It was these last words which cast a chill. The merry game of inserting a young girl into the King's affections was over, for who could tell if she was as chaste as she pretended? And if not, then the Tower at best and the axe at worst awaited her unlucky family and friends.

As for marrying abroad, there were obvious difficulties in view of the fact that Henry VIII had now executed two of his wives, as well as divorcing two others. Yet a King, however decrepit his health, however terrifying his temper, still needed a Queen. The problem was not easily solved. There was one convenient option, of course: the King could take back the Lady Anna of Cleves.

The identity of the
sitter in this portrait on
a panel of a sixteenth-
century woman has
been much debated.
For many years it
was thought to be a
likeness of Lady Jane
Grey, but recent work
by Susan E. James
has re-established it
as a portrait of
Catherine Parr.

That at least was the opinion of her supporters. The Lady Anna had not managed to conceal her pleasure at the downfall of her supplanter – and former dancing partner – not so much out of spite, as because the position of Queen was once more vacant. Olisleger, the envoy of Cleves at the English court, absolutely refused to take 'no' for answer. Finally the English council had to issue a formal refusal, begging Cleves never to issue such an embarrassing request again. The King had fully determined never to restore his 'sister' to his bed since 'what was done was founded upon great reason, whatever the world might allege'.

Early in 1543 courtiers noticed a new zest and energy in their King, as though the black shadows of the previous year had at last been cast off. Feasts were held again, at which the King's daughter the Lady Mary 'in default of a Queen' presided. Military victory over the troublesome Scots the previous November was one kind of tonic. But the King also had another private reason to feel contented. If he had not exactly fallen in love again – it is doubtful whether this rampant emotion, responsible for so many of the cataclysmic events of his life, troubled him further after the debacle with Katherine Howard – he had at least viewed with affectionate approval an English lady now at court. She was known as 'my lady Latimer', but she had been born some thirty-one years before as Catherine Parr.

Of all the good qualities Catherine Parr Lady Latimer possessed to fit her for being the King's sixth consort, none was more satisfactory than the fact that she was a widow. After all, even the most paranoid of sovereigns could hardly expect her, a woman previously married, to be 'a pure and clean maid' in the sense of being a virgin. So her supporters and relations could safely advance her cause without fear of reprisals under the notorious provisions of the 1542 Act of Attainder.

Catherine Parr was the eldest child of Sir Thomas Parr of Kendal and Maud Greene, a Northamptonshire heiress. The year 1512 is the most likely year for her birth; a brother William was born in August 1513 and a sister Anne in 1514. The Parrs were a distinguished northern family in origin, even though their lives had mainly been led in the south since the late fifteenth century. Sir Thomas Parr – knighted at the coronation of Henry VIII – was a companion-in-arms of the young King and, like Sir Thomas Boleyn and Sir John Seymour before him, was present at the Battle of Spurs in 1513. Maud Lady Parr was attached to Catherine of Aragon as a lady-in-waiting: it is possible at least that her first child was named for her mistress and that Catherine of Aragon even stood godmother to Catherine Parr. Then what looked like two promising careers at court were cut short when Sir Thomas Parr died in 1517, leaving Maud Parr with three young children.

Given the early death of her father, it is very likely that Catherine Parr was mainly brought up in Northamptonshire with her relations. In later life, she would show much devotion to her uncle, another Sir William Parr, and his

William Parr, Marquess of Northampton, Catherine Parr's brother. Drawing by Holbein.

daughter, another Maud, later by marriage Lady Lane. There, too, she would have been educated – up to a point. There is an optimistic theory that Catherine Parr was educated along with Catherine of Aragon's daughter Mary, possibly by the great Vives himself, and as a result learnt 'fluent' Latin as a girl. On the one hand, the age gap between herself and Mary – four years – makes this extraordinarily unlikely (and there is no reference to Catherine Parr in the quite detailed accounts of Princess Mary's youth). On the other hand it is clear from Catherine Parr's own later history that she was by no means fluent in Latin in 1543 when the King's eye fell on her.

There is another myth about Catherine Parr, that she had been already married to two old and sickly men before 1543, the first of them actually insane. In fact her first bridegroom, whom she married at the age of seventeen in 1529, was a young man, probably not much older than his bride, and certainly not

Snape Castle in Yorkshire where Catherine Parr lived with her second husband John Neville, Lord Latimer.

insane, even if his health was poor: Edward Borough, son of Thomas, Lord Borough, chamberlain to Queen Anne Boleyn. He died in 1532, leaving Catherine a childless widow of twenty. Her second bridegroom was indeed an older man. John Neville, Lord Latimer, was a northern grandee who had already been widowed twice, leaving him with a son, also called John, and a daughter Margaret. Lord Latimer was then about forty. This marriage, concluded in 1533, marked the real beginning of the upward mobility of Catherine Parr. At the age of twenty-one, she was now in charge of an extremely large household, as well as a step-daughter; in both cases she succeeded triumphant-ly. Margaret Neville, far from resenting Catherine, proved to be the first in the long line of younger women who would respond to her maternal warmth and friendship.

Nevertheless, it was not to prove an easy life. Catherine Lady Latimer was obliged to develop other qualities while in the north. That 'prudence' on which all observers commented was first forged at the time of the Pilgrimage of Grace, when her husband was taken hostage by the rebel Robert Aske in front of his wife and children and forced to act as his mouthpiece, thereby enraging the King who demanded that he reject Aske and 'submit to our clemency'. In December 1537 Latimer went south, leaving his wife and children in the north, and tried to explain that he had acted under duress. It was now Catherine and her step-children who were put under house arrest by the rebels in order to make sure of Latimer's return. Between threats of death to his family and accu-sations of treason, Latimer – and Catherine too – had to tread a delicate path. Latimer's health never really recovered from the strain.

In the last years of his life Catherine spent more and more time in her London house in Charterhouse Yard, and less in the north. Here she renewed her con-nections with the court where her sister Anne, now married to William Herbert, had been in waiting on Queen Katherine Howard. Catherine was also beginning to be in touch – in a mild way – with those interested in the more evangelical aspects of the Anglican religion. That was something that would obviously commend her more to the reforming Archbishop Cranmer than to the reactionary Bishop Stephen Gardiner of Winchester, but it was not thought worthy of note at the time of the King's courtship.

At some point during the final stages of her husband's long-drawn-out illness Catherine also fell in love – with Sir Thomas Seymour. For Catherine was a more complicated character than observers, obsessed by the stereotype of the prudent woman and virtuous widow, realized, and her nature was by no means devoid of passion. At this point too – still before the actual death of Lord Latimer – the King began to express an interest in her. The shadow of this vast cumbersome galleon, royal pennant flying, fell across plans which would cer-tainly have been on a personal level far more agreeable.

The King's first presents to 'my lady Latimer' were dated 16 February 1543, two weeks before Lord Latimer died on 2 March. Later, Catherine Parr would be quite candid about what happened next. She was, in the time-honoured fashion of a romantic heroine, torn between love and duty. In the end duty won. She told Thomas Seymour: 'As truly as God is God, my mind was fully bent … to marry you before any man I know. Howbeit, God withstood my will therein most vehemently for a time, and through his grace and goodness, made that possible which seemed to me most impossible; that was, made me renounce utterly mine own will, and to follow his will most willingly'.

Thomas Seymour dropped back, with what – if any – assurances for the

future cannot be known. The triumphant Parrs stepped forward. On 12 July, in 'the Queen's closet' at Hampton Court, the King and the twice-widowed Lady Latimer were married. Unlike certain of his weddings, it was not a secret ceremony. On the contrary, both the King's daughters were present, as well as his niece Margaret Douglas and others including Catherine's sister. The Ladies Mary and Elizabeth had recently undergone a pleasant reverse in their fortunes: a new act of parliament on 14 June restored them officially to the succession, after Prince Edward and his future direct heirs. As for the King himself, it was remarked that when the now familiar words of the marriage service were pronounced, an expression of real happiness momentarily crossed that bloated face.

The new Queen Catherine Parr was never described as a beauty. 'Pleasing' and 'lively', 'kind' and 'gracious' were the most flattering epithets. It is true that Catherine's age and status may have been responsible – widows of over thirty were not expected to be beauties – but when Anna of Cleves indignantly exclaimed that the new Queen was 'not nearly as beautiful as she', Chapuys, passing on the comment, did not see fit to contradict it. But if the new Queen was not a beauty, she was neither dull nor austere. She enjoyed dancing. The Spanish Duke of Najera reported that in 1544 when the Queen was 'slightly indisposed', she still came out of her room to dance 'for the honour of the company'. She was well set up – the tallest of King Henry's wives – and her height would have enabled her to cut a regal figure since her conception of her role as consort included a great deal of ornate dressing-up.

The Duke of Najera also noticed how magnificent her costume was: the brocade kirtle beneath an open robe of cloth of gold, the sleeves lined with crimson satin, the train more than two yards long. Two crosses hung from her neck, as well as a jewel composed of fine diamonds, and there were more diamonds in her headdress; pendants hung from her golden girdle. Quite apart from the clothes that she commissioned for herself, Queen Catherine inherited a vast collection of the dresses of Katherine Howard. This may seem macabre to us and redolent of Bluebeard's household arrangements was, in fact, a perfectly practical measure in the sixteenth century, when rich gowns were pieces of

Detail from the portait of Catherine Parr on p. 215 showing her elaborate rings..

valuable property. Shoes were a particular passion of Catherine Parr's – forty-seven pairs ordered in one year alone.

Queen Catherine was fond of music and had her own consort of viols, with musicians from Venice and Milan, paid 8d a day. Painting, at least portraiture and especially miniatures, was a more unusual interest. She had John Bettes limn the royal portraits and probably patronized the Dutch-born painter, Hans Eworth, if he is to be identified with 'Hewe Hawarde' – the name Eworth gave the English a lot of trouble – to provide miniatures of herself and the King at 30s each. Her own portrait was also probably painted by a female artist, Lucas Horenbout's widow Margaret. In other ways, with her love of her greyhounds (fed on milk), her parrots (fed on hempseed), her feeling for flowers and herbs, her affection for her dwarf jesters and her female jester, 'Jane Foole' as she was known, with a special 'red petticoat' bought for her, Queen Catherine Parr comes across as someone who enjoyed the small pleasures of life.

As for her Parr relatives, they were the gainers on many different levels. Anne Herbert, also praised by Roger Ascham for her learning, was placed in her sister's household, as was her cousin, Maud Lady Lane, and her step-daughter Margaret Neville. Her uncle William was to be her Lord Chamberlain. Her brother-in-law William Herbert entered the Privy Chamber, was knighted and was set on his way to build a massive fortune centred round the lands of the former Abbey of Wilton, and other estates in Wales. Queen Catherine's brother William Parr of Kendal, had found favour with the King already: he had come to court with a recommendation from the Duke of Norfolk in 1537 and his uncle and namesake had asked Cromwell to find him a place in the Privy Chamber. In 1539 he was created Baron Parr of Kendal and in April 1543 – when his sister's rise had already begun – he was given various appointments in the north, as well as being made a Knight of the Garter and, in December 1543, being created Earl of Essex.

As Queen Catherine Parr had fulfillled her duty to her own family by marrying the King, she was now bound to fulfil her duty to the King by tending to his family. It is greatly to her credit that she managed to establish excellent loving relationships with all three of her new step-children, despite their very different ages. Of course she did not literally install them under one roof: that is to misunderstand the nature of sixteenth-century life when separate households were more to do with status than inclination. At the same time, the royal children were now all together on certain occasions under the auspices of their stepmother. The real point is that Catherine was considered by the King – and the court – to be in charge of them, an emotional responsibility rather than a physical one.

Gold medal dated 1545. The inscription refers to Henry as 'Supreme Head of the Church'.

Another duty of the Queen Consort was to act as Regent in her husband's absence – if the situation demanded it (and her qualities justified the appointment). On 7 July 1544 the minutes of the Privy Council recorded that 'The Queen's Highness shall be regent in his grace's absence'. Despite the King's plethora of wives, the only precedent was in fact that of Catherine of Aragon who had acted the part with considerable verve when King Henry went to France in 1513 and the Scots were troubling the borders. In 1544 King Henry was once again taking to a French campaign, and the Scots were once again threatening trouble.

It was, of course, no longer a glorious young prince who was to lead his Englishmen towards Boulogne, but an unwieldy invalid who had to be winched aboard his horse with his armour cut away from around his swollen leg. The King had been ill shortly before embarkation and there is a touching vignette of Queen Catherine sitting with his painful leg in her lap. She also moved out of her queenly apartments into a small bedroom next to his. She was well equipped for the role of a nurse. Her apothecaries' bills reveal lists of cures, from suppositories made from olive-oil ointment and liquorice pastilles, to cinnamon comfits, as well as plaster and sponges for the administration of fomentations. The King now took to wearing reading-glasses with gilt frames – very likely on the suggestion of his wife.

By now a nurse was probably a greater necessity than a bedmate. As the King prepared for the campaign, he saw to it that parliament acknowledged the place of Catherine Parr's children, if any, in the succession: that is, after Prince Edward and his issue but before the Ladies Mary and Elizabeth. But this must be regarded as an optimistic piece of legislation at best by the 1540s. No coronation appears to have been suggested for Queen Catherine Parr. Certainly references to a future 'Duke of York' died away during the course of the King's sixth marriage.

The King was back in England by October. (Boulogne had surrendered on 13 September and Henry had decided not to pursue his campaign as far as Paris.) By this time Cranmer and the Queen had been in close contact over matters to do with the regency for three months, Cranmer being a member of the Council. Together, accompanied by those members of the Privy Council who had stayed in England, they had made a progress through Surrey and Kent, where some of the Queen's jointure properties were situated, and stayed together in Cranmer's former palace at Otford. King Henry did not expect that such propinquity would have any effect on the character and belief of such an admirably balanced woman as his newest wife. Still less did it occur to him that there was more than one way in which his authority might be challenged by a Queen. So far as he was concerned, in late 1544, following the terrible debacle with Katherine Howard, vice in a Queen was strictly connected to adultery; and of that there was certainly no danger from his dutiful and virtuous spouse.

There is no doubt that the household of Queen Catherine was seen at the time as standing for exceptional piety. Her court stood however for evangelical piety. Just as

Katherine Willoughby, Duchess of Suffolk, third wife of Charles Brandon, Duke of Suffolk. She was the daughter of Maria de Salinas and had been one of the mourners at Catherine of Aragon's funeral in 1536. In the 1540s the Duchess encouraged Queen Catherine Parr towards Protestantism and probably introduced her to the reformer Hugh Latimer.

Catherine, the widow of Lord Latimer, had seethed with passion for Thomas Seymour beneath her calm surface, so Catherine, the consort of Henry VIII, harboured surprisingly subversive views despite an outward appearance of conformity. The chaplains appointed, and the high-born ladies such as Anne Countess of Hertford and Jane Lady Denny who attended her held opinions very far from those of the Catholic and reactionary party in the Privy Council. One of these ladies – Katherine Duchess of Suffolk – was especially influential and had both the opportunity and the inclination to encourage the new

Charles Brandon, Duke of Suffolk, a portrait of him in old age by an unknown artist. Seven years older than Henry VIII, he had been a figure at court throughout the reign.

Queen in her natural tendencies towards reform. The Duchess was the heiress-daughter of the favourite lady-in-waiting of Catherine of Aragon, Maria de Salinas. She had been married off at fourteen to the Duke of Suffolk as his third wife and was even now only in her late twenties. But as the power of the Duke of Suffolk, King Henry's old jousting companion and trusted servant, waned, that of his young wife waxed. Duchess Katherine was regarded as something of a tigress: 'a lady of sharp wit, and sure hand to thrust it home and make it pierce when she pleased'.

The views of Queen Catherine Parr's chaplains and ladies were almost certainly far removed from those of King Henry, although in the remaining years of his life no one ever knew for sure what the old King's real religious views

were, perhaps because, in a state of constant pain and thus irritability, he did not quite know himself. We are on much firmer ground with the religious beliefs of Queen Catherine, for she left behind a modest but interesting body of devotional writing – one among only eight women who had books published in the sixty-odd years of the reigns of the first two Tudor monarchs. *Prayers and Meditations*, first published in 1545, was intended in Queen

Left: A manuscript version of Catherine Parr's Prayers and Meditations, *supposedly in her own handwriting, now in Kendal Town Hall.*

Catherine's own words to 'stir' the mind 'patiently to suffer all afflictions here, to set at nought the vain prosperity of this world, and always to long for the everlasting felicity'. Its main thesis is the redemptive nature of the Passion of Christ. Beyond that, the tone is one of simplicity and sincerity, devoid of any

A Protestant allegory: Girolamo da Treviso's painting The Four Evangelists Stoning the Pope, *c. 1540. This is the only surviving work of art which can be identified as one of the paintings in any of Henry VIII's houses. It hung in his gallery at Hampton Court.*

The title page of Cranmer's great Bible, printed by Richard Grafton, showing Henry, the Supreme Head of the Church, in the image of God.

kind of radicalism. Certainly Queen Catherine's *Prayers and Meditations* were sufficiently anodyne to go through nineteen editions by the end of the century, undeterred by the various doctrinal changes which followed.

But *The Lamentation, or Complaint of a Sinner, made by the most vertuous and right gratious Ladie, Queen Catherine*, would not have been acceptable to Henry VIII. Nor was it in fact printed during his lifetime, but was first published in 1547. It is not difficult to understand the delay. This was a time of feverish uncertainty where doctrinal matters were concerned, further complicated by the struggle for dominance among the King's advisers, in which religion, politics and feuds among the nobility were inextricably enmeshed. Once again *The Lamentation of a Sinner* is marked by simplicity and sincerity. But it does have a distinct doctrinal slant. King Henry is paid tribute, not only for being 'godly and learned', but also for being 'our Moses' who 'hath delivered us out of the captivity and bondage of Pharaoh' (Rome). Anti-papalism apart, however, the strongest message of the book is the crucial need for the laity to benefit from personal study of the Bible.

Yet in May 1543 the Council had decided that the 'lower sort' did not benefit from studying the Bible in English. The Act for the Advancement of the True Religion stated that no one who fell into this category could in future read the Bible 'privately or openly'. In a sermon in the City of London the next year it was suggested that the study of the scriptures was making the apprentices unruly. Women (in the sense of women of the people), yeomen and apprentices – all these led lives far removed from the court where Queen Catherine was apparently in the habit of holding study groups among her ladies for the scriptures and listening to sermons of an evangelical nature. Although a later clause in the 1543 act did allow any noble or gentlewoman to read the Bible, this activity must take place 'to themselves alone and not to others'. In her emphasis on the individual, her ignoring of the effects of grace through the sacraments, and her concentration on salvation through Jesus Christ alone, Queen Catherine had thus travelled a long way down the road to heresy – even if she did not actually cross the boundary.

Beyond authorship, Queen Catherine's role as a patroness recalls that of Queen Anne Boleyn. She encouraged the translation of Erasmus' paraphrases of the scriptures, if she did not carry it out personally. Nicholas Udall, who had written the coronation ode for Queen Anne, benefited from this encouragement. He dedicated his translation of the Gospel of St Luke to Queen Catherine; it was completed in 1545, though publication was again delayed until after the King's death. Like Queen Anne Boleyn, again, Queen Catherine exercised her influence to protect reformers who had got into trouble. In 1544, for example, she sent her own servant Robert Warner to plead for the reforming schoolmaster Stephen Cobbe before the Court of Aldermen in the City of London. She also encouraged reformers not only in her own household but in that of Prince Edward, such as John Cheke, Anthony Cooke and William Grindal, with obvious significance for his character and the future of the kingdom.

The last years of Henry VIII were marked by a series of struggles for power within the Privy Council and at court: once more Howards vied with Seymours. But now it was the regency of the future King rather than the marriage of the present one which was the fundamental issue. In these struggles, the Howards, not only the Duke of Norfolk but his son, the soldier-poet the Earl of Surrey, were represented as before by the 'Catholic' party headed by Bishop Gardiner. The Seymours' camp headed by the Earl of Hertford and including his younger brother Sir Thomas Seymour and Archbishop Cranmer, tended towards reform. The Parrs also favoured reform, not only the Queen but William Lord Parr of Kendal and the Herberts. But whereas the Duke of Norfolk represented the most distinguished family in England, and the Earl of

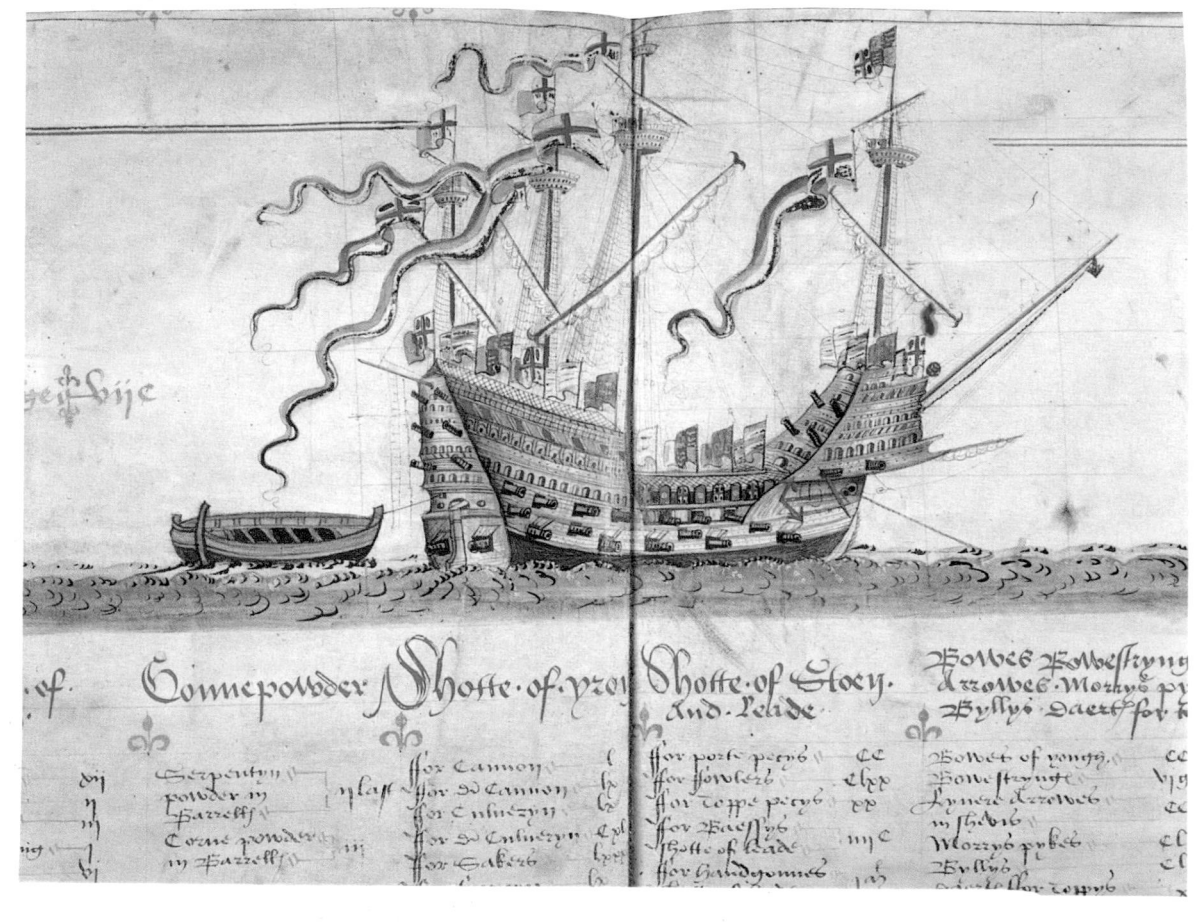

The King's great ship The Mary Rose that sank in July 1545 while he and Catherine Parr watched helplessly from the shore.

Opposite: Edward Prince of Wales wearing a jewel with the Prince of Wales's feathers. Portrait by an unknown artist.

Hertford was the blood-uncle of the future King (as well as having much enhanced his military reputation in Scotland and France), the Parrs could advance no such claim. This might have kept Queen Catherine and her family free from hostility. But unfortunately her religious views made her an excellent target for attack, in order to mount an indirect assault on the reformers in the Privy Council. In the complicated diplomatic manoeuvres of these years, Queen Catherine was not a major figure. She was recognized to be a reformer, but nobody thought she had the kind of influence that had been attributed to Catherine of Aragon (or for that matter to the dominating Anne Boleyn). Tributes to her graciousness drew attention to her true role in the King's life as Queen-Manager, a smoother-over of tricky situations, not a maker of policies.

The summer of 1545 was a testing time for the English King. The Scots had managed to inflict a defeat on him at Ancrum Moor in the early spring. Now the French avenged the loss of Boulogne by sailing along the south coast of

England, landing on the Isle of Wight, with the declared purpose of invading to end King Henry's tyranny and restore the rights of the church. The King was present on the south coast himself, at Portsmouth, where he arrived on 15 July, with the Queen, to oversee defences. There, four days later, he had the appalling experience of watching his favourite ship, *The Mary Rose*, suddenly heel over and sink, probably due to an ingress of water when its gunports were opened, ready for action. Meanwhile on land his subjects were enduring inflation, levies and taxes, a debasement of the coinage (in 1544), their plight compounded by a series of bad harvests. In the pursuit of the military glory which had brought him such happiness in his youth, this new Henry V spent nearly two million pounds in his last years – and wasted in effect the vast revenues he had derived from the dissolution of the monasteries.

At least the young heir to the throne Prince Edward – 'the greatest person in Christendom' – now had the benefit of an experienced step-mother to guide him with her 'tender love' which her step-daughter Margaret Neville had praised. The young prince's correspondence shows that in his relationship with the Queen he evinced a warmth and liveliness not elsewhere displayed by this formal princeling. She is *'Mater Charissima'*, 'My dearest mother' – his familiar form of address for her – and held 'the chief place in my heart'. From 1546 onwards, Queen Catherine was also in direct charge of the twelve-year-old Lady Elizabeth. It is unlikely that Elizabeth could remember her real mother, a Queen to whom no one now referred: she had been just over two and a half when Anne Boleyn was executed. After that she had encountered a series of step-mothers whose main concentration had been on forging bonds or otherwise with her half-sister Mary (with the honourable exception of the briefly installed Anna of Cleves who had taken a fancy to the wary, intelligent seven-year-old child). Now in Queen Catherine Parr Elizabeth found not only an experienced adoptive parent but one whose intellectual interests and reforming tendencies fitted with her own.

In 1546 the pace of persecution towards heretics gathered speed. Sir Thomas Wriothesley, now Baron Wriothesley, had succeeded the milder Lord Audley as Lord Chancellor in May 1544; he was now ardent in his pursuit of those heretics with connections to the court. There were rumours about the instabilty of the Queen's position. It is difficult to know how much weight to attach to them; the idea, floated abroad, of the King getting rid of her in order to marry Katherine Duchess of Suffolk is an unlikely one, and the rumour-monger himself admitted that the King showed no alteration in his behaviour towards his wife.

A key arrest was that of Anne Askew on 24 May. She was a young woman in her early twenties, of strongly reformist views – with a love of biblical studies like the Queen's. Undeniably she had many connections to the court. Anne Askew's sister was married to the steward of the late Duke of Suffolk; her brother Edward had a post in the King's household. She had been briefly married in her native Lincolnshire and had borne children, but had come to London after her husband apparently expelled her for crossing swords with local priests. In 1545 Anne Askew had already been cross-examined for heresy and had responded to her accusers with vigour. She survived the experience. She could not survive the renewed assault of 1546, although she never gave in to her accusers. Her remarkable spirit, maintained even under the torture which was illegal for a woman of her degree, did at least gain her reverence as a Protestant heroine of the next reign. On 16 July Anne Askew, horribly crippled by her tortures but without recantation, was burnt for heresy. Alongside her died, also for heresy, John Lascelles – he whose scandalous revelations had led to the downfall of Katherine Howard.

Sir Thomas Wriothesley (later Earl of Southampton). He became Principal Secretary of State in 1540 and Lord Chancellor in 1544. He was a ruthless opponent of 'heretics'.

It remained to be seen whether Queen Catherine Parr would follow her predecessor to the Tower of London: if for a very different reason. Ironically it was Queen Catherine herself who contributed the vital missing element, enabling her religious enemies to attack her standing with her husband. The King's health – 'the anguish of a sore leg' – made him extraordinarily irritable at this time, as even his smoothest supporters had to admit. In an emollient version of events Lord Herbert of Cherbury simply related how, in his agony, the King 'lov'd not to be contradicted', especially, as he said, in his old age and by his wife. It is clear from this, as from the account by the Protestant martyrologist John Foxe which is the real source for the story, that Queen Catherine had indulged in the impermissible where Henry VIII was concerned: she had lectured her husband, and even 'in the heat of discourse gone very far'. She should have known better. The King put up with the existence of those radical preachers in her apartments because in every other way Queen Catherine behaved so admirably; above all she showed 'that wonderful care about the King's person, which became a wife that was raised to him to so great an honour'. It was no part of a nurse's duty to contradict a difficult patient.

On 4 July the Privy Council ordered the Queen's auditors to produce her estate books. That probably meant that the charges to be brought against her were completed, since it indicated that her extensive properties might shortly be forfeited. Publicly the King's mood continued to vary: he paid a visit to the Queen when she in turn fell ill, and treated her very graciously; yet experienced courtiers knew that, along with his explosive rages, King Henry also possessed a delusive ability to extend politeness to those he was about to destroy.

Then at the last minute, everything was thrown into confusion. The King confided to his doctor, Thomas Wendy, what was about to take place. A copy of the charges was subsequently dropped by an anonymous councillor outside the passage in the Queen's chamber. Whatever the King's real intentions at this point, there is no doubt that the Queen herself was devastated, but she did not panic. Instead, she took that particular way out which was open to her as a woman, involving complete self-abasement combined with acknowledgement of her sex's weakness. Rushing to the King, the Queen found him in the mood to set about a discourse on religion. This was a test – a crucial one. Queen Catherine did not flunk it. In Foxe's account she declined to take part in the discourse but answered instead 'that women by their first creation were made subject to men'. She went on, 'Being made after the image of God, as the women were after their image, men ought to instruct their wives, who would do all their learning from them'. She herself had an extra reason to wish 'to be taught by his Majesty, who was a prince of such excellent learning and wisdom' – a graceful and tactful allusion to that theological expertise on which the King prided himself.

The battle was not quite won. 'Not so by St Mary', replied the King. 'You are become a doctor [of the Church] able to instruct us and not to be instructed by us.' But this pointed reference was met with an inspired explanation by the Queen. It seemed that the King 'had much mistaken the freedom she had taken to argue with him'. She had only done it to distract him from his pain, and of

KATHARINE PARRE

course to take the opportunity to learn from him herself. 'And is it even so?' asked the King. 'Then Kate, we are friends again.' The next day when Lord Chancellor Wriothesley came with forty guards to arrest the Queen, he was met with an outburst of the royal temper and cries of 'Knave!' 'Fool!' and 'Beast!'

Catherine Parr, c. 1545, by an unknown artist.

Queen Catherine Parr lived to breathe again.

Nevertheless Queen Catherine's withdrawal from her previous assertive position was not merely expedient. Along with her intellectual curiosity, she also continued to demonstrate the modesty suitable to a female – even where learning itself was concerned. In February, before her troubles, she had answered a request from the University of Cambridge for her intercession with the King (they had asked for a stay of their possessions and it seems the Queen was successful in securing it). The terms of her answer would have satisfied the most tyrannical husband that she did not set herself up as 'a doctor'. Derogatory references to her own lack of education abounded. The submissiveness of Queen Catherine, the more conventional side of her nature which enabled her to live – mainly – at ease with the demanding King, was also genuine. When Queen Catherine had given up her plan of marrying Thomas Seymour in 1543, she had interpreted the will of the King as being the will of God. Three years later, it is not difficult for the same woman to make the same equation, and abandon her new-found taste for theological discussion as being not only dangerous but also contrary to the divine order of things.

Queen Catherine's role was now predominantly that of nurse. A fever in the spring of 1546 had shaken the King badly; observers noted how terrible he looked. In September the fever recurred, although officially termed a cold. The King's apothecary's bill for August included payments for two 'urynals' sent to Hampton Court as well as 'eyebright' water for his eyes, and liquorice for his hands. Although the King was hardly moribund at this point – he was able to take outdoor exercise as late as 7 December – none of the courtiers who surrounded him were in any doubt that his days were numbered. On about 10 December King Henry fell dangerously ill again. Publicly the Privy Council did not admit the gravity of the situation. Wotton, for instance, the ambassador in France, was carefully instructed to play it down. It was true that the King had had a fever 'upon some grief of his leg', but he was now 'thanks be to God, well rid of it'. The reality was different. The King was dying, but he was dying very slowly. On the actual timing of his decease a great deal depended in the inner world of the Privy Council in which the religious radicals, headed by Hertford and John Dudley, recently created Viscount Lisle, were now rising.

But more than that hung on the exact moment of the King's death. It turned out that this reign, so bloodily stained with the judicial murders of the King's close relatives, ancient colleagues and lifelong servants, would end with yet more deaths – unless the King himself died in time for them to be saved. On 2 December Henry Howard Earl of Surrey, Norfolk's son, was arrested. As a poet Surrey was a perfect courtly knight, but as a man he was both arrogant and reckless and, at the age of thirty, still acted the 'foolish proud boy'. The crime with which he was charged was one of 'improper' (and thus treasonable) heraldry: he had used the arms of Edward the Confessor (from whom he was descended), a privilege which belonged 'only to the King of this realm'. Surrey

Henry Howard, Earl of Surrey, son of the Duke of Norfolk, sat for his portrait more often than any other Tudor courtier. The royal arms of England can be seen in the shields. This was painted the year before he was charged with 'improper' heraldry.

was sent to the Tower where his father, unable for once to avoid the taint of treachery, followed him. Improper heraldry was one thing; Surrey's real mistake was to have quarrelled violently with Hertford, who took over his command in France and whose military triumphs aroused Surrey's jealousy. He made no secret of his dislike of the 'upstart' Seymours. In the context, his 'improper' use of the royal arms could be construed as a deliberate advancement of the superior Howard claims to the Regency.

At Christmas, Queen Catherine and the Ladies Mary and Elizabeth were sent away to celebrate the season at Greenwich, leaving the King in London, busy with these wearing power struggles. The Queen departed on Christmas Eve.

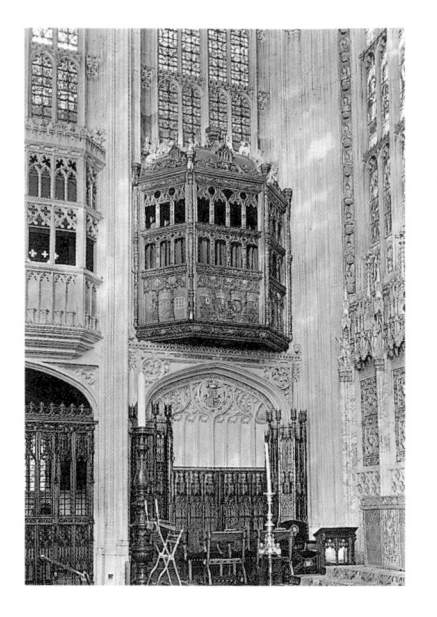

The Queen's Closet, St George's Chapel Windsor, named for Catherine of Aragon whose pomegranates can be seen among the ornamentation. From the closet Catherine Parr watched the funeral of Henry VIII.

She never saw her husband again. The royal party returned to London by 10 January, and the King could still receive ambassadors six days later, but he did not send for his wife. On 19 January Surrey was executed, leaving Norfolk still in prison, condemned to follow him to the block. Once again, however, the Duke was to survive. His master fell into a coma before the execution could take place; under the circumstances it was not thought prudent to carry out the sentence, and Norfolk was left for the time being to languish under attainder.

King Henry VIII died in the small hours of the morning of 28 January 1547. He was fifty-five years old and had reigned for nearly thirty-eight years. In his will the King expressly desired that his body should be placed with the bones of 'our true and loving Wife Queen Jane'. So Queen Jane's tomb in St George's, Windsor was opened up again after nine years. On 16 February the King's enormous coffin was let down into it 'in a vice' with the help of sixteen yeomen of the guard of exceptional height and strength. Queen Catherine watched the proceedings from the so-called Queen's Closet above, first named in honour of Catherine of Aragon. Her feelings of grief were no doubt sincere. Nevertheless they may be compared to those of Hamlet's mother after the death of Hamlet's father, an event which she soon learnt to regard philosophically. For like Queen Gertrude, Queen Catherine, a woman who believed in being 'obedient to husbands', would shortly be looking to another one.

The deathbed of Henry VIII, an anti-papal allegory painted in about 1548. Henry gestures to his successor Prince Edward. To Edward's left are members of the Council of Regency: Edward Seymour, John Dudley, Cranmer and William Russell. The Pope is shown being crushed by the Prayer Book and in the background soldiers are destroying religious statues.

CHAPTER 11

Queen Dowager of England

CATHERINE PARR WAS now the Queen Dowager of England, but until her stepson Edward married she was still the first lady in the land. This precedence over all others, including the King's daughters, had been explicitly granted by statute. She was also left handsome provision in the will of this, her third husband, to add to her Latimer inheritance: ten thousand pounds' worth of plate and jewels and household stuff, as much 'apparel' as she wanted to take away, as well as what she possessed already, and 'one thousand pounds in money', an extremely substantial sum. All this, on top of her liberal royal jointure which included properties at Hanworth and Chelsea, was a reward, in the words of the late King, for Queen Catherine's 'great love, obedience, chastity of life, and wisdom'.

If Queen Catherine was still the first lady in England, the position was purely symbolic: she had no other role in the new government. For she was not included in the Regency Council headed by the Protector, Edward Seymour Duke of Somerset; although both her position and her performance as Regent in 1544 entitled her to expect it. This effective marginalization – as a childless and thus superfluous dowager – was not something to which Catherine Parr was accustomed. It may well have played its part in urging her towards the embraces of Thomas Seymour.

Thomas Seymour was now approaching forty, about four years older than the Queen. Unlike Catherine, he had never been married, although his name had been linked with that of Mary Duchess of Richmond. Gifted with charm and intelligence as well as a handsome appearance ('one of the prettiest men of the court'), Seymour

The Parr Pot, made of milk glass. The silver mounts are marked 1546-7 and the coat of arms shows the pot to have belonged to Sir William Parr.

Sir Thomas Seymour, brother of Jane Seymour and fourth husband of Catherine Parr.

had been a favourite of the old King who had made him Lord High Admiral in 1544. Later he would be much attacked: a servant would refer to his 'slothfulness to serve and his greediness to get' (although another employee called his service 'ever joyful'). But in 1547 he showed no greater greed than the rest of the nobility round him. Seymour's real weakness was his morbid jealousy of his elder brother Somerset.

Seymour's name and the Queen's were never linked during the years of Queen Catherine's marriage to the King. Seymour had been much abroad while Catherine, in the words of the King's will, had been famed for her 'chastity of life' in a court where malicious tongues would certainly have reported otherwise.

This does not preclude the possibility that in 1543 Catherine, while resigning herself to God's will and a royal marriage, may have been woman enough to wonder just how long God would wait before gathering King Henry to 'happiness and eternal beatitude'.

However the situation had been left in 1543, with feelings dormant perhaps rather than extinguished, in 1547 passion rapidly flared up between the pair again. The word 'passion' is used advisedly, since it is clear that a full-blooded love affair began very shortly after the King's death. By 17 May Thomas Seymour was describing himself in one letter to Queen Catherine as 'him whom you have bound to honour, love, and all things obey' and in another as 'him that is your loving and faithful husband during his life, T Seymour'. These are clear references to a marriage which had either taken place already, or would do so very soon. The exact date of the wedding of Thomas Lord Seymour and the Queen Dowager cannot be known for certain: on balance of probabilities it took place at the end of May. In an age before registration existed, such dates did not need to be revealed if circumstances dictated prudence.

If we do not know the precise date of the wedding, we do know some of the details of the courtship. It took place, romantically enough, by starlight in the riverside gardens of the Queen's Chelsea Manor. (The lack of domestic privacy in the sixteenth century meant that the garden was often a convenient rendezvous for such clandestine meetings.) To judge from the engravings – it was pulled down about 1700 – Chelsea Manor, although sometimes described as a palace, was not particularly grand. But it did have beautiful gardens with a river setting, on which a great deal of money and labour had recently been spent. Catherine gave her lover instructions for his arrival which leave little doubt about the nature of their relationship: 'When it shall be your pleasure to repair hither, you must take some pains to come early in the morning, that you may be gone again by seven o'clock.' She signed herself: 'By all that is and shall be your humble and true and loving wife during her life. Kateryn the Quene. KP'.

Some of the Queen's friends and relatives were, of course, in the secret. But breaking the news to the titular ruler of England, King Edward, and its effective governor, the Duke of Somerset, was another matter. It is clear that the Protector was not inclined to encourage the 'tender love' between the Queen Dowager and her step-son, just as he was not disposed to admit her to the Regency Council: to him she was a woman without any overt power,

An engraving of Chelsea Manor House. This had been acquired by Henry VIII in 1536 and after his death it became the residence of Catherine Parr. It was later used by Anna of Cleves who died there in 1557.

whose influence must therefore be curtailed. Since the actual marriage was still a secret, the first idea was to pretend that Seymour was still wooing the Queen.

For this the help of the Lady Mary – who had left Catherine's household in mid-April – was enlisted. Seymour wrote to her, diplomatically as he supposed, asking her to plead his cause. He received a frosty reply. Mary described the proposed alliance as 'strange news'. She declined to be 'a meddler in this matter' considering, she wrote pointedly, 'whose wife her Grace was of late'.

It was time to turn to the young King, already disposed to be fonder of this generous, rollicking uncle than he was of the austere Protector. This time the approach was more subtle. John Fowler, servant to King Edward, was to be the double-agent. Fowler prepared the ground by wondering aloud: 'I marvel my Lord Admiral marryeth not'. He then proceeded to ask the King: 'Could your grace be contented he should marry?' When Edward, falling into the trap, replied: 'Yes, very well', Fowler instantly asked the prepared question: 'Whom would his Grace like to his uncle to marry?' But at this point matters looked like going wrong: 'My Lady Anna of Cleves', answered Edward innocently, already aware of the problems of the expensive family incubus. And when he thought about it a little more, he got the answer wrong a second time: 'Nay, nay, wot you what? I would he married my sister Mary to turn her opinions'. Fortunately, with tact and time, the boy was brought round to see the match between his uncle and step-mother as something he himself had initiated to solace her bereavement.

The reaction of the Protector was not so benevolent. As King Edward recorded succinctly in his journal: 'The Lord Seymour of Sudeley married the Queen, whose name was Catherine, with which marriage the Lord Protector was much offended'. Any offence the Lord Protector felt was compounded by the reaction of his Duchess. Anne Stanhope, formerly Countess of Hertford, now Duchess of Somerset, had needed the patronage of Catherine Parr in the reign of King Henry when Catherine had interceded for Hertford at his wife's instigation to get him back from Scotland in time to join the King in France. Their shared religious sensibilities had seemed to be a further bond. Unfortunately Duchess Anne had one of those imperious natures which found memories of previous inferiority intolerable. She now openly 'jostled' with Queen Catherine for precedence on the quite unjustified grounds that, as the wife of the Protector, she was the first lady in England.

This ludicrous struggle was merely the visible manifestation of a series of rows that broke out between the Somersets and the Seymours. Jewels were one topic for heated discussion as the Protector attempted to distinguish between what were Catherine's own and the jewels of state (which he kept), while his brother furiously rebutted his claims. The Protector even hung on to Queen Catherine's wedding ring, presented to her by King Henry. Catherine's letters reflect her combative mood: Duchess Anne was referred to as 'that Hell'. As for the Protector, at one point Queen Catherine's feelings ran so strong that she declared: 'It was fortunate we were so much distant for I suppose else I should have bitten him'.

And then an extraordinary thing happened. Queen Catherine, at the age of thirty-five – 'which barren was before' (despite three husbands) – conceived her first child. It was not only extraordinary but unlooked-for: one hopes that the happy surprise compensated for Seymour's less than satisfactory career after their marriage. As jealous in his own way as Duchess Anne was in hers, Seymour allowed his differences with his brother to cloud his judgement. Now the laziness and greed mentioned by his servant did play their part. He failed

Queen Catherine's room in Sudeley Castle.

to command the fleet aginst the Scots in 1547 and 1548, preferring his country estate at Sudeley. Even more inexcusably, he made pacts with the very pirates in the English Channel he should have been eliminating, in order to share the booty. The Queen however expected to spend the months of her pregnancy – the child must have been conceived at the end of November 1547 – tranquilly enough at her properties of Chelsea and Hanworth near Hampton Court, as well as at Sudeley.

She was not without companionship of the sort she had always enjoyed: younger women she could mother. One of these was the Lady Jane Grey, the eleven-year-old daughter of Lady Frances Brandon and Henry Grey, Marquess of Dorset. Another was her step-daughter, the Lady Elizabeth, now just fifteen years old. Among those who already appreciated the latter's appeal was her step-mother's husband, Thomas Seymour. Boisterous by nature, conscious of the effect of his charms on women, it may have seemed natural to Seymour to indulge in sexy horseplay with his wife's young charge. By Whitsun of 1548 when matters came to a crisis, Queen Catherine would have been nearly six months pregnant; given her condition, Seymour may have also found it natural to look for diversion elsewhere. For a married man to approach the next-but-one heiress to the throne was not only perilous, but scandalous.

Seymour formed the habit of entering the girl's room before she was fully dressed, patting her 'upon the back or on the buttocks familiarly', snatching kisses, and even pocketing the key of the room so she could not escape. Then he would appear himself, bare-legged and clad only in a short night-gown. Elizabeth's servant Katherine Ashley would tell tales of the Lord Admiral flinging back Elizabeth's bed curtains to bid her 'good morning' while the girl herself burrowed back (whether in modesty, ecstasy, or a combination of the two, Elizabeth never revealed). On one occasion Catherine, with the 'mirth and good pastime' for which she had been noted during her marriage to King Henry, joined in. She held the girl down while Seymour cut her black gown into a hundred pieces. It was however Queen Catherine who finally decided that enough was enough and sent the girl away. Katherine Ashley gave as a reason the Queen's dismay at finding Elizabeth in Seymour's arms, but later withdrew the story. Since Catherine and Elizabeth remained on affectionate terms, the Queen was probably animated as much by concern for her charge's reputation as by jealousy.

Fear of the plague drove Queen Catherine from Chelsea to her estate at Hanworth in June 1547. From here she exchanged cheerful – and frank – letters on her advancing pregnancy with her husband. 'I gave your little knave your blessing who like an honest man stirred apace after and before. For Mary Odell being abed with me had laid her hand upon my belly to feel it stir. It hath stirred these three days every morning and evening so that I trust when you come it will make you some pastime'. Later that month the Queen retired to Sudeley Castle where she intended to give birth, taking with her Lady Jane

Grey. On 30 August Queen Catherine went into labour. The child was born and it was a girl. She was named Mary and Lady Jane Grey stood godmother. On 1 September Seymour received an amiable communcation from his brother who expressed himself glad that 'the Queen, your bedfellow' had had 'a happy hour', and, escaping all danger, had made Seymour a father of 'so pretty a daughter'.

Then Queen Catherine, like Queen Jane Seymour before her, fell desperately ill of puerperal fever. Her delirium took a painful (but not unusual) form of paranoid ravings about her husband and others around her. This cast a terrible blight over the last days of a marriage which had originally been made, in some sort on both sides, for love. When Seymour tried to soothe her by lying down at her side and saying, 'Why Sweetheart, I would you no hurt', the poor deluded woman answered, 'No, my Lord, I think so' and whispered in his ear about the many 'shrewd taunts' she had received. This distressing episode allowed those accusations of poison – so familiar to this period over any unexpected death – to be brought against Seymour afterwards. But the charge was quite untrue: mercifully for Scymour, the Queen's own behaviour at the last gave it the lie.

Monument to Catherine Parr in the chapel at Sudeley Castle.

For as the Queen began to sink towards death, her fever fled. She dictated her will calmly, revealing that same attitude of trust and loyalty towards Seymour, not only her 'married spouse and husband' but the great love of her life, which she had always felt. Queen Catherine, 'sick of body but of good mind', left everything to him, only wishing her possessions 'to be a thousand times more in value' than they were. She died on 5 September at the age of thirty-six, six days after the birth of her daughter. Lady Jane Grey acted as chief mourner at Queen Catherine's funeral, after which her body was buried in St Mary's Church, adjoining Sudeley Castle, According to custom Seymour, the widower, was not present.

The baby Mary Seymour lived on for a while. She was still alive in the summer of 1550, on the eve of her second birthday, but after that there is no record of her. A wealthy 'Queen's child' who lived to adulthood in the 1560s would not have escaped remark. It can safely be assumed that the contemporary curse, death in early childhood, provided its own solution to the short sad life of Mary Seymour.

There was one relic of the reign of King Henry VIII who did live on and on, the Lady Anna of Cleves. She was the witness to those events in England which toppled heads during the reign of King Edward, recorded by the boy himself laconically in his journal for January 1548: 'Also the Lord Sudeley, Admiral of England was condemned to death and died the March ensuing'. Three years later the Protector himself fell victim to a power struggle. On 22 January 1552 the King wrote: 'The Duke of Somerset had his head cut off upon Tower Hill between eight and nine o'clock in the morning'.

On 30 September 1553 Anna of Cleves rode in a coach with the Lady

Mary Tudor, painted by 'Master John' in 1544 when she was twenty-eight.

Elizabeth at the coronation of the triumphant Queen Mary at which 'there was one blowing of the trumpet all day long'. The new Queen's carriage went first, drawn by horses 'trapped with red velvet'. The royal ladies followed her in 'a rich chariot covered with cloth of silver', with the Lady Elizabeth facing the front 'and at the other end with her back forward, the Lady Anna'. This coupling with Elizabeth continued at the state banquet that evening. The two of them sat together at the end of the table, Elizabeth now heiress-presumptive to the throne, and Anna of Cleves' precedence moved up to that of the third lady in the land.

After Mary ascended the throne, Anna of Cleves even attempted to resurrect her long-buried marriage to Henry VIII and get it declared 'legitimate' so that she might enjoy the treatment, especially in the realm of finance, of a Queen Dowager. She would also be able to get her dowry paid, 'even if absent from England'. This of course would have superseded the careful arrangements made at the time of the divorce in 1540 by which the dowry was conditional on her not going 'over the sea'. The Lady Anna was simply told that there were too many other pressing matters for the Council's attention. So she continued to petition, and worry, and write anguished letters back to the country she still regarded as her home.

The tomb of Anna of Cleves on the south side of the High Altar in Westminster Abbey.

It is obvious that the Lady Anna's real desire was now to return to Cleves, a feeling that had been growing on her since the King's insulting marriage to Catherine Parr. In April 1551 she wrote wistfully about the prospect: 'And so I

ANNO DÑI · 1 5 4 4 ·

LAD MARI   DOVGHTER TO
THE MOST   VERTVOVS PRINCE
KING HENRI   THE EIGHT

THE AGE OF   XXVIII YERES

might come to life again among my friends. For as I think my friends down there have by now all forgotten about me, I should think that I will re-enter their memories again, once my friends' eyes have seen me'. But nobody was prepared to rescue this princess from her predicament, as superfluous a female in her own way as Catherine Parr had been as a Dowager. So Anna of Cleves lived on in England until 1557. She was allowed the use of Chelsea Manor, that small but delightful 'palace' where Thomas Seymour had courted Queen Catherine Parr. It was here that she fell ill in the spring of 1557 and here that she spent the months of her decline. She died on 16 July 1557, in her forty-second year. She did not live to see the accession of King Henry's last child, Elizabeth, the girl whom she had once petted, on 17 November 1558.

A tomb of black and white marble was made for her in Westminster Abbey. The design was in the Grecian style and was 'executed in a masterly manner'. A native Clevian, Theodore Haeveus, a minister at Caius College, Cambridge, who designed there for Dr Keys, may have been responsible. Two tiers of panels

The Family of Henry VIII: an allegory of the Tudor succession painted c. 1570. Mary I and Philip of Spain are followed by Mars, god of war. Elizabeth I is followed by Flora and the fruits of prosperity. Edward VI kneels by the side of Henry VIII.

ornamented the sides of the tomb. The upper tier contained innocuous medallions with the initials A C surmounted by a ducal coronet (for Cleves). But the lower tier revealed a series of skulls, with crossbones, on a black background. In this appropriately sombre manner, the fourth wife and last surviving consort of Henry VIII was commemorated.

ILLUSTRATION ACKNOWLEDGEMENTS

The author and publisher would like to thank the following individuals, museums and photographic archives:

3 British Library, London (Roy. 11 EM f.2v) (The Bridgeman Art Library); 7 Bibliothèque Nationale, Paris (The Bridgeman Art Library, London); 14 Musée Condé, Chantilly (The Bridgeman Art Library); 16 The Royal Collection © 1996 Her Majesty The Queen; 17 Kunsthistorisches Museum, Vienna (The Bridgeman Art Library); 18 Christie's, London, (The Bridgeman Art Library); 19 above and below The Royal Collection © 1996 Her Majesty The Queen; 20 The Trustees of the Victoria & Albert Museum, London; 23 Kunsthistorisches Museum, Vienna (The Bridgeman Art Library); 24 Private Collection, by courtesy of Philip Mould, London (The Bridgeman Art Library); 25 Private Collection (J. B. Archive, London); 26 above National Portrait Gallery, London; 26 below The Mansell Collection, London; 27 Master and Fellows, Magdalen College, Oxford; 28 A. F. Kersting, London; 30 A. F. Kersting, London; 31 The Mansell Collection, London; 33 A. F. Kersting, London; 34 The College of Arms, London; 36 Burghley House, Stamford (The Bridgeman Art Library); 37 left The Board of Trustees of The Royal Armouries; 37 right The Board of Trustees of The Royal Armouries; 38 British Library, London (Roy. 11 EM f.2v) (The Bridgeman Art Library); 39 Private Collection (The Bridgeman Art Library); 40 above British Library, London; 40 below The Vyne, Hampshire (The National Trust Photographic Library/Derrick Witty); 41 Caters News Agency, Birmingham; 42 The College of Arms, London; 43 The College of Arms, London; 46 British Library, London (Cott. Vesp. B ii f.7v); 47 By courtesy of the Trustees of the Bedford Estate and The Marquess of Tavistock, Woburn Abbey; 48 The Wellcome Trust, London; 50 National Portrait Gallery, London; 51 Musée du Louvre, Paris (Giraudon, Paris); 52 Weidenfeld & Nicolson Archive, London; 53 Master and Fellows of St John's College, Cambridge (Weidenfeld & Nicolson Archive); 54 By courtesy of The Marquess of Salisbury; 55 Musée Condé, Chantilly (The Bridgeman Art Library); 56 left National Portrait Gallery, London; 56 right Fitzwilliam Museum, University of Cambridge (The Bridgeman Art Library); 58-9 The Royal Collection © 1996 Her Majesty The Queen; 60 Bibliothèque Nationale, Paris (The Bridgeman Art Library); 61 British Library, London (Cott. Augustus IIIa); 62 By courtesy of Brian Pilkington; 63 The Mansell Collection, London; 64 Hever Castle, Kent (The Bridgeman Art Library); 65 Victoria & Albert Museum, London (The Bridgeman Art Library); 66 Prado, Madrid (The Bridgeman Art Library); 67 Fitzwilliam Museum, University of Cambridge (The Bridgeman Art Library); 68 The Royal Collection © 1996 Her Majesty The Queen; 69 National Portrait Gallery, London; 70 The Master and Fellows, Magdalene College, Cambridge; 72 A. F. Kersting, London; 73 The Royal Collection © 1996 Her Majesty The Queen; 74 Musée Cluny, Paris (Giraudon); 77 National Portrait Gallery, London; 78 Private Collection (Weidenfeld & Nicolson Archive); 79 Private Collection, on loan to the Victoria & Albert Museum, London; 80 Public Record Office, London; 83 National Portrait Gallery, London; 85 The Bodleian Library, Oxford; 87 National Maritime Museum, Greenwich (J. B. Archive); 88-9 British Museum, London (The Bridgeman Art Library); 90 above British Museum, London (Roy. ms. 13 Bxx); 90 below The Trustees of the Victoria & Albert Museum, London; 90 right The Trustees of the Victoria & Albert Museum, London; 91 right Christie's Images, London; 91 above right The Trustees of the Victoria & Albert Museum, London; 91 left British Museum, London (The Bridgeman Art Library); 92-3 The Royal Collection © 1996 Her Majesty The Queen; 94 The Royal Collection © 1996 Her Majesty The Queen; 95 left above British Museum, London; 95 left centre Ministry of Works; 95 left below Private Collection (Weidenfeld & Nicolson Archive); 95 right The Royal Collection © 1996 Her Majesty The Queen; 99 Belvoir Castle, Leicestershire (The Bridgeman Art Library); 101 National Portrait Gallery, London; 104 Ashmolean Museum, Oxford; 105 Frick Collection, New York (The Bridgeman Art Library); 106 Frick Collection, New York; 107 Musée du Louvre, Paris (Giraudon/Bridgeman Art Library); 110 The Royal Collection © 1996 Her Majesty The Queen;

111 The Vatican, Rome (Scala, Florence); 112 Staatliche Museen Preussischer Kulturbesitz, Berlin (Weidenfeld & Nicolson Archive); 114 British Library, London; 115 The Mansell Collection, London; 116 British Library, London; 118 British Museum, London; 119 A. F. Kersting, London; 121 Weidenfeld & Nicolson Archive, London/photo. Bob Harding; 122 Public Record Office, London; 123 above King's College, Cambridge (Weidenfeld & Nicolson Archive); 123 below Angelo Hornak, London; 124 Royal Botanical Gardens, Kew (The Bridgeman Art Library); 125 above Knole, Kent (National Trust Photographic Library/Angelo Hornak); 125 below Hever Castle, Kent (The Bridgeman Art Library); 126 The Trustees of the Victoria & Albert Museum, London; 129 A. F. Kersting, London; 131 Kunsthistorisches Museum, Vienna (The Bridgeman Art Library); 133 By permission of the Duke of Buccleuch and Queensberry KT; 136 The Trustees of the Victoria & Albert Museum, London; 138 Pitkin Guides/photo. Sidney Newbury; 140 The Royal Collection © 1996 Her Majesty The Queen; 143 Christie's Images, London; 145 N. W. Jackson/Weidenfeld & Nicolson Archive; 146 Ashmolean Museum, Oxford; 147 Crown Copyright. Historic Royal Palaces; 148 The Trustees of the Victoria & Albert Museum, London; 150 Thyssen-Bornemisza Collection (The Bridgeman Art Library); 151 University of East Anglia/photo. N. J. More; 152 British Museum, London; 153 The Bodleian Library, Oxford; 155 By permission of the Archbishop of Canterbury and the Trustees of Lambeth Palace Library, London; 156 National Gallery of Art, Washington D.C. (The Bridgeman Art Library); 157 The Royal Collection © 1996 Her Majesty The Queen; 159 The Trustees of the Weston Park Foundation (The Bridgeman Art Library); 161 The Royal Collection © 1996 Her Majesty The Queen; 162 Crown Copyright. Historic Royal Palaces; 165 Musée Crozatier, Le Puy en Velay (Giraudon/Bridgeman Art Library); 166 The Royal Collection © 1996 Her Majesty The Queen; 168 National Gallery, London; 170 AKG, London; 171 British Library, London (Roy. 2A XVI f.63v) (The Bridgeman Art Library); 173 Musée du Louvre, Paris (Giraudon/Bridgeman Art Library); 174 British Library, London (Cotton MS. Augustus Iii 64); 175 A. F. Kersting, London; 176 Christie's Images, London; 178 British Museum, London; 179 President and Fellows, St John's College, Oxford; 180 The Folger Shakespeare Library, Washington D.C.; 181 The Trustees of the Victoria & Albert Museum, London; 182 The Burrell Collection, Glasgow; 183 The Burrell Collection, Glasgow; 184 Hardwick Hall, Derbyshire/The National Trust (Weidenfeld & Nicolson Archive); 186 Uffizi, Florence; 187 Mauritshuis, The Hague; 188 British Museum, London; 189 British Museum, London (The Bridgeman Art Library); 190 National Gallery, London (The Bridgeman Art Library); 191 The Royal Collection © 1996 Her Majesty The Queen; 192 above Musée du Louvre, Paris (Giraudon/Bridgeman Art Library); 192 below Ashmolean Museum, Oxford; 192-3 National Gallery, London; 195 The Royal Collection © 1996 Her Majesty The Queen; 196 By courtesy of the Provost and Fellows, King's College, Cambridge (photo. Dr H. G. Wayment); 197 above By courtesy of the Provost and Fellows, King's College, Cambridge (photo. P. A. L. Brunney); 197 below Kunstmuseum, Basel; 199 Christie's Images, London; 202 The Board of Trustees of The Royal Armouries; 203 British Library, London (Roy. 2A XVI f.3r) (The Bridgeman Art Library); 205 Public Record Office, London; 206 National Portrait Gallery, London; 207 British Library, London (Cott. Aug. 1ii 13) (J. B. Archive); 212 Geoff Langan/Weidenfeld & Nicolson Archive; 215 National Portrait Gallery, London; 217 The Royal Collection © 1996 Her Majesty The Queen; 218 A. F. Kersting, London; 220 The Royal Collection © 1996 Her Majesty The Queen; 221 National Portrait Gallery, London; 222 British Museum, London (Weidenfeld & Nicolson Archive/Ray Gardner); 223 British Museum, London; 224 National Portrait Gallery, London; 225 above By courtesy of the Mayor and Town Council of Kendal/photo. Edward Geldard; 225 below The Royal Collection © 1996 Her Majesty The Queen; 226 The Bible Society, London (The Bridgeman Art Library); 228 Master and Fellows, Magdalen College, Oxford; 229 The Royal Collection © 1996 Her Majesty The Queen; 231 Private Collection (Weidenfeld & Nicolson Archive); 233 National Portrait Gallery, London; 235 Arundel Castle, Sussex (The Bridgeman Art Library); 236 above A. F. Kersting, London; 236 below National Portrait Gallery, London; 237 Museum of London; 238 National Portrait Gallery, London; 239 The Mansell Collection, London; 241 A. F. Kersting, London; 243 The Royal Collection © 1996 Her Majesty The Queen; 244 A. F. Kersting, London; 245 By courtesy of the Dean and Chapter of Westminster, Westminster Abbey; 246 National Portrait Gallery, London; 248 Sudeley Castle, Gloucestershire (The Bridgeman Art Library). 256 President and Fellows, St John's College, Oxford.

INDEX

Page numbers in *italics* refer to illustrations